TRIUMPH
B O O K S

BUILT
TO LOSE

BUILT TO LOSE

How the NBA's Tanking Era Changed the League Forever

Jake Fischer

TRIUMPH
BOOKS

First Triumph Books paperback edition 2022

The Library of Congress has catalogued the previous edition as follows:

Names: Fischer, Jake, author.
Title: Built to lose : how the NBA's tanking era changed the league forever
  / Jake Fischer.
Identifiers: LCCN 2021003598 (print) | LCCN 2021003599 (ebook) | ISBN
  9781629378718 (board) | ISBN 9781641256070 (epub) | ISBN 9781641256087
  (kindle edition) | ISBN 9781641256094 (pdf)
Subjects: LCSH: National Basketball Association. | Basketball players—Recruiting—
United States. | Basketball draft—United States. | Basketball—Moral and ethical
aspects—United States.
Classification: LCC GV885.515.N37 F57 2021 (print) | LCC GV885.515.N37
  (ebook) | DDC 796.323/6406—dc23
LC record available at https://lccn.loc.gov/2021003598
LC ebook record available at https://lccn.loc.gov/2021003599

This book is available in quantity at special discounts for your group or organization.
For further information, contact:
  Triumph Books LLC
  814 North Franklin Street
  Chicago, Illinois 60610
  (312) 337-0747
  www.triumphbooks.com

Printed in U.S.A.
ISBN: 978-1-63727-173-5
Design by Patricia Frey

To Mrs. Crawford and Mr. Gagliardi

INTRODUCTION

In its heyday, the NBA's Orlando Pro Summer League was a gold mine for reporters. Unlike the lucrative carnival that, during the late 2010s, emerged in Las Vegas on the campus of UNLV, the Orlando Pro Summer League excluded fans from attendance. Just team personnel, agents, and credentialed media were allowed to attend. If you were there, you were at least—kind of—somebody who needed to be there.

Roughly eight franchises would participate every July, but even a 19-year-old intern at *SLAM* magazine could wander around the bowels of the Amway Center and rub elbows with executives from any team. You were able to approach first-round picks who were just leaning against the wall, casually waiting for their game to start, like their team had next during a pickup run. You'd wind up, just accidentally, sharing a lunch table in the media room with team owners. You could sit courtside behind your laptop and be broadcast nationwide as a bona fide member of the basketball press. NBA Entertainment even mic'd me one year—to this day, I have no idea why—and we filmed a supposedly candid conversation about player scouting, theoretically mimicking the whispers that echoed all week throughout those back halls.

In 2013, two months or so into said internship at *SLAM*, I handed the new Philadelphia 76ers president of basketball operations, Sam Hinkie, a business card that I'd made myself on VistaPrint. It was gawky and obviously unofficial. I had tried, and failed, to match the font listing my contact information to *SLAM*'s masthead. But Hinkie accepted my amateur attempt at networking nonetheless. This was Orlando, after all. I was there. I was, at least kind of, somebody.

Philadelphia hired Hinkie that May. I remember learning the news via Twitter alert, sitting in my 2008 Honda CR-V and following NBA Twitter's reaction on the screen of my iPhone 4s. If you recall, the "s" stood for "Siri," which first introduced the now-widespread, voice-activated personal assistant to mobile devices. Blackberrys, suddenly, were no longer cool. These were the early days of being ridiculed for not having iMessage. If your texts showed green instead of blue, you were lame. And, perhaps not so coincidentally, a flavor of big tech had also started blending into the NBA's ecosystem.

The Sixers scooped Hinkie from the famously data-driven Houston Rockets, steered then by Daryl Morey, who was widely considered basketball's version of Billy Beane—the number-crunching executive who shrewdly built the "Moneyball" Oakland Athletics into a World Series contender, even on a hamstrung budget. Houston fully entrusted Morey to pilot its basketball operations in 2007. That same year, the soon-to-be Oklahoma City Thunder tapped analytics-minded Sam Presti as its own franchise leader.

The Rockets won. And won. Each season, Morey's teams seemed to push the limits of mathematical tactics, both in roster construction and in playing style. They shot more and more three-pointers, while many opponents still posted up giant centers on the block. Presti's regime, meanwhile, methodically drafted superstar after superstar, his young Thunder quickly reached the 2012 NBA Finals, and the wave of NBA analytics seemed to crash on shores across the league.

The Orlando Magic, soon after, hired Rob Hennigan from Presti's Thunder to serve as their chief basketball mind. The following year, as Philadelphia empowered Hinkie, Phoenix hired Ryan McDonough as the Suns' new general manager. He was a respected talent evaluator from Boston's own analytically minded front office that first brought Morey himself into professional basketball. The Sacramento Kings named Pete D'Alessandro their general manager, a numbers guru who was known for his mastery of the salary cap. These were not former players with an innate feel for the game.

These men were, frankly, nerds rushing the NBA's storied fraternity of life-long hoopers.

This was an unmistakable trend. And any trend in any industry sparks unforeseen ripple effects. When Apple eliminated headphone jacks from its cell phones, Bluetooth products blossomed in turn. When NBA clubs equipped these young, analytical acolytes, a new team-building theme emerged across the league's landscape. The numbers were obvious: if your roster was average, and your record was mediocre, you had a near-impossible path toward a championship.

To make a long story short, Hennigan, Hinkie, and McDonough understood that losing, sinking down the standings, and earning higher lottery odds for landing top draft picks, was the surest way for a franchise to add superstar talent that could one day deliver a title. Boston set out to do the same that 2013–14 season. So while the NBA is ostensibly about competing for championships, a new race to the bottom grew maybe even more contested than the battle taking place at the top.

One year into Hinkie's tenure, the mass of at-least-kind-of somebodies flocked back to Orlando. All season, skeptics had lamented the losing culture fostering in Philadelphia. Basketball lifers wondered, aghast, how the Sixers' young players would learn about professionalism. Across the Delaware Valley, Hinkie's strategy clearly polarized his franchise's fanbase. Largely, it seemed younger supporters, fatigued by Philly's years of mediocrity, cheered Hinkie's brazen scheme with abandon. Older Sixers fans were loudly complaining about the team's terrible nightly product. My father, a longtime season-ticket holder, abandoned his seats. And I was an aspiring sportswriter, with those VistaPrint business cards, so his friends demanded an explanation whenever we crossed paths. They'd make fun of Hinkie's spreadsheets and call him "Scam Hinkie" over pointed emails and Facebook messages.

This was why I reapproached Hinkie inside the Amway Center in July 2014. I had to *actually* meet this man. I needed to put a personality and a conversation to the caricature that many were painting him as. I also needed to give him one of the glossier, more-official-looking-but-still-unofficial

SLAM business cards that I printed this time around, now no longer an intern, but still a 20-year-old "Contributing Writer" that was far more "kind-of" than "somebody." So I asked Hinkie if he wanted to meet for a meal that week. He had absolutely no reason to say yes. But the executive, infamous for undercutting NBA tradition as we knew it, promptly invited me to dinner.

I followed him outside the arena and into the murky Florida rain. We speed-walked across the street and into a parking garage. His rental car for the week was a black Chevy Suburban. Country music played quietly on XM radio while I rode shotgun.

We ate and spoke in the lobby restaurant of Orlando's Grand Bohemian Hotel. He was as charming as he was guarded, insisting, as is his custom, the conversation remained off the record. But the 36-year-old before me that evening was nothing like the cold and calculated parody many believed him to be. He won me over. And as a young reporter, finding my footing in the cutthroat business of basketball, I certainly struggled to maintain an objectivity when discussing Hinkie and his process to build Philadelphia into a perennial contender.

Later that week, I bumped into Isiah Thomas in the Amway Center media room. We shared a few mutual acquaintances, so I struck up a conversation with him while waiting in the buffet line. Thomas was in Orlando to provide color commentary for NBA TV's game broadcasts. He, of course, was a decorated point guard and a two-time champion with the Detroit Pistons. Then Thomas became both a coach and served as a team executive. He was by all accounts Hinkie's direct foil; he not only played but starred in the league. He wasn't a 30-something whiz kid—he'd been around the NBA for more than 30 years.

And yet Thomas' failures as a front office leader—muddying the New York Knicks' cap sheet, throwing lucrative contracts at unproven players, gambling on his basketball acumen alone—were the exact shortcomings by traditional NBA executives that encouraged owners to start entrusting the Moreys and the Prestis, the Hinkies and the McDonoughs. So as we chatted in that media room, Thomas expectedly lambasted Hinkie's ideals. Thomas didn't believe in losing. He couldn't possibly subscribe to tanking. Thomas played, and players are winners. You don't build a roster that you expect to drop game after game. That wasn't how the NBA, his NBA, always worked.

This larger ideological clash waged onward. Hinkie's Sixers kept losing. Critics kept calling for his head. I was covering the league from Boston, masquerading at night as an NBA reporter inside TD Garden while studying journalism at nearby Northeastern University. When the Sixers made their twice-annual visits to Massachusetts, those games felt like marquee matchups, essentially mirror images of the same abstract. Boston Celtics faithful believed in their front office. Boston would tank, draft future stars, and emerge as a contender, just like ardent Hinkie supporters staunchly defended his rebuild. But the Celtics' losing still pained many, just as the defeats stung countless around Philadelphia.

I often found myself somewhere in the middle. It was impossible to deny the math: tanking presented clear benefits. And the NBA's lottery system obviously helped porous teams springboard past those stuck in the middle; just look at Presti's Thunder. Yet inside those locker rooms, the coaches I'd begun to know started growing increasingly frustrated. The concept of hitching an organization's wagon to ultra-talented 19-year-olds seemed to ignore the fickle nature of 19-year-olds, especially when those 19-year-olds were paid millions of dollars.

Covering the league's race to the bottom called for a journalistic pragmatism that a young reporter, roughly the same age as those 19-year-old phenoms, couldn't possibly embody. It was a true battleground to develop reporting ethics and an as-close-to-an-objective lens as humanly possible. I believed in Hinkie's approach, but I also acknowledged the shortcomings of his plan and his leadership style.

If anything, this book is an ode to those years, what I've come to call the NBA's tanking era. Losing games for the sake of ultimately winning came in vogue, and eventually spurred the league office and Board of Governors to change the lottery system, hoping to dissuade future front office leaders from fumbling nightly contests in search of more ping-pong balls. Covering those tankers helped me find my footing in the industry. That early work helped me land my first job at *Sports Illustrated*, where the company actually made business cards on my behalf. Sorry, VistaPrint.

The Orlando Pro Summer League sadly is no more. Almost all of the general managers chronicled in these pages no longer steward franchises. But this fascinating epoch of NBA history launched my career. I'm a better reporter and, I believe, a smarter individual from interacting with those nerds—during the 300 original interviews for this storytelling—who shook the NBA landscape forever.

ONE

"Andy!" John Calipari demanded. "Where's he going?"

Kentucky's men's basketball coach leaned over their clothed table, prominently positioned inside the Barclays Center green room.

Nerlens Noel sat two chairs to Calipari's left. He declared pro after one collegiate season, and despite tearing his ACL in February, the 6-foot-10 big man expected to hear his name called first in the 2013 NBA Draft. "Nerlens wanted to be the No. 1 pick," says a member of Noel's initial representation team. "We thought there was a good chance," says Frank Catapano, one of Noel's early agents.

When the draft's premier prospects first flooded the Brooklyn arena with their families that evening of June 27, Calipari milled about the premises, confidently telling anyone in his path Noel was still due first. Kentucky's head coach, dark hair slicked back, always exudes a suave enthusiasm. Yet Noel's torn left ACL cast a shadow over the entire event. Noel possessed what some scouts deemed generational defensive ability—the athleticism and innate shot blocking prowess to anchor a franchise for a decade. His rookie year, however, would be largely spent rehabbing his knee on the sidelines. Would waiting for Noel's promise be worth another poor season for the 24–58 Cleveland Cavaliers, picking No. 1?

For some time NBA evaluators had largely dismissed the other talents in 2013's draft pool. "That class wasn't full of difference-makers," says Rod Higgins, then Charlotte's president of basketball operations. Once Noel shred those ligaments in his knee, the injury also tore apart any certainty of

15

June's first pick. Medical concerns followed other touted players too. And so few teams selecting atop the draft targeted specific prospects with much conviction, although several youngsters did stand out.

Kansas freshman Ben McLemore looked the part of a prototypical modern wing. He weaponized a gorgeous shooting stroke, could bound past opponents closing out on his jumper, and appeared malleable as a perimeter defender. Victor Oladipo's junior campaign skyrocketed the Indiana guard up scouts' draft boards. What intrigue McLemore packed in his potential to guard, Oladipo already cemented on tape and in spades. Many team executives labeled Oladipo the safest selection near the top of the draft, hopeful his shooting would continue to improve. Georgetown swingman Otto Porter projected as a versatile, bigger wing, capable of scoring from most angles on the floor. Still, each prospect also brought his obvious foibles. The air of uncertainty filling downtown Brooklyn bothered John Calipari.

"Andy!" Kentucky's coach pleaded again. "Where's he going?"

Calipari's questioning cut across the table toward powerbroker Andy Miller of ASM Sports, one of Noel's agents along with Frank Catapano and Chris Driscoll, a Boston-area basketball figure long affiliated with Noel's family. The Cavs revealed little preliminary information to Noel's camp. With two decades of agenting experience, Miller understood exactly what Cleveland's lack of transparency foreshadowed. Cavs officials playing coy with his client suggested Noel probably wasn't going No. 1. Even worse: the day prior, a quiet, yet reliable whisper from a Vegas oddsmaker reached ASM rumoring Cleveland's strong interest in Anthony Bennett. The UNLV freshman forward presented an equally athletic marvel with the grace of a guard. "What he was able to do, there were a lot of teams that were getting excited about him," says Dave Rice, the Rebels' head coach. Very little Bennett-to-Cleveland speculation had leaked publicly, but if the rumor was accurate it spelled doom for Miller and company.

Noel only met with the Cavaliers and the Magic leading up to the draft. Orlando expressed strong interest in selecting him second. Noel's quick hands and rim protection could have fortified the Magic's porous defense that finished 2012–13 bottom-five in the league. But Victor Oladipo also enamored Orlando executives. He brought equal brilliance hounding rival guards on the perimeter while at Indiana. Making matters more precarious for Noel, the Washington Wizards, picking third, never expressed much regard for his services. Washington long coveted Otto Porter. And yet throughout the pre-draft process, Miller rebuffed any request from teams picking lower to meet with his star client. Permitting such contact with Noel would have admitted he may slip from the No. 1 slot. "The agents are as powerful as ever," says Rod Higgins, Charlotte's then-president.

Miller scheduled a meeting with Higgins' Bobcats, who owned the fourth pick, only to cancel before Noel could ever sit down with an executive from the franchise. "Andy and Chris said, 'No, don't let him go. That would show weakness,'" Frank Catapano recalls. "I don't believe in all that bullshit." Phoenix, having pick No. 5, made numerous efforts to visit with Noel too. Again, Miller and Driscoll refused.

Cleveland maintained its own dialogue embargo. "Our information was pretty solid on the Nos. 2, 3, and 4 picks, and we didn't know about No. 5," Catapano says. With Noel's uncertain status growing abundantly clear, his group decided to appease the Suns at long last. Just hours before the draft began, ASM finally connected Phoenix with the physical therapy chief overseeing Noel's early rehabilitation. Creative agents can effectively hold their clients' medical info hostage, only revealing it to the highest-drafting teams. Miller hoped the phone call would create an opening for Noel at the Suns' fifth pick, stopping their bleeding at a $4.8 million loss in guaranteed money from the No. 1 selection.

His calculus proved wise when NBA commissioner David Stern strolled to the podium and declared the Cavaliers' first choice.

Chris Grant, Cleveland's general manager, oversaw the Cavs' pick while staring down the final year of his contract. Noel indeed faced a months-long rehabilitation process, and one may be surprised how an executive's job security can influence transactions in pro sports. "[Grant] wasn't taking a kid that was gonna miss the entire season," says a member of Noel's representation team. Cleveland's GM needed to build a playoff contender and end the Cavs' postseason drought ever since LeBron James migrated to South Beach during July 2010 free agency with fellow All-Star Chris Bosh. James announced the decision during an hour-long ESPN special. Then he, Bosh, and incumbent Miami Heat All-Star Dwyane Wade each took less salary to afford Miami the flexibility to flush out a contending roster. "I want to be able to compete to win championships," James explained, emphasizing the plurality.

Never before had three franchise players shifted the NBA's balance of power with such individual effort, much to the chagrin of many within team ownership ranks. Cavs proprietor Dan Gilbert furiously penned an open letter on the team's website, blasting James' decision as a "several day, narcissistic, self-promotional build-up." Gilbert even vowed Cleveland would claim a title before Miami ever captured a ring.

James ultimately left via sign-and-trade. He technically inked his new contract with the Cavs, before heading south—it's typically more cost-effective for NBA teams to acquire expensive players rather than sign them in free agency. And for their trouble, Cleveland received two future first- and two future second-round draft picks in return. That draft capital was sorely needed to back Gilbert's bold prediction.

While old-school basketball decision-makers valued building playoff teams by any means necessary, modern strategy suggested truly chasing championships was more worthwhile than merely constructing a decent postseason participant. And the most efficient way to turn a mediocre team into a bona fide championship contender was actually to *lose* more games. The further a franchise falls out of the playoff picture and down the standings, the higher that team would likely pick in the draft—typically where All-Star-caliber players like, in 2003, James (first), Bosh (fourth), and Wade (fifth) were still available.

Weather and market aside, the Heat largely landed James and Bosh because the organization wisely drafted Wade. And unlike Cleveland and Toronto, Miami helped shape a title team around him by 2006, then retained the All-Star long enough for him to help recruit other alphas. By

2010, as Miami's trio showcased, all-world talents never boasted greater agency within the NBA marketplace. With player salaries at an all-time high, it became less important which team signed their paychecks, and more about which starry counterparts were their teammates, and what their lucky franchise's market could provide in terms of off-court lifestyle and business opportunities. The best way for the Cavs to ascend back where James had brought them, and past Miami: Cleveland needed to strike gold again at the top of the NBA Draft Lottery, featuring the league's non-play-off teams, and then select another future superstar.

And, boy, did the Cavaliers get lucky. Not only did Cleveland win 2013's drawing having just 15.6 percent odds for No. 1, the Cavs first improbably defied a 2.8 percent chance in the 2011 lottery—a pick originally acquired from the Los Angeles Clippers—to win the right at drafting electric point guard Kyrie Irving. Cleveland paired Irving with its own selection at No. 4, big man Tristan Thompson. Yet the young Cavs hardly won under head coach Byron Scott. They returned to the lottery in 2012, picking Syracuse guard Dion Waiters fourth at the behest of Gilbert, only to miss the playoffs again in 2013.

LeBron James, meanwhile, powered Miami to consecutive titles in 2012 and 2013. The footing quivered underneath Cleveland's front office as Ohio's native son erected a budding dynasty in Florida. The Cavs remained nothing short of bad. June's NBA draft approached. With Chris Grant's contract details known widely around the NBA, never before did the top of a draft feel so truly fluid.

Cleveland held numerous discussions for its first selection, at one point pitching Portland on a package that would have sent All-Star forward LaMarcus Aldridge to Northeast Ohio. Throughout the week before that Thursday night draft, league gossip suggested Cleveland's focus had shifted onto name after name—Noel, Oladipo, McLemore, nearly every prospect projected in the top 10. "Hell, we thought *he* could go No. 1," says Mark Turgeon, who coached Noel's positional competition, Alex Len, at Maryland. "They were putting all these hooks in the water to try and get a trade," says one Magic executive.

Just as agents such as Noel's play coy with teams, executives design their own smoke screens. The NBA's draft ecosystem has evolved into an irreparable game of telephone where most whispers are presumed to be false. "What's right? What's wrong? What's fake? What's not fake? Social media, what's out there—it's crazy," says longtime executive Artūras Karnišovas. "There's a lot of information there. So you gotta be very careful."

Orlando's front office, for example, regrouped that Tuesday morning, 48 hours before draft night, attempting to pin down Cleveland's preference. Brian Wright, the team's scouting manager, observed only one name had yet been linked to the Cavaliers: Anthony Bennett. "We were like, 'They're gonna take him!'" says a Magic official.

Cleveland's chicanery didn't draw greater trade proposals. The best deal in exchange for their slot would have netted one of the lower returns for a No. 1 pick in league history. The Cavs themselves offered to empty their war chest for New Orleans' top pick just a year before. But just as Cleveland experienced this June, no rival front office wanted the pressure of choosing the best prospect in a dubious 2013 class either. With it, more than ever, came a strong chance of one day being proven quite wrong. These are the failed decisions that cost executives their jobs and careers.

The morning of the draft, while Noel's camp lingered in the dark, Cleveland waffled between Bennett and Oladipo. The latter had previously expressed his lack of interest in joining the Cavaliers. Would Gilbert risk drafting another phenom who planned to later walk in free agency just like James? Cavs officials ultimately cast a final vote. And Bennett came out as their consensus. It is said Chris Grant represented a nod in favor of Oladipo, yet Cleveland still stunned most NBA evaluators and even Bennett himself by grabbing the Running Rebel first.

The Cavs tipped their hand to virtually no one outside of their draft room. When commissioner David Stern announced Bennett's name, audible gasps pierced the arena. "Everybody in the draft class was surprised," says Ben McLemore, Kansas' guard. "Even him."

The news may have startled Kentucky's head coach the most.

"Andy!" John Calipari implored. "Where is he going?"

Miller and Noel's other agents frantically worked their phones, searching for any bit of valuable intel. Noel was far too talented to go undrafted—"This guy had Bill Russell–like physical tools," Frank Catapano says—but no member of Noel's management knew how low the center could fall. Alex Len's camp remained calm. Maryland's 7-footer heard Phoenix would likely be his destination at No. 5. But as a worst-case scenario, Oklahoma City promised it would scoop Len at No. 12 should he improbably slide that far. It was the safety net Noel's reps chased, especially when Stern announced the Magic's selection at No. 2.

Orlando hired its general manager, Rob Hennigan, the previous June, making the 30-year-old, former San Antonio intern the NBA's youngest chief basketball executive. After graduating from Division III Emerson as its all-time leading men's basketball scorer, Hennigan rose up the fabled San Antonio Spurs' front office ranks. When the soon-to-be Oklahoma City Thunder named Spurs executive Sam Presti, a fellow Emerson alum, as its new GM in 2007, Hennigan followed as his deputy, helping them reach the 2012 NBA Finals before garnering his own shot in Orlando.

Naturally, Hennigan hired another Spurs disciple, Jacque Vaughn, as the head coach to launch his Magic tenure. Vaughn spent three final seasons of his 12-year playing career in San Antonio before joining the esteemed Gregg Popovich's bench as an assistant. And from the first day of Orlando's 2012 training camp, he preached a familial atmosphere integral to the Spurs' vaunted culture, deemed by many as the main ingredient to winning four championships from 1999 to 2007. Vaughn hopped in and out of drills alongside the Magic players. "In the beginning it was kind of funny," point guard Jameer Nelson says. "But then it's like, 'Okay, this dude is real.'"

Both San Antonio and Oklahoma City famously incorporated advanced data into their decision-making. So Hennigan instituted a series of conditioning tests he would implement each preseason in Orlando. He called for players to run up and down the court, varying the number of required touches at each baseline in whatever allotted seconds, such as slapping the endline 10 times in a minute, then completing that exercise four more separate instances. Orlando's more-established players raised an eyebrow at the practices. "I'm just a guy who was used to, 'Hey, let's go play basketball,' you know?" Nelson says. "When you have a guy like Rob, who was extremely analytical—I understand you've got to have analytics, but I'm more of a feel guy."

A 10-game losing streak beginning in mid-December spiraled any hope of success for Orlando in the first year of its new regime. "We had a lot of young guys who had to be taught a lot how to win," Nelson says. A 12-game drought stretched from late January into early February, and by the trade deadline, Hennigan prudently dealt forward Josh McRoberts to free up future salary cap space. Then, four minutes before the horn, the GM flipped a package surrounding sharpshooter J.J. Redick, facing a surely pricey free agency in July, to Milwaukee for a return highlighted by second-year forward Tobias Harris, whom the Magic believed had All-Star potential. It was the type of savvy transaction modern, empirically driven front offices sought while restructuring. Why not leverage a rival's wish to add reinforcements for the postseason, trade them a veteran likely to leave on the open market anyway, and in return receive young players with upside?

Hennigan completely reshuffled the Orlando roster he inherited, once tailored to surround Dwight Howard with a championship-caliber supplementary cast. Instead he traded the All-NBA center to Los Angeles back in August 2012 and the Magic now boasted ample financial flexibility for future moves. "We had a really good run there from a player transaction cycle for the first two years," says a Magic exec. Orlando also entered the 2013 lottery with the league's worst record and a 25 percent chance at landing the No. 1 pick. The Magic wound up second to Cleveland following the May drawing, but nonetheless felt players of Victor Oladipo's caliber were worthy of the top selection. Plummeting to the bottom of the NBA, remember, offered many rewards.

Oladipo first enamored Hennigan in November at the Legends Classic as he blanketed rival teams' best players. The Magic thought his significant spikes in production during his junior season in Bloomington indicated a work ethic that would spark further improvement alongside Tobias Harris, just like OKC accomplished with Kevin Durant, Russell Westbrook, and James Harden. The Thunder drafted three future NBA MVPs from 2007 to

2009, and their collective competitiveness bred OKC's 2012 Finals appearance. Now Hennigan planned to acquire another crew of tireless athletes in Orlando. "Can we develop them? Can we grow them together and then allow that to manifest?" he mused. Magic staffers attended roughly six of Oladipo's games that year, and directly chose him over Ben McLemore. Hennigan valued Oladipo's versatility and potential to play both guard positions, envisioning his transformation at the point like Westbrook before him.

Back in downtown Brooklyn, David Stern made Orlando's No. 2 pick official. Oladipo relished his open opportunity in the backcourt. Fully aware of the Magic's positioning following the Dwight Howard blockbuster, he wrapped his arms around the upstart organization. "I'm just glad they chose me so I could be a part of that," Oladipo told reporters inside Barclays Center. Of course, John Calipari didn't agree with Orlando's decision.

"Andy?" Kentucky's coach asked once more. "Where is he going?"

With each query, Miller's anger and stress ran hotter. This situation was out of the agent's control. Every team was positioned inside their war rooms. All the work was done. Nerlens Noel simply had a bum knee. What more could Calipari want?

The Wizards, long prioritizing Otto Porter, selected Georgetown's local star third. Washington projected Porter as a perfect complement to their budding All-Star backcourt pairing. When Wizards brass met with C.J. McCollum before the draft, Lehigh's senior guard even asked, "Why are you guys meeting me? You have John Wall and Bradley Beal." Calipari resumed his line of questioning as Porter shook David Stern's hand on stage.

"Andy, where's he going?"

Noel wasn't headed to Charlotte at No. 4, either. Slighted by Miller's pre-draft tactics, the Bobcats preferred Oladipo's frontcourt teammate, Indiana forward Cody Zeller.

Charlotte believed it already rostered franchise pillars in Kemba Walker at point guard, Michael Kidd-Gilchrist on the wing, and Bismack Biyombo in the frontcourt. "We were looking for a guy who could fit in," says Rod Higgins, Charlotte's president.

The Bobcats valued that Zeller returned to Indiana for a second national championship pursuit instead of entering the 2012 NBA Draft. He wanted to win. "Vic and I agreed to give it one more shot," Zeller says. Then he tested as an elite athlete at the draft combine. His pre-draft workout in Charlotte previewed a shooting stroke that could stretch opposing defenses to the NBA three-point line. He seemed like the missing piece from the Bobcats' playoff puzzle.

Charlotte called its new forward in Brooklyn to celebrate. Zeller returned a giddy gratitude. Struggling to contain his excitement, he mistook the first voice on the line for that of Bobcats executive Rich Cho. "Okay now," the person said. "I'm going to hand the phone over to…Rich Cho, our general manager." Zeller's eyes widened. A lump bulged his throat. At that moment the 20-year-old realized he had actually been speaking to Charlotte's owner, NBA luminary Michael Jordan, arguably the game's greatest player ever.

"I thought I recognized his voice," Zeller now says sheepishly. "It was actually MJ."

A legendary grinder, Jordan appreciated Zeller's unwavering motor at Indiana. Charlotte's intel, meanwhile, indicated Noel's pre-injury work ethic at Kentucky leaned more toward being lazy than tenacious.

"Andy," John Calipari asked Miller once again. "Where are *we* going?"

Phoenix general manager Ryan McDonough had been clear. Even after consulting Noel's medical team, he would choose another prospect at No. 5, the first draft pick of his Suns reign. McDonough arrived from Boston that May, having originally joined the Celtics' new 2003 regime once local investment titans Wyc Grousbeck and Steve Pagliuca purchased the franchise. Amongst even the most impassioned sports families across New England, McDonough's stands out. His father, Will, was a storied columnist for the *Boston Globe* and his brother, Sean, an ESPN announcer. Another sibling, Terry, spent years in NFL front offices. McDonough found his start at 23 when he spun an introduction to Grousbeck and Pagliuca into an entry role within Boston's expanding basketball operations.

He knew ownership supported the league's early emphasis on data analysis. Grousbeck and Pagliuca tapped former player Danny Ainge to lead their charge as general manager. Ainge would drop into Boston's video room to poll lower-level staffers like McDonough and ask questions about the tape he was cutting. Impressed by their discussions, Ainge soon elevated McDonough into the Celtics' scouting ranks, where the rising executive watched Boston's senior vice president Daryl Morey create computer models to better evaluate players. Morey famously introduced the metric "true shooting percentage," which measures a player's overall efficiency by combining his two-point, free-throw, and three-point percentages into one, more-accurate calculation. "There's no question Daryl's been the most public face of analytics in the NBA," says Aaron Barzilai, who joined the Memphis Grizzlies as a data consultant in 2009.

By 2006, the Rockets lured the 33-year-old Morey to Houston to head their front office—assuming the role of general manager come May 2007—despite traditional basketball thinkers and longtime personnel men mocking the hire. Morey never played the game at its utmost levels of competition, and now he was set to become the Rockets' general manager? He was a nerd with a computer, not a basketball lifer. Fear may have underscored those jeers. "There was probably some element of understanding: What does this mean for their long-term job opportunities?" says Barzilai. "Is it forcing different archetypes who used to work in the league out of positions of power?"

Spurs executives, after all, used their own empirical analysis throughout their dynasty, and San Antonio captured its fourth championship in 2007. Morey's reengineered Rockets then launched to the top of the Western Conference during the 2007–08 campaign. At one point Houston took 22 straight, then the second-longest winning streak in NBA history. Sam Presti's success in Oklahoma City later paved the way for Rob Hennigan to steer Orlando. More and more, franchises were empowering statistical-driven basketball executives. A 33-year-old Ryan McDonough billed as the 2013 archetype to resuscitate the Suns' former contender. Now here was his first crack, picking No. 5 in the 2013 NBA Draft, and McDonough needed to connect.

Unlike Hennigan's situation in Orlando, Phoenix possessed no All-Star for McDonough to trade and recoup future assets; Steve Nash had already left in 2012 free agency. "There wasn't going to be enough talent around him," says Bill Duffy, his longtime agent. Nash's pick-and-roll partnership with All-Star big man Amar'e Stoudemire was long in the rearview. Gone, too, was head coach Mike D'Antoni and his groundbreaking offense that spurred Nash's back-to-back MVP awards and morphed Phoenix into a viable title threat. Nash contemplated reuniting with Stoudemire in New York before shockingly joining Kobe Bryant's quest for a sixth title in Los Angeles instead.

It made most financial sense for Nash to become a Laker through a sign and trade, just as it did for LeBron James when he went to Miami. "The quandary was that Phoenix didn't want to trade him to the Lakers," Duffy says. Los Angeles, mind you, bested the Suns in the 2010 Western Conference Finals. So Phoenix coerced the Lakers into giving the Suns two first-round draft picks, the first of which came in 2013, as well as two second-round picks.

All week Ryan McDonough dangled that No. 30 pick in trade talks with Orlando, hoping to acquire pick No. 2. He once thought the additional first could be enough ammo to slide up and nab Victor Oladipo, but Hennigan's Magic were unwilling to really negotiate. "Phoenix had a lot of interest if they could have swung a deal," says Tom Crean, Oladipo's coach at Indiana.

McDonough alas made good on his word to Alex Len's camp and selected the Ukrainian giant. Len still faced three to five months of rehab before his return from May surgery on his left ankle, but Nerlens Noel's medical worried the Suns far more. Their background intel on both prospects also pointed to Len as the safer, more trustworthy selection at No. 5. When he arrived at Maryland, Len stood a skinny 7-foot-1 and hardly spoke English. "'Gatorade' and 'chicken wings,' that's the only words he knew," says Terrapins head coach Mark Turgeon. A full summer of grueling strength training later fueled his growth as a sophomore. Len would run to a trash can in between exercises. "He'd go throw up and come back for more," Turgeon recalls.

Phoenix's intel, meanwhile, mirrored that of Charlotte's when it came to Noel's approach. And with Len's newfound muscle, he imposed his will on Noel during Maryland and Kentucky's clash at Barclays Center that fall, scoring 23 points and adding 12 rebounds. Now back in that very arena mere months later, he bested Noel once more. Phoenix favored Len's soft touch at such size.

"Andy!" John Calipari shouted at Miller one final time. "Where's he going?"

Frustration at their green room table reached full tilt. "Shut the fuck up!" one agent finally sniped back at Kentucky's coach. Noel's camp, of course, had no significant contact with New Orleans regarding its sixth pick. Miller and Driscoll never fathomed Noel slipping out of the top five. An imperfect storm had swept him this far down the draft. With each passing selection, Noel's face dropped closer into his lap, his gaze deeper into his cell phone. And the New Orleans Pelicans, having just drafted their talented center Anthony Davis at No. 1 in 2012, didn't appear in need of Noel's interior presence either.

"Everybody was in a panic," says Frank Catapano, one of Noel's representatives. "It's amazing how intense they get." Each passing minute on draft night can feel like an hour. The agents needed some stroke of good fortune, a franchise to pull the trigger, one that could afford the patience to wait on a potentially generational defensive talent's recovery. Then with two minutes remaining on the clock, a phone call finally broke the tension.

The Pelicans informed Miller that New Orleans would, against all odds, choose Noel sixth. Calipari at last had his answer.

David Stern promptly stepped toward the podium to announce Noel's name, only the commissioner paused before making the reveal. A fire still burned behind the 70-year-old's glasses. Stern was iron-willed and audacious, his shrewd business savvy having morphed the NBA from merely a league into a billion-dollar, global entertainment industry. Stern smirked and beckoned the heckling fans in the Brooklyn arena to scream louder. Where most figures would lament the jeers, he encouraged anything that drummed excitement for his association.

He could perform any public character so long as it made for a great show. It was Stern, for example, who instituted the NBA Draft Lottery in 1985 and turned its reveal into must-watch television each May, where he originally drew envelopes representing all non-playoff teams. As much as the lottery drew fan interest, it also aided Stern's efforts to decrease incentive for teams to lose on purpose. Houston closed the 1983–84 season just 5–17 over its last 22 games while Stern's tenure as commissioner began that spring. Rival teams accused the Rockets of tanking games in hopes of drafting nearby Houston Cougars center Hakeem Olajuwon No. 1. If true, the Rockets utterly manipulated the league's rulebook.

The NBA's top pick had been determined by a coin flip between the worst teams in each conference since 1966. And from No. 3 and down the board, the remaining non-playoff clubs followed in reverse order of win-loss record. But under Stern's watch, he began pawing envelopes containing undisclosed franchise logos out of a giant contraption, awarding picks in descending order. Come 1990, Stern and the league adopted its first weighted lottery system, which, after a tweak in 1993, awarded the worst team in the NBA—such as Orlando in 2013—just a 25 percent chance at landing the top pick.

Even with limited odds attempting to dissuade tanking, front offices and coaching staffs still pulled subtle strings to plummet down the standings, hoping for the greatest chance at winning the lottery. Stern and the NBA couldn't force teams to rush to replace superstars, for instance. After LeBron James left for Miami, Cleveland spent years not prioritizing winning. Orlando was bad enough after trading Dwight Howard to land Victor Oladipo. New Orleans was two seasons removed from dealing star point guard Chris Paul to the Los Angeles Clippers, and here were the Pelicans, still picking near the top of the draft one year after selecting No. 1.

The NBA could only hope teams used these high picks to soon rebound into the playoffs. Young stars, like Nerlens Noel perhaps, were necessary to challenge the game's current alphas. Would Noel do so in New Orleans?

After Stern finished riling the crowd and announced the pick, Noel rose with a toothy grin. He exhaled and splayed his gray jacket to reveal a white No. 3 Kentucky jersey stitched into the lining of his suit. "When he got picked, I said, 'It doesn't matter where you got drafted,'" Catapano says. "'It matters how you play.'" Noel pulled a navy Pelicans hat over his trademark high-top fade. He slapped hands with Calipari and Miller and began marching toward the stage. Once considered a wonky pairing between Noel and Davis, scouts were now praising the Pelicans' imposing band of rim protectors.

Only New Orleans hadn't drafted the center with intent to keep him. Few of the league's most knowledgeable insiders had yet learned of Noel's true destination. "We didn't know Philly was gonna 'pick' him," Catapano says.

TWO

When Leslie Alexander sought someone new to pilot his Rockets, he instructed a headhunter to search for Houston's own "*Moneyball*-type," referring to Michael Lewis' 2003 book. The famous story chronicled how the Oakland Athletics used sabermetrics to build a competitive MLB roster in spite of the franchise's miniscule budget. Lewis' book brought analytics into the mainstream. And by 2006, Houston's owner fully envisioned the Rockets becoming the NBA's Athletics.

Alexander had already begun restructuring Houston's basketball operations the year before, when he hired Sam Hinkie as a full-time special assistant out of Stanford business school. Hinkie chose Stanford over Harvard, allured by the school's relationship with NFL franchises. And sure enough, he worked part-time for the nearby San Francisco 49ers and the Houston Texans soon after. Hinkie then persuaded Alexander he could assist in the neighboring Rockets' decision-making, by flying from California to Texas each week for one day of meetings so he could still finish his MBA.

A multi-sport athlete in high school, Hinkie also harbored natural fluency with numbers and especially with basketball data. His comb-over and daily, simple business attire actualized the investment-banker identity that veteran executives had stereotyped analytical thinkers rising around the NBA. Hoopheads wore sweats, not blazers. But it was impossible to deny Hinkie's value to Alexander's operation. He spent countless hours fiddling with the Rockets' internal databases, running hundreds of simulations to develop a greater understanding of how certain players in certain positions impacted the team's overall results.

Alexander believed in Hinkie's contributions, but the young executive couldn't yet lead a front office. If Alexander preferred a "*Moneyball*-type" as chief of the Rockets' basketball operations, Daryl Morey made clear sense.

Word had spread around the NBA of Morey's player-evaluating brilliance in Boston. "If we combine the best information with our basketball people, we should be able to make the most informed and best decisions in the NBA," Alexander declared upon Morey's hire. The owner soon elevated Hinkie to vice president in 2007, making the 29-year-old the youngest to hold that post in the NBA. Alexander yearned to contend once again, and believed Houston could possibly calculate the Rockets' first championship since Hakeem Olajuwon powered consecutive titles in 1994 and 1995—quite a byproduct of Houston's alleged 1984 tanking efforts, no?

Under Hinkie and Morey, Houston utilized cost-effective maneuvers to build a complementary supporting cast around the Rockets' two All-Stars: 7-foot-6 center Yao Ming and prolific scoring wing Tracy McGrady. And when that duo's window effectively closed in 2009, Morey and Hinkie were steadfast in accumulating draft capital, plus young players on inexpensive deals, to eventually trade for their next star. Houston bided its time. The Rockets then pounced when OKC fell $4.5 million short of the maximum salary James Harden sought in early talks for a contract extension. Morey and Hinkie believed the reigning Sixth Man of the Year was worth more than every penny.

Once the Rockets exchanged a hoard of players and future picks for Harden, the 23-year-old rewarded their gamble. He exploded into an All-Star throughout the 2012–13 campaign, scoring at a rate almost as voluminous as his trademark bushy beard.

Philadelphia's ownership took note, inviting Hinkie for dinner in New York. He brandished a laptop upon entering the restaurant. Majority partner Joshua Harris wanted to learn what Hinkie's plan for a rebuild would look like. So Hinkie presented an extensively detailed PowerPoint, diagramming all 17 small transactions that snowballed into the amalgamation of assets Houston cashed in to acquire Harden from Oklahoma City, two months after the Sixers—to Hinkie's correct estimation—overpaid for Andrew Bynum's troubled knees.

Three days after the Suns hired Morey's former Celtics colleague Ryan McDonough that May, the 76ers named Hinkie their new president and general manager.

Philadelphia hadn't operated in previous years like a patient organization, resulting in nearly a decade of lottery appearances and first-round playoff exits. After the Sixers' budding core reached Game 7 of the 2012 Eastern Conference semifinals, they acquired All-NBA center Andrew Bynum that August in the four-team blockbuster that sent Dwight Howard to the Lakers. But instead of finally elevating Philadelphia to the top of the East, Bynum's lingering knee issues forced him to miss the entire campaign and left his teammates out of the postseason.

Bynum's absence at least allowed point guard Jrue Holiday to emerge as a bona fide All-Star, providing Philly with its first unquestioned franchise cornerstone since the Sixers began rebuilding from the Allen Iverson era way back in 2006. Holiday was just 22 years old, and rival teams expected the Sixers would use their No. 11 pick in the 2013 draft to add another running mate for their blooming floor general. Yet Hinkie convinced ownership that Holiday had more value to Philadelphia as a trade piece.

He'd determined the Sixers' core group—also featuring Evan Turner, Spencer Hawes, and Thaddeus Young—lacked the superstar talent to blossom into a legitimate title contender. Their years of pedestrian basketball had entrapped the Sixers on professional sports' treadmill of mediocrity, Hinkie explained. And if a team isn't truly competing for championships, data suggested the best option to improve for the long haul was playing the league's lottery. Holiday was indeed an All-Star, but if the Sixers could move him for two first-round picks, perhaps Philadelphia would draft a pair of future All-Stars, several years younger than Holiday, and inch ever closer to creating a contender for the Delaware Valley.

On Wednesday afternoon before the draft, talk of a trade with Philadelphia filtered throughout New Orleans' facility. Many Pelicans staffers expected they would not keep their sixth choice the following night. Word in Philadelphia, though, was mum to say the least. Hinkie previewed his approach during his introductory press conference. "First, I'll do a lot—a lot—of listening. To the staff here, about the way they see the team now, about the players that are under contract, and about all of the upcoming decisions that are coming in the draft and in free agency," he said.

Hinkie doesn't reveal any of his cards upon first encounter; he hardly suggests he's even holding a hand. He believed any parcel of information he sacrificed, in even the most casual conversation, could have detracted from the franchise's leverage in an upcoming transaction. "It wasn't his job to come in and sit down with us and drink wine and tell jokes," says Aaron McKie, a Sixers assistant coach.

The executive made no initial efforts to restructure the Sixers' scouting strategy. When Philadelphia's owners purchased the 76ers in 2011, the group conducted a statistical analysis that re-selected the previous 10 NBA drafts. Ranking each prospect by their ultimate production over their NBA careers, the study calculated Philadelphia had extracted the highest value per pick over the entire decade. Longtime talent evaluators Courtney Witte and Tony DiLeo played major roles in selecting Jrue Holiday 17th in 2009. Moe Harkless and Nikola Vučević, shipped in Philadelphia's eventual trade package for Andrew Bynum, were also drafted later in the first round.

And while Bynum never dressed for the franchise, his degenerative knees and pricey contract would be mercifully wiped from the Sixers' books when he reached free agency on July 1, four days after the 2013 draft. More than $15 million in cap space awaited, and DiLeo once expected a promotion to team president as a reward. Managing partner Joshua Harris even promised the job to DiLeo in late March. "Everyone just assumed it was going to be his," says Tony Dutt, Jrue Holiday's agent at the time.

Yet the morning of Friday, May 10, DiLeo received a phone call saying Philadelphia was going in another direction. Harris hired Hinkie as the Sixers' new president of basketball operations and general manager that afternoon. "I felt terrible for him," says Sixers center Lavoy Allen, who played at Temple with DiLeo's son.

Ownership retained Courtney Witte, Philadelphia's longtime director of player personnel, and former Sixers president Rod Thorn, still with the franchise in an advisory role, as part of Hinkie's early operations. The afternoon of the draft, Hinkie summoned both executives to his office. Sachin Gupta, a former Rockets staffer he trusted as his right-hand, sat at Hinkie's side. Gupta had originally mastered the intricacies of the NBA's collective bargaining agreement while coding ESPN.com's famous online trade machine as an engineer for the website.

Hinkie began the meeting giving Witte and Thorn each a massive binder overflowing with data and intel on each 2013 prospect. That's when they learned of Hinkie's agreed-in-principle Holiday swap with New Orleans. Not only would Philadelphia acquire the Pelicans' sixth pick, but also New Orleans' 2014 first-round pick as well. Hinkie cautioned the information was not permitted to leave the room, and that Witte and Thorn would rejoin him and Gupta in the president's office during the draft while the rest of Philadelphia's staffers remained in a connected conference room, separated from his office by a doorway similar to adjoining hotel suites.

Noel was absolutely a prospect Hinkie was willing to exchange Holiday for. "There was this sense that we got this discounted asset and we could afford to get him because we had the longest timeline in the league and leveraged our unique situation," says Aaron Barzilai, the early analytics mind now with Philadelphia. Barzilai and other Sixers staffers only learned of the trade while watching ESPN's draft broadcast from the adjacent room.

Hinkie had pulled the first block of many he planned to yank from the Sixers' wavering Jenga tower.

"That was crazy," Philadelphia swingman Evan Turner recalls.

"Evan and I texted each other like, 'Welp, this shit's over with,'" says Spencer Hawes, the Sixers center.

Swapping Holiday for a future pick and Noel, set to miss much of 2013–14 rehabbing his torn ACL, certainly sent a declarative message to the league at large.

After ESPN's broadcast announced the trade, a group message among the players Philadelphia still had under contract whirred to life. "Everyone was like, 'What the fuck is going on?'" guard Jason Richardson says.

Thaddeus Young was home in Memphis, watching the draft in his living room, expecting the only organization he'd ever played for to add another strong rotation piece. "You just traded our franchise player for somebody who is hurt right now?" Young recalls of his reaction. "I kinda thought I was gone after that."

Hinkie indeed made calls to evaluate Young's value on the trade market, as well as that of Turner and Hawes. The fickle reality also set in for the other two veterans, who continued messaging privately outside of the team's group text.

"We were just kind of, 'Welp, who's next?' Beginning of the end kind of thing," Hawes says.

Turner understood this was the business of professional basketball. "I didn't know Sam Hinkie from anything, and he didn't owe me anything," he says.

Word fully permeated rival front offices around the NBA. The Sixers were selling, attempting to acquire another 2013 first-round pick while still holding their own No. 11 selection. "That was kind of the signal like, this is where this team is going," longtime Brooklyn Nets assistant GM Bobby Marks says. "I don't think any of us really knew what the master plan for Sam was gonna be. But that was kind of the first inclination."

It served as Jrue Holiday's first notion as well. The All-Star was in the car, packed with family, heading to a Dodgers game in his hometown Los Angeles, when Hinkie rang. Hinkie apologized the two had never met in person, but expressed his belief in Holiday's continued emergence nonetheless. It was simply business. "You just take the call," Holiday says. He dialed his wife after getting off the line. Holiday told Lauren, a champion U.S. women's national team soccer player, she could end her house shopping in Philadelphia that evening.

Holiday's next call went to Turner. "Evan wasn't too happy," Holiday remembers. "We definitely thought that we'd be backcourt mates for our careers." In the background, Holiday's brothers began reading off the Pelicans' roster. New Orleans of course featured the immensely talented Anthony Davis. After an entire season of hoping to play with an All-Star center, Holiday found solace in his new pick-and-roll partnership as their car sped down the freeway. "I think, quickly, I realized this is kind of how it goes for some people," Holiday says. NBA transactions don't stop for anyone.

"The challenge in front of us is not for the faint of heart," Hinkie had cautioned during his introductory presser. And with Noel finally off the board, the seventh pick of the 2013 NBA Draft put another franchise in transition, Sacramento, on the clock.

Vivek Ranadivé spearheaded a new ownership group that acquired the Kings from the Maloof family at the end of May. It took until June 16 before Ranadivé hired Denver executive Pete D'Alessandro to lead Sacramento's front office, but the tech mogul believed he'd found the Kings' own analytics acolyte. Bald and bespectacled, standing under 6-foot, D'Alessandro looked the part of a new-age basketball executive even more than Sam Hinkie. He forayed into the sport as a video coordinator at St. John's before working seven years at a DC-based sports agency. D'Alessandro joined the Golden State Warriors' front office next in 2004 and was elevated to assistant general manager by 2007, boasting a reputation for mastering the league's complicated salary cap restrictions. Ranadivé then granted D'Alessandro the opportunity to run his own team after a successful stint in Denver.

The seventh pick in the 2013 draft marked D'Alessandro's first high-profile decision as a general manager. If all went to plan, he prepared to select Lehigh product C.J. McCollum. The senior guard had recently recovered from a fractured foot, but McCollum notably led a stunning upset over Duke in the NCAA men's basketball tournament a season prior. He proceeded to visit with 10 franchises eager to check the status of that foot before the draft, even venturing to Sacramento twice for group workouts with the Kings. "He was really impressive," says Chris Jent, then a Sacramento assistant coach. "We needed shooting. That was definitely the emphasis."

When McCollum had his first individual workout in Philadelphia, he flashed his full skill set and then some. "When you think of a Lehigh basketball player, you would think that this kid was gonna come in and be shy and just to himself," says Aaron McKie, the Philly assistant coach. "Just right off the bat, you could tell this kid had personality and could flat-out play."

McCollum carried himself like a future franchise focal point during his time in Sacramento as well. Only one caveat remained in D'Alessandro's plan. Should Ben McLemore still be available at No. 7, Kansas' freshman would be the Kings' pick instead of McCollum. McLemore had struggled mightily during his workouts for the Magic and the Suns. He appeared out of shape to some and looked lethargic to most. Rumor suggested he arrived late to one workout and even forgot to bring sneakers to his visit in Phoenix. Even still, the possibility of McLemore's slide excited D'Alessandro's front office.

McLemore was once considered 2013's top prospect for several reasons. He packaged a gorgeous shooting stroke some scouts compared to that of Ray Allen, the legendary marksman, with elite athleticism and the beginnings of an off-the-dribble attack. And while McLemore ultimately slipped further down the draft than Nerlens Noel, he sat calmly for well over an hour after Cleveland chose Anthony Bennett. "I just knew my time was gonna come," he says. "I stayed patient. I didn't get nervous." Once Noel came off the board at No. 6, Sacramento officials erupted with cheers. Kings brass ecstatically nabbed McLemore over McCollum, believing Sacramento acquired the draft's highest-upside perimeter prospect to pair with rising center DeMarcus Cousins.

In the bowels of Barclays Center, McLemore followed the selected prospects on an hours-long media tour winding throughout the arena. Hysteria around Noel's fall, and Philadelphia's about-face into a full-scale rebuild, underscored most of the evening's unfolding drama. Noel still wore a Pelicans hat, waiting for the trade to become official, unsure of his true destination and new teammates. "I missed celebrating with my family, just sitting back there not really knowing what's up," Noel says. "It really [puts a damper] on your excitement." What appears on television as a glossy, seamless event can be a tiresome circus behind the scenes. When Noel at last reached the press conference podium to meet assembled reporters, finally wearing a 76ers cap, he was asked about being traded to Philadelphia, and the center mistakenly remarked how excited he was to play alongside Jrue Holiday.

All the while, pick No. 11 inched closer. Philadelphia scouts situated outside Sam Hinkie's office draft room hoped to possibly add McCollum, perhaps the versatile point guard of the future, to replace Holiday almost as quickly as he was dealt. They watched Detroit pass on the Lehigh star for Kentavious Caldwell-Pope at No. 8 and Trey Burke go to Minnesota at No. 9, although the Timberwolves soon swapped Burke to the Utah Jazz for pick Nos. 14 and 21. Burke going as high as No. 9 shocked Portland's front office, impatiently waiting to pick at No. 10.

Trail Blazers officials spent all week fretting their target wouldn't still be available. But hearing Burke's name, their war room exhaled a collective sigh of relief. Not only did Burke's shoulder injury worry some teams, Portland had projected him far below their own choice—where McCollum still waited as David Stern declared the Blazers were on the clock. Portland point guard Damian Lillard and a large contingent of fans had emphatically greeted McCollum at the airport before his pre-draft visit. Now the reigning Rookie of the Year texted McCollum, "Uh oh!"

Lillard and McCollum were already bonded. Aside from starring at smaller schools, both players suffered long-term injuries during college. Lillard first documented his rehab process at Weber State in a brief video series. And after McCollum's foot landed him on the shelf, he devoured each of Lillard's clips over multiple watches. Portland envisioned them sharing an NBA backcourt for years. Knowing of the Blazers' affinity for McCollum, Sam Hinkie had readily prepared for McCollum landing in Oregon.

The binders Philadelphia's new president handed Courtney Witte and Rod Thorn that afternoon included endless outcomes stemming from each pick before No. 11. At No. 7, for example, Hinkie and Sachin Gupta predicted several of Sacramento's most likely selections, and what those possible picks would trigger at Nos. 8, 9, and 10. Hinkie and Gupta had pages of decision trees continuing throughout the first round, detailing numerous trade frameworks for Philadelphia to acquire more future draft capital. Hinkie at one point called Brooklyn offering a chance to move off expensive contracts, happy to eat salary at the cost of the Nets' No. 22 pick. Brooklyn, however, declined.

He sprang into action bartering with other teams. As the draft ticked onward, sometimes Hinkie or Gupta would poke out from behind the adjoining door and call individual personnel into Hinkie's office for last-minute clarifications. Hinkie held a phone to each ear at one point, conducting a three-way call manually with a mobile and a landline. His tie was loosened, sleeves rolled up his forearms. "I was like, 'This motherfucker is Jerry Maguire,'" says a Sixers staffer invited into Hinkie's office at that moment. It's said during a finance undergraduate class at the University of Oklahoma, Hinkie once satisfied a negotiation presentation requirement by ordering roughly 50 pizzas to a filled lecture hall and convincing the delivery guy to hand over the stack of pies free of charge.

Owner Joshua Harris' young son sat outside in Philly's larger quarters, repeatedly chiming the Sixers should draft 7-foot-1 French center Rudy Gobert 11th, despite his projection toward the end of the first round. "Everyone laughed at him," says Aaron Barzilai, Philly's incumbent analytics czar. While the gathered scouts once hoped Philly could land McCollum, only those inside Hinkie's office knew full well they were focused on gangly, 6-foot-5 point guard Michael Carter-Williams at No. 11. "It was incredibly tight," Barzilai says.

Veteran Philly staffers felt uncomfortable sitting in the dark. The old regime voted on a consensus big board about a month before draft night. They ranked prospects from 1 to 60, listed the order on a giant white board, and reconvened every two or three days to make subtle tweaks. When their pick arrived, the Sixers simply selected their highest-ranked player still available. That process worked systematically for over a decade. And while Hinkie encouraged group debates throughout the weeks before the 2013 draft, he only participated by asking questions. Hinkie and Gupta never revealed their opinions to the rest of the room. "They were pretty cautious about biasing the group," Barzilai says.

Hinkie did lob his queries with noticeable enthusiasm. He polled staffers hoping to make the group's preparations more efficient and even sought different ways to set up Philly's conference room to better facilitate debate. Hinkie, after all, wore a white dress shirt, blazer, and jeans most days to streamline his decision-making each morning.

Many Sixers officials felt empowered by the executive's listening. He worked at the team's meager offices inside the Philadelphia College of Osteopathic Medicine until midnight each evening, ordering Chick-fil-A catering for whoever still burned their candle. He'd return to work by 5:00

AM and intentionally sit next to a different person that day, inquiring about their family.

Proximity played a key factor in developing his kinship with Gupta back in Houston, where they originally worked in adjacent cubicles. Now they made the second move of Hinkie's reign in Philadelphia. David Stern indeed strolled back to the podium and announced Carter-Williams' name at No. 11. He had led Syracuse to the Final Four that March, and advanced defensive metrics projected the supersized ball handler as a potential NBA lockdown guard.

As the draft continued in Brooklyn, trade chatter hung in the air. At No. 12, Oklahoma City selected Pittsburgh center Steven Adams. The pick originally belonged to the Toronto Raptors, but arrived in OKC via Houston as part of the James Harden blockbuster Hinkie helped swing the previous October. And as Stern announced the Dallas Mavericks were on the clock at No. 13, the Atlanta Hawks ramped up efforts to finalize their own deal to acquire a potential franchise-altering phenom.

Atlanta general manager Danny Ferry dreamed of landing Greek teenager Giannis Antetokounmpo for quite some time, despite the prospect's background leaving other front offices far less convinced. The son of Nigerian immigrants, Antetokounmpo and his four brothers hustled bootleg sunglasses, hats, and bags on the street while their father picked up whatever work he could as a handyman and their mother babysat. Eviction notices forced the family from place to place. Giannis and his brother Thanasis, two years his senior, would race to the basketball court at their nearby park looking for moments of respite.

A coach at the local academy one day stumbled across the duo. And struck by their raw athleticism—each bounce toward the rim a burst of obvious potential—he invited them to join his academy. By 2011, the two brothers launched their pro careers with Filathlitikos' junior division club teams. Word quickly spread of the 6-foot-9, 18-year-old athletic wonder Giannis had become. Personnel from NBA teams soon packed Filathlitikos' tiny practice gym to scout a possible first-round pick.

Even still, many NBA talent evaluators were skeptical of Antetokounmpo's level of competition. Grainy footage appeared to highlight the prospect galloping past defenders half his size. Daryl Morey gave his film and information to Houston's analytics interns for evaluation. But the Hawks, and Danny Ferry in particular, truly championed Antetokounmpo's talent level. Ferry thought Giannis' inherent vision spelled future stardom, regardless of whom he'd played against. You either see the right pass, the right play, or you don't.

Atlanta pleaded with Antetokounmpo's representation to hold their prospect from all basketball events as early as four months before June's draft. If they couldn't keep the hype around Antetokounmpo subdued enough, the Hawks believed he could have risen as high as the top five. Ferry was ready to promise a selection at Atlanta's first pick, which became No. 17, so long as they were able to bring Antetokounmpo to Atlanta for a physical.

The Philadelphia 76ers also sent a handful of scouts to Greece. Yet when Sam Hinkie and Courtney Witte visited, the situation quickly devolved. Witte got into a heated exchange with one of Antetokounmpo's handlers. He felt like the Greek agents wanted all NBA executives to shower praise upon their client and offer assurances like Ferry had. "I'm not putting up with that shit. It's bullshit," Witte sternly told the handler.

The Hawks did manage to bring the Greek wunderkind for a visit in Atlanta under cloak and dagger. When Antetokounmpo walked through Philips Arena, lights half-on, his eyes widened before welling with tears, envisioning his game taking such a stage after once haggling on the street. "It was pretty amazing," says one Hawks staffer. "It gave you goosebumps."

Atlanta didn't want to just fly the kid into town and put him up in a hotel, as per common practice. Instead, Ferry hosted Giannis and Thanasis at his home, ordering in chicken and pasta from a favorite Italian spot and watching his children interact with, hopefully, the next franchise player of the Hawks. The final step: Antetokounmpo's physical not only came back clean, but Atlanta's doctors said his growth plates were "wide open," and suggested the long-armed teen might not yet be done growing. Antetokounmpo's visit couldn't have gone any better.

Milwaukee, though, was prepared to select Antetokounmpo 15th, should he still be on the board, regardless of hosting him for an official visit. Some wondered if Larry Drew, Atlanta's former coach and the newly hired head man in Milwaukee, had tipped the Bucks of his former employer's interest. But Milwaukee had sent a contingent to Greece. "We just kind of stayed close to the vest with him," GM John Hammond says. "Had we overexposed ourselves, we may not have gotten him." The executive recalls Antetokounmpo's agents never contacted Milwaukee again, so they, too, remained silent, keeping their zeal secret. "This guy could be special just based on his extraordinary length, his extraordinary big hands, his extraordinary great feel for the game that he had," Hammond remembers thinking.

Fear of losing his dream prospect emboldened Ferry to call Dallas as time waned for the Mavericks' decision at No. 13. OKC rebuffed Ferry's offers to move into No. 12, before the Thunder selected Steven Adams. At the 14th selection, Utah had already agreed to trade that pick and No. 21 to Minnesota in exchange for the rights to Trey Burke at No. 9. Milwaukee posed a serious threat to swipe Antetokounmpo two slots before the Hawks. "I know Atlanta was a team that was obviously extremely interested in him and had him on their radar, to say the least," says Hammond.

Ferry phoned Dallas one last time. He pitched numerous trade packages. The Hawks held the No. 18 choice in addition to No. 17, but in a draft widely considered to be a weak class, Ferry's best offers never got the attention of the Mavericks. Dallas maintained No. 13 wasn't for sale. So when news broke the Mavericks actually sent Kelly Olynyk to Boston after drafting the Gonzaga big 13th, Hawks officials sunk inside Atlanta's war room. "Everyone was disappointed," says the former Hawks executive. "Some of the front office couldn't think of what was next."

While Atlanta mourned, Utah selected Shabazz Muhammad at No. 14 as part of the swap with Minnesota. Muhammad had not received a green room invite, but the UCLA product later strolled onstage to shake David Stern's hand after the commissioner announced the 20th pick. Travel complications prevented Muhammad from arriving on time, but he desperately wanted to greet Stern in his final NBA draft. After 30 years as commissioner,

Stern was set to retire in February 2014, giving way to his successor, deputy commissioner Adam Silver.

Back at No. 15, the Bucks came on the clock with Milwaukee's best-case scenario coming to fruition; Atlanta hadn't jumped to grab the Greek phenom. "With the 15th pick," Stern began, "the Milwaukee Bucks select…" He paused, appearing to ready his much-rehearsed pronunciation, "Giannis Antetokounmpo!" The young prospect had flown to New York on Wednesday from his Atlanta visit the day before. He also hadn't been invited to the green room, but cameras circled Antetokounmpo at his seat among fans in the Barclays Center stands. He was now a Buck, with Thanasis by his side, big brother proudly waving their national flag as David Stern announced their last name for the world to learn.

"We struggled a lot in the past to have a better life," Antetokounmpo told reporters that evening, a thick accent blanketing each word. "And I think in the past, make me sad. And now that I get drafted in the NBA, for sure we're going to have a better life." He declared his immediate commitment to join Milwaukee, unlike many European prospects who were drafted at the time and then stashed overseas. The practice both allowed players to develop their skills on another team's dime and provided present-day cap flexibility for the NBA club.

Another international prospect sure enough came off the board at No. 16. Boston selected Brazilian center Lucas Nogueira to trade Dallas in exchange for Kelly Olynyk, who himself hailed from Canada. The Hawks regrouped to select German point guard Dennis Schröder at No. 17. Utah soon after completed its trade with Minnesota by nabbing Louisville center Gorgui Dieng, a product of Senegal, at No. 21. A total of 12 overseas players were selected in the opening round, setting a new NBA record.

"We've had to explain to our international audience that the 'boo' is an American sign of respect," Stern joked. He'd egged on the crowd's antics all night. And by his final appearance at the podium to reveal pick No. 30, fans rose to salute the commissioner. "Stop it, you're ruining all the fun," he cooed. Adam Silver emerged to relieve Stern and announce the second round, but the deputy commissioner prevented his predecessor from quickly walking off. That's when Hakeem Olajuwon slipped out from backstage.

TWO

He wore a dapper tuxedo and red bow tie, mirroring his draft night outfit from 1984, when Olajuwon marked the first pick Stern ever announced as commissioner.

Thirty years later, player and commissioner were still as connected as franchises had continued tanking around the league.

THREE

Doc Rivers knew.

Standing in the silence sweeping Boston's somber locker room, the Celtics' Game 6 loss to New York not only ended their 2013 postseason but palpably closed their championship window. Rivers, Boston's head coach, knew full well that Danny Ainge eyed a plummet in the standings—similar to when Rivers endured 18 straight losses coaching a miserable 2006–07 tanking effort under the direction of Ainge's front office.

The Celtics lingered among the league's basement that season eying greater odds at the No. 1 pick in the 2007 NBA Draft. Fans were spotted in the stands wearing paper bags over their heads. But lottery fortune evaded Boston once again, as the Celtics emerged with June's fifth pick. Ainge forged forward nonetheless. He shipped No. 5 along with Wally Szczerbiak, Delonte West, and a 2008 second-rounder for All-Star guard Ray Allen, perhaps the greatest three-point shooter in NBA history, plus young forward Glen Davis. Ainge returned next to talks with Minnesota lead executive Kevin McHale. With Allen now joining the Celtics' franchise face Paul Pierce, Ainge sold Timberwolves All-Star Kevin Garnett on forming a formidable Big Three rivaling Boston's original fabled troika of Larry Bird, McHale himself, and Robert Parish.

Garnett inked a three-year, $51 million extension with the Celtics once the blockbuster trade was processed. In a matter of weeks, Ainge had morphed a sullen roster into the East favorite. "We were a bunch of A-type-personality guys," Ray Allen says.

A powerful brotherhood formed in Boston. "We got into arguments, we got into fights, we wrestled. We were a team full of barbarians. We were like *300*. It was us against the world, straight out," Kevin Garnett says. "If you ask anybody from that team, we felt like we were straight-up warriors and straight-up Greek Gods and Goddesses and all this other shit."

Boston raced out to an 8–0 start and finished the 2007–08 regular season 66–16—a remarkable 42-win improvement from the previous year's slog. The Celtics then marched their way through the Eastern Conference and defeated the Lakers in six games to capture the franchise's 17th banner.

Five years later, Boston's outlook appeared far murkier. The Celtics didn't roster a healthy, in-his-prime alpha like Pierce to build around. Age truly derailed the Celtics' 2013 playoff push, but losing All-Star point guard Rajon Rondo to a torn ACL that January had already clouded his and the team's overall future. There was no off-season makeover that could yield an instant contender. Bottoming out made even more sense than in 2007. "That was the only direction that the organization had to go in," says Courtney Lee, a veteran Celtics guard.

Boston had actually discussed trading Pierce to Brooklyn the previous fall, after Ray Allen departed in 2012 free agency, spurning his own Big Three counterparts to help Miami's trio instead. The Celtics escalated Pierce conversations once more before February's trade deadline after Rondo tore his right ACL, but Boston fell short of reaching an agreement with Brooklyn yet again. "I think they got cold feet at the time to move Pierce, but it would have cost you half of the package of what happened four months later," says Bobby Marks, the Nets' longtime assistant general manager.

In late May, Celtics assistant GM Mike Zarren phoned Marks to rehash their negotiations. Now the 37-year-old Garnett debated retirement as Boston's championship footing continued to crumble. If the Celtics didn't move Pierce during the 2013 off-season, Ainge's front office might never have received the assets necessary for an effective rebuild.

Doc Rivers whiffed the smoke billowing from that fire. Rivers couldn't withstand another painful rebuild like 2006–07, regardless of the 2008 payoff. With one championship ring already on his finger, he yearned to keep coaching a contender. And while Rivers' preference initially irked his longtime counterpart in Ainge, the executive eventually collaborated to find an outcome that would benefit both coach and team.

At one point, the Celtics and Clippers discussed a megadeal that included Rivers and Garnett for center DeAndre Jordan and two first-round picks, but the league's collective bargaining agreement bars teams from trading players and coaches in the same transaction. After weeks of haggling, Los Angeles surrendered an unprotected 2015 first-rounder on June 23 in exchange for Rivers, just four days before the 2013 NBA Draft. "Now that was weird," says Celtics forward Jeff Green. "I mean, you never hear of a coach getting traded."

Most of Green's teammates were stunned. "I was just like, wait...you can trade coaches?" says Jared Sullinger, another Boston big.

Relative precedent existed. After Stan Van Gundy resigned in Miami and became Orlando's next head coach, the Magic sent a 2007 second-round pick to the Heat and offered the choice of swapping 2008 first-round picks. That deal only occurred, however, because Miami maintained Van Gundy's rights throughout the remaining year of his contract. Boston plainly moved their head coach like any impending free agent player on an expiring contract. And Ainge expertly recouped future draft capital in return. Two days later, talks intensified as well with the Nets to move not only Pierce but also Garnett to Brooklyn. The rebuild Rivers hoped to avoid was well underway.

While Boston fell to New York, Brooklyn also faltered in its opening-round matchup against Chicago. Nets management still faced the lofty expectations ownership first assigned in 2010, demanding a contender for the franchise's move from New Jersey to Brooklyn. "That kind of laid the foundation for the Boston talks," Bobby Marks says. "But it really did not pick up until, I would say, a week before the draft."

Brooklyn's interest in Garnett only sweetened the opportunity. "That deal started small and then it got big," says Billy King, then Brooklyn's general manager.

Mike Zarren continually asked for more compensation in the form of draft picks, and Nets ownership kept green lighting each version of the trade more costly than the last. "Our mindset was always about Miami," Bobby Marks says. The Spurs nearly defeated the Heat in the NBA Finals had it not been for Ray Allen's clutch three-pointer in Game 6. "We had felt Miami was in a bit of a decline," Marks says, "and the opportunity to catch LeBron and that group was there for the taking."

Celtics and Nets officials went to sleep Wednesday night confident in the framework of a massive blockbuster. As Thursday's draft loomed, both Pierce and Garnett appeared headed down I-95 to New York. The only work left: Zarren needed to get the notoriously cagey Garnett to waive his no-trade clause. The Nets even pleaded for Pierce to help contact his Hall of Fame teammate. "That day was such a freaking whirlwind," Zarren recalls. "That was one of the craziest days of my career."

The trade wouldn't become official until July, but its terms were reported early during the first round of that June's draft. News of Boston's megadeal with Brooklyn shook the NBA landscape as loudly as Ainge's 2008 trade for Garnett. While Sam Hinkie pulled the rug out from another regime's mediocre playoff contender in Philadelphia, Ainge had imploded the remains of a champion he once built. And either way, two of the NBA's most storied franchises were publicly punting on the upcoming season with obvious eyes toward the 2014 NBA Draft.

The Nets, meanwhile, celebrated their haul inside their Barclays Center war room, as the draft event unfolded on the nearby arena floor. Once Garnett agreed to the trade, Brooklyn finally added him and Pierce to a starting lineup already featuring three All-Star-caliber talents. In exchange, Boston received a package of players that brought significant financial flexibility, and a staggering surplus of future Nets draft ammo.

Brooklyn surrendered unprotected first-round picks in 2014, 2016, and 2018, and what would ultimately become a fateful dagger: the Celtics also received the right to swap first-rounders with the Nets in 2015 and 2017. It was shocking to some how wealthy teams, willing to pay, could so easily wield draft capital to land stars. If Brooklyn's experiment flopped, Boston suddenly loomed as a dangerous candidate to rebound back into contention. The valuation of first-round picks across NBA front offices immediately skyrocketed. "Our trade with Brooklyn scared a lot of people," Zarren says.

Ainge continued dealing throughout draft night. While Atlanta bad-gered Dallas for the Mavericks' No. 13 pick, hoping to position itself to nab Antetokounmpo, Boston sent No. 16 and two 2014 second-round selections to move up for Gonzaga big man Kelly Olynyk. Ainge knew Dallas prioritized salary cap space for July's upcoming free agency period, so sliding down three spots would pay less guaranteed money to Dallas' rookie, and Boston's two 2014 seconds wouldn't impact the Mavericks' books for another year—unlike Atlanta's offer of picks Nos. 17 and 18 bringing two more guaranteed contracts immediately onto Dallas' payroll.

Olynyk enamored Celtics staffers during a three-on-three pre-draft workout with Boston, scorching the nets in their Waltham practice facil-ity with his pretty shooting stroke. As a data-driven emphasis on firing three-pointers swept the league, 7-footers like Olynyk who could space the floor grew increasingly valuable.

As the second round approached, Ainge's front office worked to swing yet another deal amid an already frenetic evening across the NBA. Not includ-ing Boston's megaswap with Brooklyn, a total of 14 trades sparked chaos and confusion throughout the 2013 NBA Draft. And Sam Hinkie's keen-to-deal Sixers were also due back on the clock at No. 35.

Hinkie nearly sent Evan Turner to Phoenix for the Suns' No. 30 pick to close the first round. Freshman guard Archie Goodwin, Nerlens Noel's Kentucky teammate, wowed Philly coaches during his Sixers workout. "He could run, jump, good size, good length on him, and he was young," assis-tant coach Aaron McKie says. "When I see guys like that, I think right away, 'This kid could develop into something special.'" Goodwin remained on the board at No. 29. Yet instead of moving their 30th pick to Philadelphia, the Suns traded up one slot to nab the springy guard for themselves, equally enamored by his raw potential. Hinkie just the same flipped the pages in his draft binder. Plenty of opportunity stood abound.

He phoned the agent for Robert Covington, a 6-foot-7 forward from Tennessee State, wondering if the career 42.2 percent three-point shooter would accept a four-year, non-guaranteed, minimum-salary contract if the

Sixers drafted him at No. 35. The Chicago Bulls also rang his agent, Chris Patrick, offering the chance to nab Covington 49th if he agreed to play the 2013–14 season overseas. After years of teams drafting and stashing international prospects who could maybe, one day, develop into NBA-caliber players, front offices were widely exploring that route for American-born prospects.

The Mavericks took Mike Muscala at No. 44 before trading him to Atlanta, but he first played in Spain. Erick Green, taken by the Jazz at No. 46 and traded to Denver, headed to Siena of the Italian League. James Ennis, whom the Heat acquired from Atlanta after he was selected at No. 50, played 2013 in Australia with the Perth Wildcats. At No. 53, the Celtics managed to swing their final trade of the night with the idea of stashing their selection overseas as well; Boston sent cash to the Indiana Pacers in order to acquire Colorado State center Colton Iverson.

The Celtics, evidently invested in Iverson's growth, simply lacked front-court minutes to spare that season. Like Hinkie in Philadelphia, sending Garnett and Pierce to Brooklyn merely marked the first strike of Boston's intended rebuild. The Celtics hoped to showcase their other veteran players throughout 2013–14 for more potential trades, netting even more future draft resources. Plus they would prioritize growing the team's lottery pick, Kelly Olynyk.

"With Colton, we think he has the capability to be an elite rebounder in this league," Celtics director of player personnel Austin Ainge said that year. "Unfortunately we just didn't have the roster flexibility to make that work." Iverson inevitably delayed his Boston career to crash the boards in Turkey. Some European clubs even pay for American players' housing, replete with a private chef and a leased luxury car.

Despite the emerging trend, Robert Covington's camp wasn't interested in deferring his chances to play in the NBA. But his agent, Chris Patrick, still declined Hinkie's contract offer for the 35th pick. He believed Covington could draw more guaranteed money on the open market after the draft concluded.

Hinkie pivoted quickly. There were more calls to be made. Philadelphia ultimately selected Glen Rice Jr. at No. 35, a bouncy forward with NBA pedigree. He'd spent the previous season with Houston's D-League affiliate—basketball's burgeoning version of baseball's farm system—after being dismissed from Georgia Tech for behavioral issues. But Rice marked a high-upside, athletic prospect modern executives like Hinkie so clearly valued. If a team believed in his character, they were adding a young collegiate product that already experienced a bit of the professional ranks.

That gamble wasn't anything for Sixers brass to contemplate, however. Hinkie chose Rice knowing of Washington's interest in the prospect and soon shipped him to the Wizards for two selections later that evening. One of those picks, South Dakota State guard Nate Wolters, Hinkie immediately swapped with Milwaukee for No. 43 plus a 2014 second-round pick. And then Philadelphia traded that No. 43 pick, Providence's Ricky Ledo, to Dallas for another 2014 second-rounder. "It just kept going," says a Sixers official.

Hinkie leveraged key intel from rival front offices into greater draft assets. He relied on the same information he refused to reveal during Philadelphia's internal pre-draft debates. There would be no leaks from his organization. "Sam was very creative when it came to acquiring picks," Bucks general manager John Hammond says. "We did like Nate, we liked what he did in college as just a really tough guy who knew the game and could score."

Philly's maneuvering showcased the shrewd dealing Hinkie would deliver throughout his Sixers tenure, even on the most painstaking of margins. "If they could trade and get assets or future picks, they were going to do so," says a veteran Philadelphia staffer. "That's not normal draft behavior. I've never seen it predetermined that you're looking at acquiring all these future draft rights."

It was hard to argue with the evening's haul, even so. Hinkie pulled four of the draft's 14 trades, coming away with the rights to Nerlens Noel, at one point considered the unanimous top prospect; Michael Carter-Williams, another long athlete at point guard; and New Orleans' 2014 first-round pick. Philadelphia added two 2014 second-round selections as well, plus

Hinkie chose Oregon forward Arsalan Kazemi at No. 54, the other pick acquired from Washington for Glen Rice Jr. Negotiating his many deals over the phone, Hinkie's style impressed several onlooking Philly staffers who were occasionally invited into his office that evening. "He was aggressive," says one, "in a way that felt like the GM of a high-powered franchise should be."

Amid the bevy of activity, a report surfaced that Hinkie also tapped San Antonio Spurs player development expert Brett Brown as Philadelphia's new head coach. Team PR quickly denied the rumor, although internal damage had already been done. The assistants gathered within their coaches' office sat stunned inside the Sixers' rented portion of Philadelphia College of Osteopathic Medicine's athletic facility. Hinkie marched down the hall to apologize for any confusion. He couldn't have possibly hired Brown, the president assured. Hinkie was only beginning his expansive search for Philadelphia's vacancy, with former head coach Doug Collins having resigned in April.

Sixers assistant Michael Curry would get his fair shot. His defensive teachings were key in Philadelphia's 2012 playoff run. Hinkie already requested permission to meet Rockets assistants Kelvin Sampson and Chris Finch. He'd jetted from the NBA Draft Combine in Chicago to Indianapolis to meet with Pacers assistant Brian Shaw. In addition to Warriors assistant Mike Malone and Jazz assistant Jeff Hornacek, Hinkie also interviewed Hawks assistant Quin Snyder.

Philadelphia's president approached his job opening as an asset rather than a void, an opportunity to mine the brightest minds on benches around the NBA. "You've got nothing to lose except the cost of a plane flight and some time," says Spencer Breecker, a longtime agent for coaches and front office executives. Hinkie polled his staff for suggestions on candidates, welcoming a group brainstorm. Why not cast their net as wide as possible?

Aaron Barzilai, the holdover analytics staffer from Philly's previous regime, suggested Lloyd Pierce. They had overlapped in Memphis, and the young Grizzlies assistant impressed Barzilai on multiple fronts. Pierce probably wasn't ready to be a head coach but checked a lot of boxes for a future franchise figurehead. Once they finished an expansive list, Hinkie instructed his group to collect detailed background intel on the candidates. "That's Sam's whole M.O., right?" Barzilai says. "Leave no stone unturned, get as much information as possible and talk to as many people as possible, to really try and understand what makes them go and what kind of impact they're gonna have on your organization."

Hinkie even quizzed Jeremy Lin about Hawks assistant Kenny Atkinson. Lin and Atkinson had developed a close relationship during the guard's rapid star turn in New York, so Hinkie cold-called the Rockets point guard to conduct a lengthy conversation. They shared a level of familiarity from their previous season together in Houston, and Hinkie felt Lin would offer honest answers about Atkinson's strengths and weaknesses. "He had a lot of questions," Lin says. "He's very, very thorough."

Hinkie's Sixers weren't going to cut any corners. Philadelphia wouldn't sacrifice the quality of their decision-making for the sake of speed. "Ownership truly was driving a lot of that," says one early Hinkie hire. "Any sort of organizational leader is trying to develop a strategy and communicate that strategy relentlessly to people inside the organization."

Philly's new brain trust failed to share that vision externally, however. As July free agency began, a large portion of the Sixers' fan base longed for insight on the head coaching post that had been vacant since April. Local media swirled with impatience, demanding answers. What could possibly be taking so long to hire someone?

The Cavaliers hired Mike Brown in April. The Bucks went with former Hawks head coach Larry Drew in late May. A few days later, Atlanta had replaced Drew with Spurs assistant Mike Budenholzer. The Nets hired Jason Kidd before the draft. Even two interview candidates from the Sixers' list, Jazz assistant Jeff Hornacek and Warriors assistant Mike Malone, already agreed to coach Phoenix and Sacramento, respectively. No matter, Hinkie continued at his meticulous pace.

Spike Eskin, the program director at 94 WIP-FM, went on the Philadelphia sports talk station's morning show with curmudgeon host Angelo Cataldi to support the merits of Hinkie's lengthy process. The segment exploded into a heated debate crackling over radios across the Delaware Valley. Hinkie's long search began dividing the sand amongst Sixers faithful. "I think in some ways that started to bring together the group of people that supported Sam," Eskin says. "It showed the real difference between the people who were going to be in on this and the people who were going to write columns on what a sham this was." Boston, mind you, had already traded Doc Rivers and swiftly secured his replacement—all since Doug Collins resigned in Philadelphia.

Danny Ainge announced his hire of the 36-year-old Brad Stevens on July 3. The news emerged without even a prior whisper, stunning many around the NBA. Ainge, ownership, and assistant general manager Mike Zarren quietly met with Stevens and his wife, Tracy, while hushing any details of the meeting. The coach held a staunch loyalty to Butler University. Stevens recognized his Boston talks could ultimately stall, and where he'd be happy to remain at the university, he feared news of his NBA interest might upset his Butler players and derail recruiting efforts for future additions. "If this had gotten out, I think it very easily could have blown the situation," Ainge said at Stevens' introductory press conference.

Rival executives applauded Ainge's stealthy choice. Stevens fit naturally with Boston's longtime data-driven front office and he billed as a younger face to lead a rebuild full of recent college phenoms. Stevens piloted Butler's mid-major program to consecutive NCAA championship games in 2010 and 2011, supporting his film sessions with metrics from KenPom.com, a college analytics subscription website. He preached limiting Butler's offense to just 10 turnovers per game. When walking through scouts of upcoming opponents, Stevens could even recall foes' offensive and defensive ratings from memory, at specific spots on the floor, within particular play types.

Many college coaches before Stevens failed to survive at the NBA level. Boston had witnessed Rick Pitino fail to lead a winning season during his four-year Celtics stint after guiding Kentucky to the NCAA title in 1996. Ainge encouraged Celtics players to attend Stevens' presser and meet their new play caller. And Stevens wasted no time getting acclimated to his new surroundings. He invited Rajon Rondo to join his family for dinner during their first night in their new home. "We just went from there, started talking about the game, where we see ourselves as a team and where we were going to go in the future," says Rondo.

Stevens also visited Jeff Green in D.C., where the former Georgetown product made his off-season home. They sat in Green's living room discussing their basketball backgrounds and philosophies, finding commonalities between their two families. "Brad's a great guy, knows his craft, loves studying his craft," Green says. "You know, it was just all new for him."

Ainge retained two of Doc Rivers' assistants, Jamie Young and Jay Larranaga, hoping the veteran coaches could aid Stevens' adjustment to the NBA. Boston planned to particularly rely on Larranaga, only Sam Hinkie had requested to interview the assistant for Philadelphia's own head coaching vacancy. Stevens would start each week in part asking Larranaga if he'd heard any word from the Sixers. But after their initial conversations that July, Hinkie had curiously gone dark. "It was stressful on Brad," Larranaga says. "I just kept saying, 'Oh, well maybe I'm not involved anymore.'"

Larranaga had met with Hinkie one evening during the NBA's Summer League in Las Vegas, sharing dinner for nearly five hours. To highlight his rise up the Rockets' organization, Philadelphia's new president recounted one of his early studies. It turns out the winner of a jump ball at the start of regulation has no real impact on that game's outcome, but Hinkie uncovered the tipoff that opens an overtime period showed a significant correlation to winning those extra five minutes. "As a young person in management, that kind of helped his credibility," Larranaga says.

Any serious conversation about the Sixers' vacancy required blunt honesty. Just like in Boston, losing would not be a requirement; Philadelphia wouldn't intentionally drop games on a nightly basis, but losses were an absolute side effect of trading the team's best players like Jrue Holiday for greater draft ammo. Losing, garnering greater lottery odds, and then netting a top draft pick, they'd select high-upside prospects and mold them into champions. "That sort of flow chart was something that was talked about a lot and everyone in the organization sort of understood," says one early Sixers hire under Hinkie.

The executive wouldn't be successful, however, without the right head coach to develop those young talents into superstars. "His humility also struck me," Larranaga says. "It wasn't that, 'Hey, we're gonna get a bunch of picks and just outwork everybody and we're gonna know who the best player is in the draft.' He just said the draft is really hard and everybody's going to make mistakes, so we just want to have as many darts to throw at the dartboard as possible."

Hinkie also treated Chicago Bulls assistant Adrian Griffin to dinner in Las Vegas. Griffin feels they sparked a quick connection; he was drawn to Hinkie's approach. "It was almost like he had a master plan going that maybe no one else knew at the time," Griffin says. "He kind of reminded me of a left handed player that you're probably not used to playing against. Just a little unorthodox."

Griffin is the son of a minister and worked toward a PhD in organizational leadership. Hinkie saw how that through line could benefit a future NBA head man. "I think he really appreciates that aspect of coaching, not just the Xs and Os," Griffin says.

These interviews typically provide executives a glimpse behind enemy franchises' walls. They'd ask Griffin, for example, about the Bulls' schemes or practice structure, prying for valuable intel. Hinkie was far more invested in understanding Griffin's personal philosophies—not Chicago's—on basketball and in life. How would he lead a group of men into a battle on top of hardwood?

Hinkie described a specific hypothetical disagreement between management and a head coach and sought how Griffin would respond in that situation. By the meal's end, he even hinted at Griffin possibly joining his front office in some capacity should the coaching decision not land on him.

Hinkie then went silent, just as he had with Jay Larranaga. Throughout the summer he could go months between first meeting a prospective Sixers addition before contacting them again. And Hinkie's search for a unique basketball leader in particular, Sixers owners agreed, deserved a longer undertaking than usual. A coaching job for developing teenagers into dominant players, despite collecting nightly losses, called for a man who could maintain such a difficult balance.

Still, as August began, even Hinkie's staunchest advocates tired of defending Philadelphia's lingering vacancy against local pessimists. "Knives were out," says Michael Levin, a Hinkie supporter who oversaw the popular 76ers blog *LibertyBallers.com*. Naysayers accused Hinkie and Sixers ownership of incompetence. Trust had already eroded among many fans following the fiasco that was acquiring Andrew Bynum—and the season of his curious medical updates that followed. Bynum's No. 33 jersey now made for an ironic fashion statement.

Bynum ended that off-season in Germany undergoing a platelet-rich plasma therapy on his knees, one that former Lakers teammate Kobe Bryant recently benefited from but was not yet performed in the United States. Despite helping Los Angeles win two championships, Bynum missed scores of games having dislocated, torn, hyper-extended, and bruised one or both of his knees. Even though Bynum played in 60 games in 2011–12 and started in the All-Star Game, the treatment seemed prudent, ideally able to prevent the inevitable decline of Bynum's knee cartilage. Instead it kept the Sixers' splashy acquisition out of training camp.

Philadelphia soon announced his practice debut would be delayed three more weeks. "I personally saw the MRIs before Bynum went and then I saw them after Bynum went," says a former Sixers staffer. "It was clear that procedure did not have the positive effect that Kobe's did. It had the reverse."

While Bynum sat deep into that fall, Philadelphia ownership first met with Sam Hinkie. Hiring your own front office leader is all the rage as a new NBA team owner. Wyc Grousbeck and Steve Pagliuca picked Danny Ainge in 2003, Leslie Alexander swiped Daryl Morey in 2007, just as Vivek Ranadivé minted Pete D'Alessandro Sacramento's general manager in 2013.

Hinkie's business background streamlined a fluent conversation with Joshua Harris and David Blitzer. The Rockets exec spoke of optimizing probability and predictive data within NBA team-building decisions. Houston notably scooped contributors on inexpensive contracts like Shane Battier and Luis Scola. The Rockets also boasted a remarkable draft record, first identifying sharpshooter Steve Novak with the 32nd pick in 2006. The following June, Houston nabbed future 10-year veteran Aaron Brooks with the 26th pick and dealt cash with a 2008 second-round pick to obtain forward Carl Landry, the 31st choice, who would go on to play nine seasons of his own. There were several others to brag about.

When Hinkie diagnosed the Sixers' present cap sheet, he audaciously projected Philly's trade package might have overvalued Andrew Bynum. Hinkie predicted adding Bynum could actually decrease the Sixers' expected win total. Harris and Blitzer, of course, opposed such a notion. "We felt like [Bynum] was the guy to potentially get us over the top," Sixers assistant Aaron McKie says.

But Harris remained intrigued by the Rockets' number-cruncher. The owners further met Boston assistant general manager Mike Zarren, another stathead. "They were out looking for people. They weren't just going after the usual suspects, that was clear," says one person familiar with the search.

Harris and Blitzer did take a liking to a more traditional foil, former Charlotte/New Orleans Hornets general manager Jeff Bower, as well. They interviewed all three candidates twice. "Bower was very, very close to getting that job," says another figure familiar with the search. Although no decision, of course, was made until Harris tapped Hinkie the following May.

Bynum, meanwhile, remained sidelined well into 2013. He once tweaked his recovering knees while bowling with friends. "There'd be, like, a rumored setback and then you'd see him and then you wouldn't see him," says Sixers center Spencer Hawes. It was Philly's painfully erratic communication regarding Bynum's return that reminded the public of Hinkie's elongated coaching search.

Internally, Sixers personnel routinely heard of Bynum's return date being pushed further and further into the future. Players learned at one practice that the center's recovery period would be extended due to a minor injury sustained while walking his dogs on a gravel road near his home. Thaddeus Young beelined directly toward him.

"Big fella. Do you wanna play?" Young asked.

"Yes," Bynum confirmed. "I want to play."

"How much money do you make this year?" Young asked.

Bynum paused before answering, "$17 million."

"That means you got enough money to pay somebody to do all these different things that you need to do," Young said, his voice growing stern. "From now on, if you take the trash out, if you're washing the dishes, if you're doing anything that you can hurt yourself, just call somebody and pay 'em to do it!"

Fans grew rightfully fearful Bynum would never return, especially as the team spun out of the playoff picture. Some Philly supporters suspected the Sixers were pedaling Bynum's alleged, eventual debut as a means to sell tickets. In reality, the cartilage inside Bynum's knees had grown degenerative and simply refused to cooperate. Doctors even attempted to regrow his cartilage in a petri dish. Each morning was its own, different battle. "You don't know how much of a mind fuck it is going through that day after day, week after week, month after month," says Spencer Hawes.

Bynum would work his way up to small, half-court live scrimmages. His presence on the court commanded the whole gym's attention. The first session Bynum was permitted to participate in three-on-three, Sixers veteran Jason Richardson hung back to bear witness. "I mean, I played with Shaq and it was almost in that sense, because he was so big, nobody could guard him," Richardson says. "We were sending two, three guys on him, and he was still making turnaround hook shots, get down there dunking the ball."

Spencer Hawes guarded Bynum in many of those half-court battles. "Yao Ming was definitely the toughest guy I ever matched up against," Hawes says, "but Bynum was up there."

At the end of each day, the team waited to see how Bynum's knees would respond to the level of activity. Typically, only bad news followed. Bynum would be cleared for a heightened level of exercise, and then shut down once more by week's end. "His knee, it was just gone," a former Sixers executive says of Bynum's right joint. "It looked like slush."

Trainers then cleared Bynum somehow to scrimmage five-on-five in February. "We were literally quadruple-teaming him and he was murdering us. Murdering us. Just killing everybody," Thaddeus Young says. When possessions grinded into the half-court, there was nothing any opposing Sixers player could do to limit their would-be superstar.

Jrue Holiday saw glimpses of a dominant pick-and-roll partner. "He destroyed our whole starting five. We understood the reason why they wanted him," Holiday says. "He could pass. He could shoot. If he got on the block, he was pretty much unstoppable."

Only Bynum struggled to sprint up and down the floor. He couldn't keep pace with Holiday's transition bursts. And after that one memorable outing, his body wilted again. He complained of excruciating pain that evening. By March, Philadelphia officially announced Bynum would undergo season-ending surgery. With Bynum's contract sliding off the books and leaving ample financial flexibility, ownership wanted to successfully build a legitimate championship contender just as the people of Philadelphia wanted to cheer for one.

After four general managers and seven head coaches in 10 years, myriad playing styles, and empty promises of superstars, the Sixers struck a uniform chord within the organization. "It was such an average team," says Spike Eskin, the Philadelphia radio executive. "We knew we had no chance of winning a championship. It finally seemed like there was somebody who was smart who was going to be in charge."

Sam Hinkie's early moves had delivered Nerlens Noel and Michael Carter-Williams. More young stars would follow. For now, Hinkie was just missing his head coach, and readied to finally appease his critics.

After nearly a month without contact, Hinkie finally called Jay Larranaga, asking if the Boston assistant could fly to New York and meet with Sixers ownership. Philadelphia's second round of head coaching interviews were held the first week of August 2013 in Joshua Harris' sprawling Manhattan offices, designated solely for managing his family trust. While San Antonio assistant Brett Brown clearly hadn't come to terms with the Sixers on draft night, he joined Larranaga and Bulls assistant Adrian Griffin as Philly's final candidates, along with Hawks assistant coach Kenny Atkinson, Blazers assistant David Vanterpool, and the incumbent defensive-minded assistant Michael Curry, who had piloted Philly's Summer League outfit in Orlando that July.

Brett Brown already interviewed for Denver's opening with Nuggets general manager Tim Connelly. "He was extremely interesting. [I was] blown away with his passion, his love for the game," Connelly says. "He was a really fun guy to sit down and talk hoops with."

Hinkie's second batch of interviews began with a tour of several minority owners' offices, visiting with Art Wrubel and David Heller, before culminating in the massive glass conference room in Harris' midtown building, overlooking Central Park as the Manhattan skyline brimmed its sea of trees. "Which is pretty impressive," Larranaga laughs.

Upon arrival, knowing the number of Wharton business school alumni in the room, Griffin joked his master's degree from the University of Phoenix online had the same worth as their MBAs from Penn. "See, I told you this guy was pretty sharp," Hinkie laughed.

Griffin remembers Hinkie asking him questions that addressed the assistant's inexperience and potential shortcomings as a head coach. Then just 38, Griffin was only five years removed from his playing career. It was as if Hinkie was selling ownership on a stock. "I don't think I was ready to be a head coach at that time, but I think he felt he had found someone who could potentially be a very good coach," Griffin says. It became obvious to Griffin that Hinkie was projecting his coaching candidates like he did college players. He truly needed them ready for 2017 and beyond. "I think that was the genius of Hinkie," Griffin says. "He could foresee. He could predict the future."

Larranaga entered the discussions armed with an important question: was this billion-dollar ownership group truly willing to stomach a years-long rebuild? "I just know how difficult losing is on everybody, on the coaches, on management, on the fans, ownership, on the players," Larranaga says. He listed recent, painful examples. The Memphis Grizzlies experienced three straight years of 20 wins from 2006 to 2009 while trading Pau Gasol to Los Angeles in 2008. "I think Josh got a little bit annoyed with me, like, 'Hey, kid, we've thought a lot about this, we realize how hard it's gonna be,'" Larranaga says.

Yet the history lesson served a point. It would be, and always had been, very difficult for a coach to survive that monsoon of losses. Marc Iavaroni, for example, only lasted 123 games in Memphis from 2007 to 2009. And throughout Larranaga's interview process, only the framework of a three-year contract was discussed. It was the standard structure for a first-time head coach's deal, but Larranaga had seen firsthand how the length of a contract can impact a team, even during voluntary summer workouts.

Danny Ainge convinced Brad Stevens to join the Celtics thanks in part to a six-year offer, and that vote of confidence spoke volumes throughout the organization. Stevens wouldn't be a scapegoat when losing streaks continued. "The players respected that," Larranaga says. And so, "even in the interview, you're negotiating a little bit for a potential job offer." Philly wouldn't budge on the three-year term for most candidates. Ownership did acquiesce for one.

On August 14, the Sixers finally hired Brett Brown with a fourth year tacked onto his contract. Adrian Griffin was given the impression he was Hinkie's runner-up at the end of his long process. Brown hungered for the job but wouldn't have signed without that additional season. "The litany of how many guys in this league did the dirty work and somebody else came in," says veteran coach P.J. Carlesimo, a friend of Brown's from their time together in San Antonio. "All of a sudden, these guys look like a genius because the players had [already] improved so much. I always thought that was a danger in Philadelphia."

"We went through an exhaustive search to find the right head coach for our organization, one who had a passion for developing talent, a strong work ethic to help create the kind of culture we hope for, and a desire to continually improve," Hinkie said at Brown's introductory press conference. He and ownership made note of Brown's success coaching Australia's National Basketball Team. He won titles in San Antonio, and the reports from Spurs personnel about his infectious charisma were resounding.

"You needed someone who was an optimist," says Aaron Barzilai, the Sixers analytics staffer.

Brown appeared the perfect balance to lead a team doomed for a roller coaster of growing pains. If anyone, Sam Hinkie believed, could mold young prospects into All-Stars while maintaining a sunny environment, it was Brett Brown. "He was exceptional," P.J. Carlesimo says. "I used to argue that he was so good at player development that [the Spurs] kind of pigeon-holed him."

Hinkie finally had his answer to Danny Ainge's hiring of Brad Stevens in Boston. The Celtics were remodeling a championship roster for a new era. The Sixers began detonating a run-of-the-mill playoff team. And both now employed the head coach to oversee their rebuilds, each franchise armed with an additional first-round pick for June's draft, holding two chances to pluck a future All-Star in what many scouts considered an absolutely loaded 2014 class.

FOUR

Not since LeBron James' 2003 group had an NBA draft class been as touted as that of the 2014 talent pool.

And ever since James commenced Miami's rule of the league in 2010–11, alongside fellow '03 draftees Dwyane Wade and Chris Bosh, rival teams had been preparing to select phenoms in 2014 like Andrew Wiggins and Jabari Parker. Why bother falling short of the Heat when tanking brought such obvious rewards? "The idea that there were franchise-changing players in that draft added fuel to the fire of not improving your team too much," says a veteran NBA executive.

If a rebuilding franchise could nab one of those elite 2014 prospects, and truly solidify its young core—unlike Oklahoma City prematurely parting ways with James Harden—perhaps that team could reach the Finals in a similar short burst as Kevin Durant, Russell Westbrook, and Harden once powered the Thunder, only then return to the championship stage together, year after year. Or maybe those young talents would attract other alphas in free agency, like Miami's Big Three that bested OKC for the 2012 championship.

Come 2013, Harden himself proved once again how powerful a hammer superstars can swing on the open market. His All-Star campaign in Houston grabbed the attention of prized center Dwight Howard. In the modern NBA, superstars seek superstar teammates, and the Rockets had long coveted Howard, who conveniently reached free agency drained from a dramatic year in Los Angeles. The All-Star big man, of course, first arrived in Hollywood via the four-team blockbuster that brought Andrew Bynum's knees upon Philadelphia.

While landing Howard one year before he reached free agency was nothing short of a coup, the center marked Los Angeles' second marquee acquisition that 2012 summer. With MVP point guard Steve Nash having already left Phoenix for L.A., many pundits expected the Lakers' new duo to lift their incumbent All-Stars Kobe Bryant and Pau Gasol back toward contention, forming a superteam capable of thwarting Miami's own star power. "They anointed us champions the second the signings were done," says Clay Moser, Los Angeles' longtime director of basketball strategy.

"I was like, 'Man, I'm about to be playing in June for the next two, three years,'" says Jodie Meeks, a shooter who also joined Los Angeles in free agency.

"That was *the* superteam," adds Robert Sacre, a rookie center for those Lakers.

But from the onset their vaunted group never meshed. Bryant pined for a return toward Phil Jackson's triangle offense of the early 2000s, so the Lakers hired Eddie Jordan as an assistant coach to install his similar Princeton attack. Jordan's teachings, however, worked to no avail. "It was just kind of a round peg in a square hole," Moser says. That pass-happy style would have limited Nash's brilliance in pick-and-rolls with an athletic big like Howard.

But the bouncy center hardly had an opportunity to develop chemistry with his floor general; Howard's lingering back injury sidelined him throughout training camp. And midway through Los Angeles' second regular season game, Nash collided with Portland's Damian Lillard, cracking a small fracture in his left leg that cost Nash the next 24 games. "I think he felt like he let them down," his agent, Bill Duffy, says. "That's the type of person he is."

After a dreadful 1–4 start, general manager Mitch Kupchak axed head coach Mike Brown. The Lakers flirted with retreading Phil Jackson, appeasing Bryant's preference, but alternatively hired Mike D'Antoni to pair the trailblazing coach once more with Nash.

Los Angeles posted a 40–32 mark under D'Antoni to close 2012–13. But even with Nash's eventual return from injury, D'Antoni never managed to blend the preferred styles of his two MVPs. "We couldn't quite get the floor spread enough for [Nash] and the pace quick enough so that he could be successful," says Dan D'Antoni, Mike's brother and Lakers assistant coach. "Kobe wasn't used to running at his pace, and it just became almost an impossible situation."

And similar to his love-hate relationship with Shaquille O'Neal at the beginning of the century, Bryant's approach clashed with Howard's. Bryant had chafed at O'Neal's work ethic. With Howard, Bryant couldn't comprehend how casually the big man seemed to approach the game, chortling through practice with a personality as large as his hulking shoulders. "To be fair, some of that's pretty true," Moser says. Howard's stature certainly made his class clown antics hard to ignore. "He was an easy target," Moser adds. "Kobe, frankly, was that way with a lot of people. It just so happened that Dwight being Dwight and all that incredible ability, he was the one that the spotlight got turned on."

Howard developed solid shooting mechanics from the foul line, but aside from his rookie campaign in 2004–05, he had never converted over 60 percent of his free throws in actual games. Lakers officials say Howard would routinely make around 80 percent from the line during practices. "That was true," confirms one team source. "But when the lights were on and the popcorn was popping, Dwight was hyper-aware of every single person in the building, every set of eyeballs that were on him, and all the people at home watching on TV."

Lakers personnel believe Howard created his silly side to mask insecurities. His humble, religious upbringing strayed far from the luxuries that an NBA contract affords and the late-night lifestyle the league's schedule can permit. Los Angeles quickly learned how deeply Howard's parents were involved in his adult life, their son having first entered the league out of high school. In Orlando, he often played Magic coach Stan Van Gundy and general manager Otis Smith off each other like a clever teenager does with Mom and Dad. Still, he shouldered Orlando to the 2009 Finals nonetheless, against Los Angeles of all teams.

Now with the Lakers, Howard's impending free agency further complicated matters. His year inside their facilities could either provide a massive advantage or drive him out of town before he ever got settled. Mitch Kupchak had made re-signing Howard the Lakers' clear priority, and his directive was communicated throughout the organization. "That just put a magnifying glass on the whole deal," Moser says. Kupchak hoped Los Angeles' playoff push that spring, despite a year riddled by injury, would leave Howard wanting another taste of a Lakers postseason. If they could just make the playoffs, staffers maintained all year, they were too talented not to compete for a title.

Nash was back in street clothes near the end of the regular season, so Bryant assumed much of the Lakers' ball handling duties. And after initiating the offense, he pestered opposing guards all the way in the backcourt. "He was playing like 40 minutes a game, just taking over games," center Robert Sacre says. Bryant followers hailed the string of performances as his latest of epic proportion. Then during Los Angeles' April 12 win against Golden State, Bryant crumpled into a heap at the left wing, moving gingerly in obvious discomfort.

Bryant sat on the hardwood staring down at his left heel after drawing a foul. When Jodie Meeks walked over to help him off the hardwood, Bryant, incredulous, asked if any Warriors defender kicked him from behind to prevent his drive. "I was just like, 'Oh no!'" Meeks says. "I heard that it feels like that when you tear your Achilles." While the Lakers added Howard to bolster Bryant's sixth championship chase, the Hall of Fame scorer wouldn't even appear in the postseason after indeed tearing his left Achilles tendon. Now 34, would Bryant even be the same player upon his return?

No matter; San Antonio promptly swept Los Angeles in the first round. The Lakers began their Dwight Howard retention efforts as quickly as they were eliminated from the playoffs. Los Angeles posted billboards outside Staples Center and around the city, plastering enormous images of Howard, alongside the word "STAY" with an accompanying "#STAYD12" social media tag. Kupchak informed representatives for Los Angeles' other free agents they were focused on first re-signing Howard into cap space.

Kobe Bryant had originally welcomed Howard's Lakers tenure, telling reporters he would play two or three more seasons before yielding the franchise's mantle to his younger co-star. Now less than a year later, Bryant played a key role in Los Angeles' free agency meeting with Howard, but word of their unpleasant interaction—possibly poor enough to drive Howard else-where—trickled throughout the franchise that July.

Instead of envisioning their successful union, Bryant told Howard the center hadn't yet learned how to be a champion, and he could teach Howard those winning ways if the latter was willing to comply. "There were certainly rumblings within the walls of our practice facility that it had not gone well," says Moser, the Lakers staffer. "Kobe had dressed him down one last time. And Dwight said, 'Screw it, I'm out.'"

Unlike Bryant's lecture, Howard's meetings with other suitors were full of effusive praise. He wanted to be wanted as much as he wanted to win.

Houston owner Leslie Alexander and general manager Daryl Morey led the Rockets' dinner meeting with Howard at Hotel Bel-Air. Head coach Kevin McHale, having since left Minnesota's front office, also attended, as well as Rockets legends Hakeem Olajuwon and Clyde Drexler. Howard harbored a relationship with Olajuwon from their 2010 off-season work-outs together. The contingent pitched Houston's championship history and long-standing connections with its franchise legends. Yao Ming even Skyped into the meeting from China to join the chorus.

The Rockets already told agents around the league they were seeking shooters to space for Howard and James Harden's pick-and-roll duet. League personnel suggest the Rockets even hired Kevin McHale, back in June 2011, with an eventual eye toward the Hall of Fame low-post scorer one day helping entice Howard to Houston.

That May, Rockets forward Chandler Parsons also changed agents, from Mark Bartelstein to Dan Fegan, who just so happened to represent Howard. Not only did Parsons emerge as a viable NBA starter, but he particularly blos-somed alongside Harden in the All-Star's own 2012–13 breakout campaign. Come free agency, Parsons got in touch with Houston's target directly, calling, texting, and FaceTiming Howard every day. He often drove to Howard's house in the hills while spending his own off-season in Los Angeles. "I helped a lot in getting Dwight there," Parsons says. "It was almost like a favor."

The Rockets originally signed Parsons, the 38th pick in the 2011 draft, to an inventive four-year deal. The first two seasons were guaranteed above the minimum salary, but Houston only partially guaranteed the next two seasons—a similar structure to the contract Sam Hinkie later offered Robert Covington during the 2013 NBA Draft.

The agreement awarded Parsons more upfront money than a typical second-rounder, yet as he blossomed in Houston, the Rockets retained their investment for an extremely cost-effective salary during the latter half of the contract. "They kind of put that on the map as something that teams can use to get control of a player for the long term," Parsons says. "Why create the risk of letting them hit free agency?"

Parsons indeed found success in Houston, averaging 15.5 points with 38.5 percent accuracy from three-point land, 5.3 rebounds, and 3.5 assists by his second season, in 2012–13. The Rockets had Parsons, and the rest of their roster, practice shooting with Noah Basketball technology, software that used location-tracking data to study details such as where players' attempts contacted the rim and their shots' entry angle through the iron.

Sam Hinkie was a particular fan of Noah. "He had Daryl's ear on a lot of things," Parsons says. "A lot of the success that Houston had, I'm damn sure you can credit it back to Sam." Noah data, for example, suggested if Parsons increased the launch angle of his considerably flat shot, he could increase his three-point shooting accuracy by as much as 5 percent. "Shit like that, players would never think about," Parsons says.

In fairness, Hinkie couldn't match Parsons' free agent courtship abilities. Harden joined Parsons' recruiting efforts as well, promising a locker room chemistry that would embrace Dwight Howard's persona, not demean it. After all, with both of their All-Star talents on one roster, the Rockets would compete for championships for years to come.

Los Angeles no longer offered that guarantee. Bryant's effectiveness after Achilles rehab remained a critical question. And his aggressive nature in the Lakers' meeting with Howard certainly didn't woo the free agent like the Rockets' young cornerstones had. No suitor mustered a more appealing offer to Howard's camp. "You know what I like about Houston? They're always in on the big guys," Parsons says. "Every free agent, Houston was always in the mix. I think that's really smart."

The Rockets weren't just involved with Howard's free agency. The center confirmed on Twitter the night of July 5 he was spurning Los Angeles for Houston. Howard chose Houston's maximum offer of $88 million over four years—$30 million below and one year shorter than what Los Angeles could have paid as Howard's incumbent team.

His departure stranded the Lakers in unfamiliar uncertainty. They hadn't advanced past the second round since Los Angeles defeated Boston in the 2010 Finals. Now Kupchak's trade for Howard had officially flopped, as Bryant faced months of rehab that threatened to stretch into the 2013–14 season. Like in Boston and Philadelphia, the crossroads presented a rare occasion for Los Angeles where rebuilding suddenly seemed prudent.

The Lakers had already dangled Pau Gasol to rival teams over the past few seasons. "Dealing with Mitch Kupchak was like, you had no idea what was gonna happen," says Greg Lawrence, one of Gasol's former representatives at Wasserman.

But while Danny Ainge completely severed ties with his Celtics corner-stones, Kupchak still hoped to extend Kobe Bryant's apparent championship window, even as he faced an arduous recovery. "He's a tough rascal, but there is reality," says Dan D'Antoni, the former L.A. assistant coach.

Reality shrouded Steve Nash's own health. He'd now developed nerve damage in his back from the leg injury that derailed his first Lakers season. Both Nash's and Bryant's struggles highlighted the value in moving aged stars before it's too late. There was no guarantee when either would be healthy, despite Kupchak's persistence in building around Bryant. Besides, just as Boston would soon watch Kevin Garnett play only 54 games that season in Brooklyn, Nash's body was already failing in Los Angeles, while Phoenix began its rebuild under a new general manager.

Ryan McDonough continued his first off-season. He scored young reserve point guard Eric Bledsoe and veteran forward Caron Butler in a three-team deal with the Clippers and Bucks that July. Bledsoe was yet another product of John Calipari's Kentucky program and still had one year remaining on his rookie contract.

Acquiring such an asset, at merely the cost of taking on Caron Butler's $8 million expiring deal, was the type of transaction a tanking organization dreamed of. Phoenix faced its own low expectations for the 2013–14 season. And now the Suns would vie for a high pick in that June's loaded draft, with a blue-chip prospect like Bledsoe already in the fold.

By late August, Caron Butler's family fully relocated to Arizona. His children were already enrolled and attending school. Then a phone call from Pat Connelly interrupted one afternoon. The Suns assistant general manager developed a bond with Butler when they overlapped with the Washington Wizards. "We had a different type of relationship," Butler says. A rare honesty underscored their connection, not always present between front office executives and players.

Connelly held nothing back: Phoenix's teardown was only beginning. The Suns traded Luis Scola, moving the 33-year-old to Indiana for 25-year-old center Miles Plumlee, veteran guard Gerald Green, and a coveted 2014 first-round pick. More veterans would soon be dealt for future draft ammunition, Connelly admitted. He was straightforward about Phoenix's expectations for a poor season leading to a high lottery pick. Butler returned the candor.

"Look, yeah, I don't want to be a part of this shit," he said.

Connelly assisted in sending Butler to his preferred destination, Milwaukee, having grown up in Racine, Wisconsin. "That meant a lot, to be able to represent your state one time before I call it quits," Butler says. In exchange, Phoenix received Viacheslav Kravtsov and Ish Smith, two more 25-year-olds to develop within their rebuild.

The Suns kept selling. Ryan McDonough swung another deal in October, trading starting center Marcin Gortat and three others to the Wizards for another 2014 first-round pick, while taking on Emeka Okafor—in the last year of his contract and out indefinitely with a herniated disk. Phoenix now owned three firsts in what many league insiders considered the best draft in a decade. They'd swapped their big man for a giant who wouldn't play that season. With the Suns' inexperienced roster, a high lottery pick surely awaited.

Moving off Gortat also allowed new head coach Jeff Hornacek to reignite Phoenix's up-tempo style that once powered Mike D'Antoni's success in the Valley. D'Antoni's Suns famously looked to score within the first seven heartbeats of the 24-second shot clock, when data suggested teams had the highest overall efficiency—theoretically as defenses were still transitioning back down the court. While opposing giants routinely caught the ball on the block, their backs to the basket and a defender directly in their path, Steve Nash ran fast breaks and danced within pick-and-roll situations.

Their pace-and-space style had permeated the NBA. Players began chucking triples during three-on-one fast break situations rather than prioritizing layups. And come 2013, rivals were burning Phoenix with the barrage of quick threes Suns fans had once known as their own. "It's your job to continually bring in people that are gonna evolve your style and make you better," longtime Suns forward Channing Frye says. "I thought Jeff was that guy."

Hornacek's Suns wanted to play even faster. While the Clippers had developed Eric Bledsoe off their bench, Phoenix's data suggested the Suns would be more potent when both Bledsoe and the tenacious Goran Dragić shared the floor. Either point guard could lead a break or fill the lane, their shooting ability enough to draw defensive attention even without the ball. Hornacek hired Mike Longabardi, an assistant on Boston's 2008 championship team, to teach the Celtics' detailed defensive rotations. "We stop guys, we're gonna be able to run, and nobody can run with us," said Dionte Christmas, a rookie Suns wing.

Christmas went undrafted in 2009 out of Temple, yet Phoenix's 2013 preseason presented him with a position battle against James Nunnally, a 6-foot-7 marksman, also undrafted out of UC Santa Barbara. Christmas sparked 14 points on 3-for-4 shooting from deep during Phoenix's exhibition win at San Antonio.

When he arrived for the final day of Suns camp, Nunnally was nowhere to be found. Christmas, though, still heard nothing on his own status. "It was, like, weird," he says.

Before practice began, Hornacek gathered the remaining players to huddle around Ryan McDonough so the GM could address his motley roster. He conveyed optimism.

"I thought it was a little bullshit," Channing Frye says.

"Everybody has doubts about us, but this is the team I'm gonna go with," McDonough began. He acknowledged their roster's projection by media outlets across the nation, placing Phoenix at the bottom of the Western Conference. "I don't care what people say, we're gonna go out and play. We can run with anyone," he said. He wanted the players to represent their storied franchise by playing hard until the final buzzer.

"Don't be…too tanky," Frye translates.

McDonough brought the players closer, raising their fists in the middle of the huddle, and wished them luck.

Frye and veterans like P.J. Tucker and Marcus and Markieff Morris, identical twins out of Kansas, looked at the Suns' two-headed point guard monster and grinned. "We were like, 'Dude, they think we're just gonna tank here?'" Frye says.

McDonough walked off the court and back toward his office.

Christmas didn't understand. He jogged over to the first-year GM, tapping McDonough on the shoulder.

"Hey, what's up, man?" Christmas began, concealing his unease. "Does this mean I'm on the team?"

McDonough raised his eyebrows. "Oh my god," he said. "I forgot to tell you. Congrats!"

Four years in, Christmas finally earned his spot in the NBA, akin to the opportunity Phoenix ownership had awarded McDonough that May. And despite his gaffe in communication with Christmas, McDonough had surely conducted a sweeping off-season during his first months in Phoenix, just like Sam Hinkie had done in Philadelphia.

FIVE

When Comcast Spectacor needed to compile a presentation for prospective buyers of the Philadelphia 76ers, Comcast chairman Ed Snider enlisted the help of longtime player agent Happy Walters and Jason Levien, then an executive for the Sacramento Kings. "What we just saw was a great opportunity," Walters says.

The ensuing collective bargaining agreement negotiations were expected to net owners a significant victory in basketball-related income, slicing at least 6 percent off the players' 57 percent share—a massive piece of a multi-billion-dollar pie back onto the owners' plate. "Ownership, no matter what team it was, was gonna benefit—I thought and Jason thought—from what the economics would be," Walters says.

Joshua Harris' group bought the Sixers in July 2011 for just $280 million. And from the onset of their ownership, several voices, specifically minority partner David Heller, suggested the Sixers commence a rebuild. "They were prepared to go deep into collecting assets," Walters adds.

David Heller asked Aaron Barzilai, by then the Sixers' first analytics staffer in 2012, to run a series of analyses. He wanted to learn what quantitatively defined contenders throughout recent NBA history. So Barzilai studied how long it took homegrown superstars to reach the Finals leading the teams that drafted them, like LeBron James in Cleveland and Kevin Durant in Oklahoma City. What steps did the Cavs and Thunder take to get there?

Heller would call for weekly updates. "He was really interested in getting the information," Barzilai says.

Empirical evidence can only trump so much emotion, however. When the young Sixers pushed the champion Celtics to seven games in the 2012 playoffs, any notion of a teardown quickly evaporated. "At that point the owners said, let's keep it together and let's build on our success," says one former Sixers executive.

Andrew Bynum's knees, of course, brought that strategy to a screeching halt. Enter Sam Hinkie, exit Jrue Holiday, welcome Brett Brown, heat your practice gym to the proper temperature, and watch your rebuild rise.

Philadelphia introduced its new head coach on their stadium's concourse. Brett Brown seemed incapable of containing his excitement. He milled about following the press conference, meeting the sea of new faces comprising his new organization. Chris Heck, hired one week earlier as Philadelphia's new chief sales and marketing officer, asked Brown if there was anything he could do to ease the transition from San Antonio.

"You probably don't have a car up here," Heck assumed. "Do you need a car?"

"What do you mean?" Brown asked.

"You're going to need a car here," Heck said. "I'll get you a car deal."

Incredulous, Brown earnestly wondered: "You can do that?"

Heck smirked. Of course the Philadelphia 76ers could scrounge up some local sponsorship.

Brown paused. He was obviously dreaming up possibilities. "Any car?" the coach asked.

Heck chuckled. "Yeah. Pretty much any car."

Heck prepared for a lavish request. Brown was grinning like a boy ready to order the largest-sized ice cream. "Alright…" Brown gulped. "Can you get me a Jeep?"

Brown stopped the first workout he saw in the Sixers' PCOM practice facility. Spencer Hawes was launching midrange 17-footers out of pick-and-pops. "No. No more," Brown instructed. "You're either rolling or you're shooting the three."

Under Doug Collins, the Sixers had led the NBA in shot attempts inside the three-point arc but outside the painted area. "We wanted to switch that totally," says Lance Pearson, the Sixers' analytics-minded basketball operations assistant.

Brown long believed the data. Accessing over 4 million shot attempts across years of NBA basketball, analytics staffers around the league determined midrange shots only connect 37-39 percent of the time. Why not shoot from beyond the arc instead, worth an additional point, and where the average player can still convert 35 percent of his tries?

If a shooter converts merely 33.3 percent of his triples, that's the equivalent of scoring 0.99 points on every possession. And what if Sixers players caught fire, hitting 60 percent of their threes one night? The composite output skyrockets to an average of 1.8 points per possession. Meanwhile, teams must make 50 percent of their two-point field goals in order to average one point on every possession. Mike D'Antoni's early three-point scheme in Phoenix was on to something. "When I got Brett, I put up a shit ton of 'em," Sixers forward Thaddeus Young says.

The numbers also encouraged playing with speed, as D'Antoni's Suns showcased, and Brown wanted his Sixers to outpace all comers. Philadelphia's depleted roster would need all the advantages it could get in order to score. "The faster you play, the more easy opportunities there tend to be early in the [shot] clock," Lance Pearson says.

Brown drilled live scrimmages with only 10-second and 8-second shot clocks instead of the full 24 ticks. Pearson would later track the Sixers' shooting percentages within the four six-second increments of the shot clock throughout the season. Brown would yell "Butter!" to call out the final six seconds, a learned habit from San Antonio, as if the remaining time was melting toward zero. Philadelphia staffers got a kick out of Brown shouting the word in his unique pronunciation, a hybrid of New England flair and Australian twang, that had tickled many Spurs personnel. "His Bos-tralian accent," says longtime San Antonio guard Manu Ginóbili.

Both Brown and his father, Bob, are in fact enshrined in the New England Basketball Hall of Fame. "He's a legendary coach in Maine," veteran sideline leader P.J. Carlesimo says of Brown's old man. Bob oversaw South Portland's

29–0 record and State Class A title in Brown's 1979 senior season. His son went on to run Rick Pitino's offense for four years at Boston University, where Brown powered BU to the 1983 NCAA Tournament. He was a tenacious defender and steady floor general, with a mound of sandy brown curls atop his head.

Brown spent an additional season at BU as a grad student assistant coach, but soon departed for an AT&T sales job. He wanted to save enough over three years to quit and backpack across New Zealand, Fiji, and Australia. Those travels ultimately introduced Brown to an Aussie named Anna, who later became his wife. Now in need of work for a longer journey than he'd planned, Brown returned to basketball. He first coached Altos Auckland in 1988. By 1993, Brown filled North Melbourne's head coaching vacancy in Australia's larger National Basketball League.

Chris Jent, a 6-foot-7 forward out of Ohio State, spent the 1995 season as Brown's floor spacer. The young coach charted all of his players' shots in practice, logging each make and miss, even with just one assistant to help track the data, while guys passed and rebounded for each other. "It was the first time where all my shooting had been numbered," Jent says, having dotted the world playing for five pro clubs from 1992 to 1995. "It was different, especially with a small staff. There was no help."

Brown made sure to connect with players off the floor, eager to lend an ear about homesickness. Many were hooping a world away from home. He forbade players from lingering on their in-game gaffes. "He was always, in his way, keeping you up and keeping your spirits up," Jent says. When Brown invited figures from around the sport to a basketball camp he helped organize, Spurs general manager R.C. Buford accepted. Taken by Brown's charisma and diligence, Buford offered Brown an unpaid player development position for San Antonio's 1998–99 season.

That June, Tim Duncan led the Spurs to their first championship, unofficially launching San Antonio's dynasty. And by 2002, Buford created a full-time director of player development position to lure Brown away from his other post coaching the Sydney Kings. Brown just had a way with players. "And he was able to do that from Tim Duncan all the way down to a 10-day guy," says Carlesimo, a Spurs assistant from 2002 to 2007.

His first full season in San Antonio, Brown equally aided Ginóbili, the Argentinian then amid his first NBA campaign, and 14-year veteran sharp-shooter Steve Kerr. "There was no question about how important what Brett was doing was to our success," Carlesimo says.

Kerr played a crucial role winning four straight titles with the Bulls and Spurs between 1996 and 1999, yet he saw just 46 minutes during his final postseason in 2003. Any time the little-used reserve hoisted a jumper, Brown would howl "Why not?" in that unique accent. "I loved it," Kerr says. "He just infused me with confidence."

When the Spurs returned to San Antonio following a road trip, Brown would wade to the back of the bus. Long past 2:00 AM, he'd find swingman Bruce Bowen, proposing he rebound 500 jumpers if they could meet on the practice court by 9:00. Then he'd scan nearby seats, trying to corral as many players as possible, asking if they'd want to work out before or after Bowen. "The players only responded to that because it was Brett offering," Carlesimo says. "Otherwise they would have been like, 'Fuck no!'" Brown and Ginóbili would stay after practice comparing the cultures in Sydney and Buenos Aires.

Australia soon tapped Brown to coach its national team in 2009, and the Boomers finished 10th in the 2010 FIBA World Championships. Ahead of the 2012 Summer Olympics, Brown asked the Spurs' video coordinators and scouts to compile film on his guys playing around the world. He followed the growth of bruising 6-foot-10 forward Aron Baynes in particular. Come the 2012 London Games, Brown guided Australia to the quarterfinals and San Antonio would sign Baynes in January 2013 too.

Spurs executive Dell Demps watched every Olympic game stateside, beaming with each of Brown's victories. "This guy's going to be an NBA head coach," Demps believed. "I just thought that he had great people skills, he understood players and player development. He could talk to them. He has a passion." Demps knows Brown's zeal for teaching more than most.

The coach had spied Demps floundering in San Antonio's practice facility lap pool one afternoon. Brown's laugh echoed off the water as he entered the room. Demps could stay afloat just fine, but he moved more with a treading doggy-paddle than a legitimate stroke.

"You don't know how to swim!" Brown crowed.

"I'm just getting a workout in," Demps defended himself.

"Dell," Brown smiled. "Meet me here tomorrow morning at 6:30. I'm gonna teach you how to swim."

Brown explained the sport's many different strokes. Before their colleagues arrived for practice each day, Brown taught Demps how to cup his hands during freestyle for a stronger glide, and to swing his arms directly over his shoulders during backstroke. When other staffers began trickling in for the day, R.C. Buford, Gregg Popovich, and countless other Spurs personnel would cackle mercilessly at the two men splashing together. "I always refer to him as my swim coach," Demps says. "His patience with me, to say the least…"

Brown could have returned to San Antonio's sideline for 2013–14 as Popovich's lead assistant, but he leapt for Philadelphia once Sixers ownership acquiesced and offered that critical fourth year for his contract. It was Brown's time to build an NBA program. "Everybody knew what we were going in for. It was not going to be a surprise," says Vance Walberg, an assistant coach on Brown's staff. "I knew we were gonna be bad." Losses would follow, but Philly would play fast and play hard.

Readying for the frenetic pace, Brown implemented his own conditioning test. Players were required to sprint down and back the full length of the floor four times, first in 62 seconds, and then in 60 seconds and 58 seconds and so forth. If you finished early, you could bank that extra time for the next run. Finishing the 60-second sprint in 58 seconds and the 58-second trial in 57 seconds, you could have an additional three seconds to make the 56-second burst. "You hope you had enough stocked up," center Spencer Hawes says. "He was really emphasizing, 'You gotta be in the best shape of your career.'" Such conditioning would also yield the best numbers of veterans like Hawes' career—all the better for Hinkie's efforts to receive as much as possible for their return via trade.

Hinkie, of course, kept a close eye on the NBA trade market. He casually touted Hawes as the NBA's best three-point-shooting big man during an October appearance on *The Rights to Ricky Sanchez* podcast. Spike Eskin, the local radio executive, and Michael Levin, editor of the popular Sixers blog *LibertyBallers.com*, had emerged as Hinkie's most public supporters in Philadelphia, while ironically naming their show as a nod to NBA transaction minutiae. *The Rights to Ricky Sanchez* pokes fun at the fact a 6-foot-11 forward, first drafted by Portland, saw his NBA rights dealt four times in eight years—including once to Philadelphia—only to never play in the league. Savvy team executives like Sam Hinkie sometimes move amorphous draft rights to complete trades without surrendering any asset of greater consequence.

Hinkie naturally maintained his steep asking price as Spencer Hawes proceeded to drain 39.9 percent of his triples for Philadelphia during the 2013–14 season. Any rival team hoping to obtain Thaddeus Young and Evan Turner would also have to pay future first-round draft capital.

Turner was the No. 2 pick out of Ohio State in 2010. His dribble attacks helped Philly overcome Chicago in the first round of the 2012 playoffs. "We thought the future was bright," Jrue Holiday says. "If we would have kept our team together, we think we would have been a problem."

Then Andre Iguodala exited in the trade that landed Andrew Bynum. Hinkie sent Holiday to New Orleans on draft night. Any day now, Turner seemed like the next player due out of Philadelphia. "It came to a point where we all thought at any point we could get traded," says Sixers center Lavoy Allen.

Hinkie rarely interacted with Philly's veterans lingering on the trade block. Some Sixers personnel suggest Hinkie did so as a means to mentally separate the men from their market values. He'd be a better executive if he focused on trading contracts, not people.

Turner says Hinkie walked past him at PCOM on several occasions without introducing himself. "Sam didn't really speak much, to tell you the truth," says Turner. During one early training camp practice, Turner eyed the executive walking down the sideline. "Is that our GM?" he asked teammates, feigning animated ignorance. "What's up, bruh!" Turner shouted toward Hinkie. "We play for the Sixers!"

Turner arrived late to the team's public relations training session the morning of media day. Just 30 minutes later, a PR staffer placed him on camera for an interview with Sixers.com. "We were on our way to be historically one of the worst teams in history," Turner says. "Why would we have a media day live [stream] for who was at home?" Thousands would watch the ensuing video spread across social media.

Turner mouthed several words into the microphone, but without any discernible volume. Someone behind the camera suggested he flick the switch on. As a sound check, Turner cupped his hands around the mic and bellowed, "Motherfuckaaaa!"

What Turner assumed was a measly prank to the PR staffers had actually aired on the stream. "Oh, we're live!" Turner exclaimed. Shock stretched the grin across his face into an awkward smile.

"So they heard me say 'motherfucker'?" he whispered.

Indeed.

Turner looked back into the camera. "My bad," he apologized.

"I mean, I was gonna do something way worse," Turner says now.

His penchant for comedy did brighten the Sixers locker room. Turner brought an infectious laugh to Brett Brown's program. In between jokes, the veteran exhibited trademark NBA leadership. He noticed undrafted rookie Khalif Wyatt didn't own a suit, so Turner drove Wyatt to the King of Prussia Mall and spent over $7,000 on a new business wardrobe for the youngster. It was the least he could do amid their team's curious circumstances.

No Sixers player, whether veteran or rookie, expected to reach the postseason. Brown sat his players down individually and preached his staff was committed to helping them improve day by day. "He was ready and excited for the challenge," says Wyatt, the rookie guard in Philly's training camp. "He knew where the team was at and where it wanted to go and that it was gonna take time."

Only on opening night, the Sixers dethroned LeBron James and the defending champion Miami Heat 114–110, sending the Wells Fargo Center crowd into a frenzy. No. 11 pick Michael Carter-Williams opened the contest with a steal and rumbled down the floor for a two-handed flush. Just over a minute later, Turner charged at James in transition and dunked on the reigning Finals MVP. "There might have been a little bit of championship hangover," says Heat forward Udonis Haslem.

Carter-Williams clinched Philadelphia's narrow victory and capped his 22-point, seven-rebound, 12-assist debut. Turner led the way with 26 points and Hawes followed up with 24 of his own.

Philadelphia topped Washington two days later in the nation's capital, with Thaddeus Young leading the way with 29 points. The following night, Carter-Williams' 26-point, 10-assist effort powered the Sixers past Chicago 107–104. Brown's bunch stood atop the NBA at 3–0. "It was like, 'Holy shit, maybe we're not that bad,'" says Vance Walberg, the Sixers assistant.

"There was more optimism from the coaching staff those three games than there was the next three years," says Lance Pearson, the analytics staffer.

Carter-Williams and Tony Wroten, a 6-foot-6 point guard Sam Hinkie acquired from the Memphis Grizzlies, danced in the locker room, chests puffed and hollering. "I remember walking in and telling them like, 'Hold your horses. Don't get too hype,'" Thaddeus Young says. "They was like, 'No, we nice!' Everybody started to get too high, and then we started getting our ass kicked. And then after we started to get our ass kicked, then we started to realize that we weren't that good of a team."

Golden State smacked Philly 110–90 in the Sixers' fourth game. Washington won by 14 the following contest. "We didn't have the right pieces," Young says. "I knew it from the jump."

SIX

Boston also needed to learn how to walk before it could run. Brad Stevens and the Celtics' shallow roster dropped their first four games of the 2013–14 campaign. "He was probably nervous," says Celtics guard Courtney Lee, an Indianapolis native who knew Stevens previously.

The NBA's 48-minute setup takes far longer than the NCAA's 40-minute contests and media timeout system. "At the end of the third quarter, I was like, 'Is this game over yet?'" Stevens says. "Those extra eight minutes you can feel."

There were other little wrinkles in need of ironing. Stevens wasn't used to advancing the ball past half-court by calling a timeout after a defensive rebound. "Little stuff like that," says Celtics forward Jared Sullinger.

Stevens nonetheless maintained a steady calm on the sideline. As a boy, he idolized not only the talent but also the resolve of Celtics great Larry Bird. As a coach, Stevens projected the poise he wanted his players to emulate on the court. Don't confuse that for a lack of competitiveness. "The guy just has a fire inside him," says Ronald Nored, who spent 2013–14 assisting Boston and its D-League affiliate in Maine.

Nored saw the coach's edge playing under Stevens during Butler's back-to-back dances to the NCAA championship game. The Bulldogs won 25 straight games before falling to Duke in the April 2010 title match. Nored recalls one huddle when Stevens cracked. He snapped a clipboard in frustration and a fragment sprayed into Gordon Hayward's leg. "He went from really mad to really apologetic really quickly," Nored laughs. "This guy's so different."

When Stevens guided Butler back to the championship game in 2011, Nored saw 26 minutes off the bench. He graduated in 2012 before spending the next year coaching nearby Brownsburg High School in Indiana. And when Stevens took the Boston gig, Nored not only followed, but moved into the head coach's basement.

Every night, he returned upstairs for the evening's family meal. He attended the first dinner to which Stevens invited Celtics point guard Rajon Rondo. They'd share what Stevens' wife, Tracy, cooked while music hummed lightly in the background. "I learned a lot about being a dad and being a husband," Nored says.

After the couple put their kids to sleep, Nored would join Brad and Tracy in a bout of Rack-O. To win, one must fill their rack with 10 of the game's 60 cards in descending order, drawing new numbers like in Gin Rummy; players can only move cards within their rack if they exchange it with a card from the game's deck. Each round brings its own scoring. Stevens logged everyone's points on a piece of paper. "It doesn't matter what you're competing at, he is trying to beat you, and he's not afraid to talk trash," Nored says.

Whenever Stevens won the nightly Rack-O session, he'd autograph the scoresheet like a painter admiring his artwork.

Stevens brought several other college figures to his Boston staff. He hired former Celtics forward Walter McCarty specifically as a bridge to the pro game. McCarty played eight of his 10 NBA seasons with Boston and developed a friendship with Stevens on the recruiting trail as a Louisville assistant from 2007 to 2010. "Brad's big on acquiring information," McCarty says. "What are the differences? How do we play these certain actions, and when you teach this stuff, how are we gonna get this through to the guys?"

Stevens ultimately captured players' attention in the film room. When breaking down video, the young coach's mind for the game took center stage. He detailed opposing defense's tendencies and how to expose them. Like Jeff Hornacek in Phoenix and Brett Brown in Philadelphia, Stevens wanted his Celtics to play fast, whipping the ball around the floor in half-court settings to catch teams sleeping in rotation.

He drilled various endgame situations—trailing by two with 45 seconds left, leading by two with 45 seconds left. They simulated nearly every scenario teams can imagine facing in the final three minutes, whether inbounding from full-court or three-quarters court or already in the half-court. Boston would be prepared for any crunch time condition. "When they come up in the game, it's not the first time you've seen this," says Kelly Olynyk, Boston's rookie center.

The Celtics' November 9 battle in Miami brought such a situation. After timeouts, some coaches simply design actions to inbound the ball cleanly. Aggressive coaches like Stevens use the opportunity to craft plays targeted to score. When the Celtics trailed the Heat 110–108 with just 0.6 seconds remaining, Stevens had no choice. And his players were more than prepared for the setting.

With Gerald Wallace set to inbound on the left sideline, Stevens positioned four Celtics in a box formation, standing at each elbow and at both blocks. Through a series of chaotic screens, Olynyk held his ground and freed Jeff Green to dart toward the right wing. When Wallace flung his pass over all the action and toward the opposite corner, he somehow plopped the ball perfectly in time for Green to catch, fire, and drain a ridiculous game-winning three as time expired. The buzzer-beater delivered Boston's third straight win.

"That's when Brad got comfortable in his own skin, calling plays, making rotations, making adjustments, having great ATOs [after timeout plays]," says Jared Sullinger, Boston's young forward. Stevens would run the same plays night in and night out but instructed players to finish with different options and counters to burn the Celtics' foes. "It could be sometimes 10 games in a row, we'd run the same little pindown for Avery Bradley coming out of the timeout," Sullinger says. One game Bradley would shoot, the next he'd curl off the screen and cut toward the basket for an easy layup.

Two nights after the win in South Beach, Boston beat Orlando at home to reach 4–4 on the year. But just like Brett Brown's Sixers, the Celtics followed their winning spurt with a long stumble of their own. Young teams and inexperienced head coaches only pack so many punches in the NBA. Stevens' Celtics dropped six consecutive games to fall to 4–10. Another four-game drought soon dropped the Sixers to 5–8. Jockeying for position atop the 2014 lottery was well underway.

Brett Brown's group stopped their bleeding on November 22, vanquishing the Bucks 115–107. While executives in Boston and Philadelphia anticipated losing seasons, dreaming of top picks in the 2014 draft, the loss marked Milwaukee's seventh straight defeat—despite the Bucks originally hoping to reach the postseason. Injuries, though, plus a suspension for young center Larry Sanders, derailed that effort from the outset. It was hard for Bucks general manager John Hammond's front office to ignore the college scouting circuit. Andrew Wiggins and Jabari Parker were hooping as advertised at Kansas and Duke, respectively, just as Danny Ainge and Sam Hinkie had expected. "We didn't tank in Milwaukee," says Hammond. "[But] you do get to a point where you're saying, 'Now we have a chance at one of these guys.'"

Losses to dreadful teams like Philadelphia certainly entrenched Milwaukee in the NBA's increasingly contested race to the bottom. Spencer Hawes drilled three triples in that game's final 1:22 of regulation, including a one-legged bomb from the left corner with 1.7 seconds left, which sent the contest to overtime. He curled his hands into celebratory finger-guns. "That was probably my personal highlight of that season," Hawes says.

Especially as Philadelphia returned right back to the losing column. The Sixers' record plummeted like a sinking ship just as Hinkie expected, but much to coaches' and players' chagrin. No member of the team's bench was actively fumbling wins. "I'm not gonna be there when this thing comes full circle," Hawes says. "I'm not gonna play bad intentionally to help out the organization. That's not my job."

The Sixers still needed double overtime to outlast Orlando on December 3. And after 58 minutes, Michael Carter-Williams and Victor Oladipo became the first pair of rookies in NBA history to post triple-doubles in the same game. "We just used to go at each other," Oladipo says. With Nerlens Noel still rehabbing his torn ACL, Carter-Williams and Oladipo suddenly found themselves pitted against one another in the Rookie of the Year debate beginning across the league, despite both teams' poor records.

Rob Hennigan's rebuilding Magic were just 6–12 in their own right, equally tracking toward the top of the 2014 NBA Draft.

Magic officials still thought Oladipo could become a floor general far beyond Carter-Williams' capabilities. He started alongside Jameer Nelson and slid to point guard when the veteran rested. "We looked at it from being able to project moving forward. What was he gonna be?" says an Orlando official.

Maybe Oladipo could truly become Russell Westbrook, a brute force at point guard who Hennigan watched develop in Oklahoma City. Or maybe Oladipo would emerge like Kevin Durant, the unquestioned leading scorer for an upstart contender. "It wasn't necessarily that we had to feature someone, but rather could everyone grow together as a team?" says a Magic executive.

Hennigan operated patiently, akin to his counterpart in Philadelphia. "We really wanted to be committed to growing our youth," an Orlando executive says. Magic officials, however, never considered one variable to which Celtics and Sixers brass seemed more than attuned.

Durant and Westbrook were uniquely hard-wired, valuing diligence more than individual success. Many high draft picks, meanwhile, arrive in the NBA accustomed to certain star treatment. Their toes can feel stepped on suddenly sharing the spotlight with equally touted phenoms. Teams must implement careful player development strategies when playing time is scarce, or each youngster can hunger to be fed more than the next. "They're all trying to, not necessarily say, 'I'm the best on the team,' but it's a business. You gotta make money," Jameer Nelson says. "And sometimes everybody at the top goes on 'me.'"

SEVEN

There was no question which superstar represented the Lakers' heartbeat. On November 25, Los Angeles announced Kobe Bryant agreed to a two-year contract extension worth $48.5 million, expected to conclude in 2015–16 with his retirement. "I call it the 'golden parachute' contract," says Clay Moser, Los Angeles' longtime director of basketball strategy. "It was almost like an outgoing CEO that the company felt obligated to say, 'Hey, you've done right by us, you've made us wealthy beyond our wildest dreams, and we're gonna take care of you.'"

Whispers circulated around the franchise that Lakers brass hadn't even negotiated with Bryant's agent, Rob Pelinka. Once the representative agreed to something of a salary decrease, general manager Mitch Kupchak presented that $48.5 million starting offer and Bryant happily accepted. "He signed it and walked out the door," Moser says. And while the deal still afforded room for another star in 2014's free agency, Los Angeles staffers gossiped that Bryant would have been willing to sign a two-year agreement that paid just $25 million over both seasons. That lower number would have provided ample space for two additional superstars in July. "I heard he would have done it for half," Moser says. "They did it at the expense of flexibility and all kinds of ramifications that it caused them years to kind of pull themselves out of."

Of course Bryant's career brought historic success to the Lakers, far more than commensurate with his salary. "Kobe was worth every penny he was paid, from A to Z," says Mark Madsen, a Los Angeles assistant coach and former Lakers teammate of Bryant.

"He's filling up the stadium," says Johnny Davis, another Lakers assistant for 2013–14. "Not only in L.A., but around the league. If you computed everything in terms of dollars he generated, what he made was small in comparison."

The modern NBA, however, spearheaded by data-driven executives, valued every cent on the cap sheet. Rewarding players and roster stability were key ingredients to sustaining championship organizations, but so too was manipulating contracts and franchise assets in order to assemble the most talent for as long, and as inexpensively, as possible. The Lakers did the opposite, investing so much in a 35 year old penning his final chapter. Kupchak and executive vice president Jim Buss preached patience, spinning L.A.'s Dwight Howard loss as a way to clear their decks for an even bigger signing in 2014.

The Lakers opened 2013–14 at 10–9 while Bryant sat the first 19 games recuperating from his spring Achilles tear. As his imminent December return reignited the perennial playoff hopes in Hollywood, Lakers brass believed Bryant, again now 35, would surely bounce back from an injury that could end many careers, lead the Lakers to the postseason, and reaffirm his championship window. Then just like Shaquille O'Neal and later Pau Gasol, another All-Star would undoubtedly combine forces with Bryant once more.

Both Bryant and Gasol were due for free agency themselves in July. Only Steve Nash's $9.7 million counted a significant salary on Los Angeles' books. Hell, maybe LeBron James and Carmelo Anthony, who could both test the open market, would sign into the Lakers' bounty of cap room that summer.

Although James, Chris Bosh, and Dwyane Wade only teamed in Miami by sacrificing a chunk of their individual paychecks, Bryant saw no benefit in waiting for July. Having played 17 seasons and sustained his first major injury, he naturally sought security, unsure about the remainder of his career. "Because your window is so small, you do have to maximize your earning potential while you can," says Johnny Davis, the Lakers assistant.

Bryant's $30.4 million already marked the highest wages in the NBA. Even after trimming his 2014–15 and 2015–16 average annual salary to roughly $24.3 million, such an expensive deal immediately eliminated space to sign both James and Anthony near their own maximum salaries. More damning: the Lakers, like every NBA team, could only sign free agents into available cap space. The league's collective bargaining agreement would have then permitted Los Angeles to dip into the tax to retain Bryant—teams could exceed the 2014–15 salary cap of $63.1 million up to $76.8 million before crossing a luxury tax line. Signing Bryant so early significantly hampered the Lakers' flexibility half a year before free agency even began.

Rival NBA executives mocked the decision. Working within the confines of the CBA was already challenging enough, as many of the league's rules attempted to dissuade such big-game free agency machinations. Any youngster, for example, who either earned league MVP honors, had been named to two All-NBA teams, or was an All-Star twice by the end of his fourth season, qualified for an even higher salary than the typical maximum for a player with four years of service—but only with the franchise that drafted them. (The so-called Derrick Rose Rule.) So if rebuilding teams like the Celtics, Magic, Sixers, or Suns struck gold in the draft and developed their pick into a superstar, young phenoms would see even greater earnings if they re-signed long term.

But the Lakers, with all their championship entitlement, don't rebuild. "I never, ever heard Mitch Kupchak say we're gonna tank," says Clay Moser. Instead, Los Angeles chose Bryant over the possibility of adding two superstars years his junior. Once management struck the deal before Bryant's December return, the Lakers thought they would project their commitment to the franchise legend as well as confidence in his health—both to their fans and upcoming free agents.

"That's all politics," says former Lakers assistant coach Dan D'Antoni. "The decisions were half-brained and half-empty. That doesn't work."

D'Antoni left Los Angeles and his brother, head coach Mike D'Antoni, after the 2013–14 season. "It was just an impossible situation," Dan D'Antoni says. The push-and-pull between Bryant's preferred, methodical style and a speedy system that benefited Steve Nash merely highlighted the growing dysfunction burbling throughout the organization. Coaches looked to owner Dr. Jerry Buss for an ultimate directive, but never heard a clear message. Meanwhile, numerous former players still lingering around the Lakers were lobbying, loudly, to feature Bryant in the half-court. "And that carried weight," Dan D'Antoni says.

Dr. Buss had always been the Lakers' lifeblood, powering each department, since he purchased the team in 1979. "His personality kind of held that franchise together," says Dan D'Antoni. He simultaneously signed players' checks and rivaled their swagger. And even within an organization full of high-profile figures in a city full of celebrities, Dr. Buss' star shined brighter than most. Then as the century turned, he began divvying his sports empire amongst his four children. The eldest, John, became president of the WNBA Los Angeles Sparks and Janie, his youngest, held an executive title in the Lakers' community relations office. Dr. Buss positioned Jim, his second child, and Jeanie, his third and first daughter, to oversee the Lakers' basketball and business operations, respectively.

To Lakers insiders, the nature of Dr. Buss' nurture seemed curious at best. The relationships amongst his children were contentious at their worst. And as the health of Los Angeles' storied owner began deteriorating, not long after the Lakers' 2010 championship, a rift particularly emerged among Jeanie's business side—with the trust of legendary point guard Magic Johnson and those other outspoken Lakers alumni—and Jim's basketball regime, led by Mitch Kupchak and Mike D'Antoni. "Your control tower's not there anymore," Dan D'Antoni says. "So that created some problems getting everybody on the same page."

Hiring Mike D'Antoni alone sparked fireworks amongst the Buss children. After Mike Brown failed to blend Howard and Nash with Bryant and Gasol to start the 2012–13 season, Jim agreed to meet Phil Jackson at the coach's Marina del Rey home with Kupchak in tow. Jackson piloted all five of Bryant's championships and each of Michael Jordan's six titles in Chicago. Having also maintained a long romantic relationship with Jeanie, Jackson's reunion with Bryant and the Lakers appeared just around the corner. They chatted for over 90 minutes before leaving Jackson with the belief L.A.'s head job was his. Happily engaged to Jeanie, a few years removed from coaching, Jackson hadn't originally sought the opportunity, but now had until Monday to decide.

Yet as the coach pondered his decision, Lakers brass interviewed several other candidates. And by the time Jackson dialed his agent to accept Los Angeles' offer, Kupchak had already come to terms with D'Antoni and his representative. "I was awakened at midnight on Sunday by a phone call from Mitch Kupchak," Jackson said in a statement the next morning. Kupchak revealed D'Antoni had signed for three years, leaving Jackson and Jeanie equally stunned and wounded. They felt Jim further twisted the knife by delegating the decisive phone call to Kupchak, despite Jim having initiated the Lakers' conversations with Jackson.

All the while, Dr. Buss remained hospitalized undergoing cancer treatments. His end unfortunately seemed near as the calendar flipped to 2013. Jim says he watched most Lakers games from his father's bedside during those final days in February. Their connection mounted on myriad mutual interests, from partying to opera, and Dr. Buss trusted Jim's sense with numbers and basketball savvy to help shape the Lakers. However, Jeanie and Magic Johnson say Dr. Buss summoned them to the hospital days before his passing on February 18. And through tears, the trio shared how they always hoped Jeanie and Johnson would lead Los Angeles, as the Hall of Fame point guard who won five titles in the 1980s structured another championship roster heading the basketball operations—not Jim.

Losing their patriarch thus gutted the franchise as much as their family. "All of a sudden you rip that out," Dan D'Antoni says. "It was almost impossible to have somebody take his place."

The fissures amounting throughout the Lakers bred Los Angeles' failed attempt to retain Dwight Howard. "That's no secret," says Mark Madsen. "There were some things that happened during that transition that were tough." Howard's free agent departure not only burned that bridge to the Lakers' post-Bryant future, but potentially signaled the crumbling of their organization altogether.

If anything, maybe Bryant was in fact the lone force capable of stabilizing Los Angeles' wobbly foundation. Approving his two-year extension that November marked at least one decision on which the Buss children unanimously agreed. They were the Lakers and he was *the* Laker. And despite Jeanie remaining skeptical of Jim's foreseeable basketball operations plan,

Los Angeles forged forward into 2013–14 keeping an eye toward the summer's free agency period, while, of course, vying for the playoffs.

Kupchak finished the Lakers' roster with a slew of one-year deals. While the moves preserved cap flexibility for Bryant's extension and July's open market, Los Angeles staffers hoped the lack of security would also prompt less established players like Nick Young and Wesley Johnson, and former playoff contributors like Jordan Farmar and Chris Kaman, with added incentive to perform. Mike D'Antoni's simplified, up-tempo system provided plenty of scoring opportunities. "You should have almost already made the decision in your mind if you're going to shoot it, pass it, or drive it," says rookie forward Ryan Kelly.

Just ask Steve Nash. The two-time MVP point guard started opening night playing 20 minutes in the Lakers' 116–103 win over the crosstown Clippers. Nash, now 39, wasn't yet cleared to play in back-to-back games, and so he appeared in just six of Los Angeles' first eight contests. But the Lakers were 3–3 with their floor general.

Pain, though, still plagued him, no matter his output on the court. After Nash scored 13 points and dished six assists in the Lakers' November 3 win over Atlanta, he still experienced nerve complications in his back and hamstrings from the broken leg he suffered a year earlier. "That kind of set off a chain of events for him and he never recovered," Clay Moser says.

Nash played just over 13 minutes in his sixth appearance but couldn't finish the game. He met with a back specialist soon after and was diagnosed with nerve root irritation. "He was so frustrated," says Bill Duffy, Nash's longtime agent. He would be sidelined for a minimum of two weeks.

Bryant's November 16 return to practice lifted the Lakers' downtrodden spirits. He claimed to be capable of playing in live games but was delaying his debut until he could play at full speed, with full confidence in his body to handle his famously heavy workload. Bryant unleashed his frustration, pent up from watching on the sideline since April. In scrimmage action, defenders returned his aggressive play and bumped Bryant right back. "I was telling guys not to take too much of it," guard Jodie Meeks says.

"And of course Kobe never backed down from that," says Mark Madsen, the assistant coach. "It was a very physical day. A lot of raw emotion. And

I think there was a sense of, really from everyone, of excitement that Kobe was back."

Bryant relished the fire, spitting trash talk in between dribbles. "It brought out a different dimension in him," says Johnny Davis. He debuted on December 8 against the Raptors, starting and playing 28 minutes against Toronto. But Bryant finished with only nine points on 2-for-9 shooting from the field as the Raptors spoiled the evening, escaping Staples Center 106–94 despite their shorthanded roster.

Toronto coaches yanked big man Aaron Gray from pregame warmups and sat the center in street clothes, along with forward Quincy Acy and swingman Rudy Gay. The Sacramento Kings had agreed to trade Greivis Vásquez, Patrick Patterson, John Salmons, and Chuck Hayes to land the three Raptors, including the final two years and $38 million left on Gay's contract. It was the exact win-now type of move from the front office that Mike Malone's coaching staff read as increased pressure for Sacramento to make the postseason. "Things like that are very awkward," says Chris Jent, the Kings assistant coach. In reality general manager Pete D'Alessandro completed his latest trade at the behest of owner Vivek Ranadivé.

Amid the Lakers' palace intrigue, a tenuous power struggle also unfolded in Northern California. Superstars like Kobe Bryant and perhaps the Kings' All-Star center DeMarcus Cousins fuel championship contenders, but ownership and management truly drive the success of NBA franchises. It's why Dan D'Antoni fled Los Angeles. Instability at the top trickles down throughout an organization, leaking into the front office and spilling into the locker room until the entire dam breaks.

So when Ranadivé purchased the Kings that May and hired Malone as head coach a few weeks before naming D'Alessandro as Sacramento's chief executive, rumor sparked around the league that a change on the bench could come by season's end should Sacramento fail to make the playoffs. Just as owners like to hire their own executive, general managers like to hire their own head coach. "It was difficult," says assistant Chris Jent, who played previously for Brett Brown at North Melbourne. "It put a lot of stress on Michael."

For Malone to survive, developing an honest relationship with Cousins would be paramount. Behavioral questions followed Cousins dating back to college despite his undeniable talent. "He was a strong personality," Jent says. "You gotta have thick skin, you gotta be confident in what you do, and you'll be okay. But he's gonna talk to you and he'll let you know." While many scouts rated Cousins as the most talented prospect in the 2010 class, his dubious intangibles allowed the Kings to snatch Cousins down at No. 5. And sure enough, Cousins clashed repeatedly with his first head coach, Paul Westphal.

Midway through the giant's second season, Westphal issued a bizarre statement through the team website, criticizing Cousins' commitment to the Kings and claiming the big man had demanded a trade. But just four days later, in what would foreshadow a string of managerial decisions that placated Cousins, Sacramento curiously fired the coach. Elevating assistant Keith Smart didn't ultimately appease Cousins either; he too was ousted by the end of 2012–13. The Maloof family, just as Vivek Ranadivé would exhibit during his ownership, continually sided with Cousins, as enamored by his philanthropy and community involvement as they were his dexterity on the court.

Now Malone hoped to coach Cousins like every other member of the roster. If Malone had an expectation and a player failed to meet his demands, he held that man accountable. When Cousins, famously subpar on defense, didn't make his rotation, Malone, a noted defensive tactician, let him hear it. And Cousins seemed to respond. "He's a very competitive guy and I think that he and Malone have the same level of competitiveness," Jent says. "The guy did really hate to lose." If Cousins wanted to make the playoffs—as was Ranadivé's directive to new general manager Pete D'Alessandro—listening to Malone seemed to present a decent chance.

D'Alessandro heard the noise brewing outside of the Kings' facilities. He had no intention of firing Malone or increasing the temperature on his bench. But Ranadivé wanted an upgrade on the wing, and Rudy Gay was available. It didn't hurt that Toronto's lead executive, Masai Ujiri, had been D'Alessandro's boss in Denver, and Gay did appear to round out a potent starting attack for Sacramento. Forward Jason Thompson had complemented Cousins throughout their joint Kings tenure. Ben McLemore, D'Alessandro's 2013 first-round pick, projected as the shooting guard of the future. Gay would present the final piece to the lineup now organized by point guard Isaiah Thomas.

The Kings had used the 60th and final pick of the 2011 draft to add Thomas out of Washington. Standing at just 5-foot-9, he packed 185 pounds of sturdy muscle into that diminutive frame, delivering his unorthodox scoring touch from the beginning of his pro career. Come 2013–14, his third NBA season, Thomas scored 20.3 points per game, dancing off Cousins' screens at the top of the key. He could snipe from distance and twist around the giants stalking the paint. "It was amazing what he was able to do," Jent says.

Thomas and Cousins seemed to develop a blooming pick-and-roll partnership. The threat of Thomas' jumper often forced bigs to hedge on his shot, leaving an easy post opportunity for Cousins. Thomas could float long enough in the air, contorting for a look at the rim, then find Cousins on delayed rolls to the basket. "It was impressive," Jent says. "They were really close when we first got there."

Both players relished their shared success, but Thomas carried himself with confidence that could combust around Cousins' open fire. The swagger needed to carry oneself from the 60th pick to an unquestioned NBA starter sometimes irked the Kings' centerpiece, especially when Thomas dominated the ball in late-minute situations. "There were games you just couldn't take him out," Jent says. "Him in the middle of the floor playing pick-and-roll, he was almost unstoppable at that point in time." The point guard posted a team-high 29 points at Phoenix on December 13, despite the Suns undoing Gay's debut 116–107.

Perhaps it was the defeat, or maybe the fact Phoenix center Miles Plumlee swatted Cousins twice in the fourth quarter, but the Kings' big refused to talk to reporters postgame. Thomas leading Sacramento's scoring effort may have also been a factor. Kings staffers noted Cousins often envied

his teammates' brilliance, especially in contrast to his own subpar performances—he welcomed Gay by shooting just 5-for-16 from the floor.

Cousins, though, wasn't the only player to struggle with Miles Plumlee and
the Suns' pestering defense that fall. While new general manager Ryan
McDonough expected to battle Boston, Philadelphia, and others for draft
positioning in June, Phoenix's win over Sacramento marked the Suns'
fourth straight. After crashing Gay's Kings debut, Phoenix topped Golden
State 106–102 to reach 14–9 on the year. For a roster projected to stink,
McDonough's motley crew sure were playing like a postseason contender.
"We were underdogs. Nobody expected us to be where we were," says
forward Markieff Morris. "We just basically had a lot of fun proving people
wrong."

Morris sat out Phoenix's season opener, suspended for throwing an elbow
in an October preseason game, and watched Channing Frye instead start at
power forward. Point guard Goran Dragić could scurry off his screens while
Frye, who drained 38.8 percent of his career triples, popped for a long-range
look. "Back in the day, there was not a lot of switching, especially with the
4 position," Dragić says. "Usually they show or they're in deep zone. From
there on, Channing's such a great shooter, you just read the situation and
make the play."

When Plumlee initiated a high pick for Phoenix's other point guard, Eric
Bledsoe, his aggressive rolls to the rim presented a dangerous lob threat.
"Eric would create an opening and I knew it was coming," Plumlee says. "I
could wind up and slam it so easy." Rookie head coach Jeff Hornacek had
unlocked the up-tempo scheme he promised to employ.

The Suns brought their streak into San Antonio on December 18. Young
teams visiting the Spurs were often intimidated by the championship aura
emanating from Tim Duncan, Tony Parker, and Manu Ginóbili. "We went
in there like, 'Yo, we're trying to bust their ass,'" Channing Frye says. Phoenix
indeed led throughout the battle, yet Ginóbili scored 11 points in the final
four minutes to lift the Spurs 108–101. San Antonio's veterans promptly

greeted Phoenix's players after the buzzer with admiration. "All those guys were like, 'Oh, shit. We gotta take them kinda serious,'" Frye says.

A determined Suns team regrouped in the postgame locker room. Phoenix personnel listed a few uncharacteristic late-game mistakes that doomed the contest. When a team is fine-tuning on those margins, and recognizes it boasts shooting, playmakers, and a fierce defense, it can start to believe. "I think that was the turning point of that year," says Markieff Morris, "when we figured out, 'Yo, we can really do something.'"

Sure enough, after Phoenix fell to San Antonio, the Suns rallied off three more consecutive victories. A 117–90 demolition of a shorthanded Los Angeles squad on December 23 pushed Phoenix to 17–10. It was the Lakers who were supposed to be the team surging into 2014 like a playoff contender rounding into form, but Pau Gasol looked depleted after missing the previous outing with an upper respiratory infection. And with ball handlers Steve Nash, Steve Blake, and Jordan Farmar all sidelined, Mike D'Antoni decided to start 6-foot-6 forward Xavier Henry at point guard.

The biggest name on Los Angeles' injury report: Kobe Bryant. He scored 20 points against Phoenix back on December 10, Bryant's second game after returning from off-season Achilles rehab. By his fourth outing, Bryant resumed playing over 32 minutes per night, dropping 21 points on December 14 at Charlotte. In Atlanta two nights later, Bryant insisted on carrying the Lakers' fourth-quarter offense. He typically checked back in for the final nine minutes, replacing Xavier Henry. That evening, D'Antoni sent Bryant off the bench to retrieve Wesley Johnson. "I swear to you, Kobe called the same exact play every single time," Henry says. It was the first time the young swingman heard an NBA player discard a coach's call.

As the Lakers broke their huddle, Bryant schooled his teammate. "Every time down, this is what I'm going to do," he instructed. The Hall of Famer wanted Henry to initiate action on the right wing. Bryant would set a ball screen, forcing his man to guard Henry's drive instead while also drawing his teammate's defender, the notably slower-footed Kyle Korver, as the Hawks switched. He then wanted Henry to toss it back for Bryant's mid-post isolation. "I'll tell you when to cut," Bryant said.

Henry followed orders. "He'd look for me, and then he'd take his eyes off me and then I'd come back, and he'd want me to circle around and cut again," Henry says. The Lakers never managed to overcome Atlanta's sizable advantage, but Bryant kept calling for the same sequence, quite antithetical to D'Antoni's zippy system. "Every time we had a fast break, he was like, 'Slow down,'" Henry recalls. "He would literally have me walk that thing up and come over there and do the same thing."

Bryant's heavy workload continued the next night in Memphis. The 35-year-old scored 21 points through 32 minutes of action, showing no signs of slowing down. This was what he'd been practicing for. He would lift the Lakers into the playoffs even without Steve Nash. Then with 3:25 to play in the third quarter, Bryant was backing down Grizzlies wing Tony Allen on the right block when his left knee buckled, attempting to spin baseline for a patented fadeaway jumper. Bryant crumpled on the floor, clutching at his injury just like eight months earlier in Staples Center. He had famously refused to leave that April contest before taking his earned trip to the charity stripe. "That son of a gun stayed in the game and went and shot the two free throws and made both," Moser says.

Now one pivot in Memphis rendered a nine-month, arduous rehab all for naught. And like those free throws against Golden State, Bryant returned to the court to finish Los Angeles' win over Memphis, only for the Lakers to announce two days later he would miss six weeks having suffered a lateral tibial plateau fracture in his left knee. "When you work that hard to come back from the Achilles, it's tough," Lakers assistant Mark Madsen says.

Perhaps such rigorous playing time became futile. No Spurs player, for example, saw more than 29.4 minutes per game in 2013–14 en route to San Antonio's title that June. "The human body, quite frankly, is not built to take those kinds of punishments," says Johnny Davis, another Lakers assistant. Los Angeles won at Minnesota but promptly dropped its next six games, including that December 23 defeat in Phoenix.

Bryant's absence left a chunk of minutes available in Mike D'Antoni's rotation. Ryan Kelly, L.A.'s rookie small forward, always attempted to reach the locker room before any teammates. On a one-year deal, the Duke product hoped his commitment and punctuality would stand out to Lakers coaches.

"I tried to be the one to turn the lights on," Kelly says. Days after their Christmas Day clash with Miami, originally billed as a marquee matchup between Bryant and LeBron James, Kelly entered the Lakers' private quarters one game night and found the Hall of Famer sitting alone at his locker in silence. "You could tell, body language–wise, that was really disappointing for him," Kelly says. "When you back one injury up with another, it was devastating."

Reaching the playoffs suddenly seemed impossible. Poor health continued to plague Los Angeles overall. Nash remained on the shelf, far longer than that initial two-week prognosis, as nerve damage continued plaguing his back. Now, for the second straight season, Bryant and Nash's unavailability stood in stark contrast to Phoenix's rebuilding efforts. And here were the Suns, improbably vying for the Lakers' postseason spot, while Los Angeles' leadership quibbled like the lottery-ridden Sacramento Kings.

EIGHT

Steve Nash worked tirelessly to return for Los Angeles. He infused pliability exercises and dynamic, explosive movements into on-court workouts, as if yoga and basketball molded into an entirely different sport. He first learned the regimen from Vancouver physiotherapist Rick Celebrini during the 2004 off-season. "An incredible movement guru, so to speak," Nash says.

The floor general joined forces with Celebrini at the University of British of Columbia. They trained across forested trails and in the ocean, building ample core strength that could overcome Nash's spondylolisthesis, an aching back condition that causes vertebral slippage. "He's like a big brother to me now," Nash says. In Mike D'Antoni's system, Nash won MVP honors the next two seasons.

But as 2014 approached, each morning for the 39-year-old brought a new tweak and new soreness. That troublesome back seemed to grow worse by the hour. "He was almost hurt every day without getting hurt," Lakers forward Xavier Henry says. "It would be like shin splints or something with his fibula or something with his tibia. And then you're like, 'Wait, didn't he just practice yesterday?'"

More bodies continued to drop from D'Antoni offense that winter, as Henry went down next on December 29, straining his right knee in the first quarter against the visiting Philadelphia 76ers. "Injuries just did not allow him to reach his full potential," says Johnny Davis, the Lakers assistant.

Thaddeus Young scored seven of his 25 points in the fourth quarter to deliver Philly's 111–104 win that night. The victory gave coach Brett Brown's team just its third of December, bringing the Sixers to 9–21 on the year. "You keep hammering the rock, and one day it's going to split," Brown said postgame.

Evan Turner finished with 22, his final pair coming on an acrobatic, run-out slam just before time expired and the contest already decided. The Los Angeles crowd jeered Turner's gesture, and Philly's charismatic wing quickly walked over to the Lakers' bench and apologized. "We were upset," L.A. forward Ryan Kelly says. "That's kind of an unwritten rule."

Several Lakers ignored Turner's remorseful high-fives. Sharpshooter Jodie Meeks, having overlapped with Turner for two seasons in Philadelphia, merely offered his forearm to Turner's outstretched hand. "If I didn't know Evan," Meeks says, "it might have rubbed me the wrong way."

Xavier Henry underwent X-rays in the locker room as he watched Turner pump the ball below his waist before finishing the 360-windmill. "That was definitely disrespectful, right at the buzzer," Henry says. He would be diagnosed with a bone bruise, initially requiring a seven-to-10-day recovery, but Henry missed the next 28 games. The Lakers just didn't have enough healthy players to compete.

Los Angeles opened 2014 with an 11-point win against Utah on January 3 before dropping the next six. Any hope of a postseason push, especially with Bryant hampered, had fully faded. "When you keep waiting for someone, there's a psychological thing that takes place," Johnny Davis says. "'Well, we're missing our key guy, but he's on his way.' You have to perform at a high level, and whenever he comes, he comes. We didn't have enough wins early to put together four, five, six in a row where the guys thought, 'We need Kobe, but we can be competitive without him.'"

The Sixers, meanwhile, topped the Nuggets in Denver on New Year's Day to notch their first consecutive wins since beginning the season 3–0. Of course, instead of cheering those victories, team president Sam Hinkie spent much of December negotiating trade packages with rival executives, particularly with his former colleague and Houston general manager, Daryl Morey.

A deal framed on swapping either Thaddeus Young or Spencer Hawes for Ömer Aşık seemed to be gaining momentum.

Dwight Howard's arrival in Houston disgruntled the Turkish center, who started all 82 games for the Rockets the previous season. And while Aşık made repeated requests to flee, Thaddeus Young's agent, Jim Tanner, also lobbied Sam Hinkie to move his client. Unlike Hawes and Turner, set for free agency that summer, Young was signed through 2015, theoretically an even more enticing trade acquisition for rival teams, able to acquire Young for nearly two full seasons before he reached the open market. "I just was like, 'You know what, man? I'm not gonna be able to win, I got my deal, let's put me in a situation where I can at least have some pieces to win,'" Young says.

His request came weeks before news of Hinkie's talks for Aşık leaked publicly. Yet the stream of anonymously sourced media reports regarding Philly's negotiations with Houston irritated the Sixers veteran, when he couldn't find an audience with Hinkie himself. The news cycle also suggested Hinkie demanded an unrealistically hefty return for Young. "When you're being secretive, you gotta give people something to understand the meaning to your madness of what's going on," Young says. "He didn't understand you gotta give 'em something. We in this league, the basketball players, are entertainers. And to some extent, the GMs have to do the same thing. You have to give some type of feedback, you have to give some type of entertainment, something to talk about. He just wasn't willing to give that."

When Philadelphia departed for its annual winter road trip, spanning as long as two weeks while Disney on Ice occupied its home arena, Young saw the six-game jaunt as an opportunity. "If you didn't want to trade me, you want to hold me hostage, you know what I'm gonna do?" Young says. "I'm just gonna audition for every team out there." He scored 30 both in Milwaukee and at Phoenix before his 25 points in Philadelphia's win at Los Angeles. "I got to take every shot," Young says. He added 17 in Philly's win at Denver on January 1, then hung 28 and 30 in the Sixers' next two wins at Sacramento and then at Portland.

"I was like, 'Man, this dude really wants to go,'" Spencer Hawes says.

"He just went on a rampage," says Sixers guard Jason Richardson.

The Trail Blazers won by 34 when they visited Philly back on December 14, but Young's 30-point outburst in Portland on January 4 improbably powered the lowly Sixers to four straight road victories. "We were supposed to be a shitty team, too," he says.

At 12–21, however, reality still hung over the franchise. Young, Hawes, and Turner would surely depart before February's trade deadline. And Hinkie's moves would likely return a mix of young players, expiring contracts, and future draft assets, not postseason reinforcements like Kings owner Vivek Ranadivé hoped Rudy Gay's services would provide Sacramento.

From 1999 to 2006, the Kings made eight consecutive postseason appearances, highlighted by their controversial 2002 Western Conference Finals loss to the Lakers. Sacramento hadn't returned to the playoffs since, marking one of the longest droughts in the NBA. "Sac's been a place that, for so long, has wanted a winner," Rudy Gay says. While numerous teams had since rebuilt and rebounded into the postseason, the Kings—no matter the management in place or the coach stalking the sideline—found themselves perennially entrenched in the league's cellar. Sacramento toiled into the lottery each May yet was neither bad nor lucky enough to select higher than fourth. The Kings seemed trapped on the treadmill of mediocrity with the machine programmed to a numbingly slow speed.

DeMarcus Cousins' talent was nothing short of a coup at No. 5 but hadn't yet translated to winning basketball. In the 2011 draft, Sacramento came away with BYU's electric scorer Jimmer Fredette, but a combination of Cousins' incessant practice taunts and Fredette's inconsistent playing time prevented any confidence or early success for the sharpshooter. "He never really had any kind of opportunity," says Chris Jent, the Kings assistant coach.

With a roster in obvious need of development, Mike Malone's coaching staff joined Sacramento expecting a two-season cushion before expectations mounted. They would get their feet wet, establish a rapport with Cousins, regroup that off-season, and dive headfirst into the 2014–15 playoff picture. Ranadivé's patience, however, expired by December, when the Kings' 4–12 record sparked the owner's insistence to acquire reinforcements. "It all changed right away because we got Rudy," Jent says. "That two-year projection ended."

In Boston, Danny Ainge wasn't waiting for the February trade deadline, either. On January 7, the Celtics swapped Courtney Lee, in a three-team maneuver, for Jerryd Bayless from the Grizzlies. Two seasons and $11 million lingered on Lee's contract, as opposed to Bayless' $3.1 million deal expiring that June. One week later, Ainge sent guards MarShon Brooks and Jordan Crawford to Golden State in another three-team exchange that netted what became a 2015 second-round pick and two 2016 second-round selections—all for absorbing the final two years and $8 million on Miami Heat center Joel Anthony's contract.

This was how a team expeditiously rebuilds from a playoff era. And when the Celtics welcomed the struggling Lakers on January 17, a mid-game timeout brought Joel Anthony's first Brad Stevens after-timeout experience. The veteran center stood agape at the rookie head coach, scribbling on his whiteboard inside Boston's huddle like a student racing against the clock of a standardized test. "There were so many lines and everything going across the board and you're looking, you're like, 'That…might just work,'" Anthony says. Each timeout brought another play call. "It seemed like he always had something. Every single time. He'd draw it all up. They looked almost like he was doing it on the fly, but he understood everything in such great detail. You could see his IQ."

Stevens' group held a 104–96 edge over the Lakers with 3:12 to play, but faltered 107–104 in a rare Los Angeles win. A Lakers three-point barrage from Wesley Johnson, Jodie Meeks, and backup guard Kendall Marshall spurred an 11–0 sprint to the finish. The Celtics' offense was so dreadful down the stretch and the Lakers were so dreary, few among Boston's coaching staff found consolation in their loss. Stevens, though, had earned a new believer. "At the end of the game," Joel Anthony says, "I was like, 'Oh, he's gonna give them a shot.'"

That spring, however, Boston had no chance at the postseason. By design, Ainge had scattered veteran contributors across the league in favor of draft compensation. More deals were sure to follow. Rival teams valued both point guard Rajon Rondo and forward Jeff Green on the trade market. Having made his season debut in that Lakers loss, Rondo could play a few weeks of game action to showcase his surgically repaired knee ahead of the February 20 trade deadline that promised to be buzzing with buyers and sellers.

Sam Hinkie still waited to strike any deal for his very available veterans. Thaddeus Young's West Coast eruption prompted a series of calls from Ryan McDonough in Phoenix, a surprising buyer ahead of the deadline, yet the Suns refused to part with one of their 2014 first-round picks. Sixers faithful characteristically debated the delay in Philadelphia's trades, just like Hinkie's head coaching search that summer. Young, Turner, and Hawes all somehow still remained on the roster. What was Hinkie waiting for? Fans feared the longer their new chief executive stood pat, the lesser a return the Sixers would receive. Until that point, Hinkie had only tinkered around the back half of his roster.

Whenever a new player arrived in Philadelphia, Hinkie stashed handwritten letters inside their hotel room at the Hilton, down the street from the Sixers' PCOM headquarters on City Line Avenue. Darius Morris appreciated the warm welcome when he joined Philly that August on a one-year minimum contract. "However, I didn't know that the whole Hinkie experimentation was gonna be going on," he says. "If I knew, I probably would have made a different decision." Morris' time under Brett Brown in turn featured its share of highs and lows.

Having started 17 games for the Lakers the previous season—and scoring 24 points in one playoff outing that spring—Morris struggled to maintain the composure Brown urged his point guards to play with, even amid Philadelphia's nightly uphill battles. Morris celebrated scoring 20 points during the Sixers' 37-point loss at New Orleans in November, but drooped his shoulders during Philly's three-point defeat in Dallas the next game, when he only managed three points in just 11 minutes.

Morris synced his phone to the charter's Wi-Fi before closing his eyes on the flight back east that evening. He was looking forward to the team's day off before a text message pinged his cell. "I want to discuss roster spots tomorrow," Brett Brown sent. "Sorry," he quickly followed. "Wrong person." Morris furrowed his brow, staring into his phone deciding whether to respond. Brown's note was clearly intended for Hinkie. "I don't know if that was God giving me a heads up," he says.

The next morning before practice, Brown asked Morris to step into his office. It was tough for him to let Morris go, the coach explained. And while Brown liked Morris as a man and respected his talent, he did not appreciate Morris' body language. He needed positivity and energy to launch his Sixers program, and besides, Brown revealed, there would be plenty more casualties in Philadelphia that season. "The plan all along was to get a lot of guys in there, rotate them, and see what they got," Morris says.

Hinkie signed and later waived Kentucky center Daniel Orton, a former first-round pick looking to find a home. He added D-League guards Elliot Williams and Lorenzo Brown. They'd listen to music and do cross-word puzzles when shuttling back and forth to the Sixers' affiliate team in Delaware.

In January, Hinkie visited the D-League Showcase to scout more young talent, trekking with the rest of the NBA's evaluators to Reno for a three-day, 15-game slate. The Showcase marks the premier opportunity for all involved in the minor league—coaches, players, executives, referees—to exhibit their abilities to NBA decision-makers. Those games presented the greatest opportunity for players on the cusp of their dream, bringing each affiliate club together for a midseason tournament. By the middle of the month, NBA teams could begin auditioning D-League players on 10-day contracts. Each franchise can sign free agents to two consecutive 10-day deals before having to either extend the player for the remainder of the season or sever ties entirely.

While those margins can appear crude, those opportunities rendered more than worthwhile for players. The median D-League salary hovered just over $20,000. A single 10-day contract in 2013–14 paid rookies over $28,000 and nearly $50,000 to players already with one year of NBA experience, plus the chance to earn an NBA deal for the rest of the season. At the Showcase, though, Hinkie found himself most impressed by Robert Covington, the sharpshooter out of Tennessee State.

He'd nearly drafted Covington at No. 35 back in June, but the marks-man's agent said he would decline the non-guaranteed, four-year minimum salary contract Hinkie planned to offer after the selection. Covington instead signed with Daryl Morey and Houston for a similarly structured four-year deal front-loaded with over $500,000 guaranteed. Now here he was, scoring over 20 points per game for the Rio Grande Valley Vipers, right for Hinkie to observe.

Covington haunted Hinkie throughout the 2013–14 season as he toggled back and forth between Houston and the Rockets' D-League affiliate, instead of playing for Philadelphia. These were the margins on which Hinkie strived to beat his competitors. The executive felt he could have signed Covington back on draft night as a free agent, before Morey, if he hadn't been required to meet with the assembled media waiting at the Sixers' facilities late that evening.

When Covington wasn't stealing Hinkie's attention during that January showcase, the executive focused on finding another center to audition with the Sixers. He'd ultimately invite Dewayne Dedmon, Jarvis Varnado, Hamady N'Diaye, and Kyrylo Fesenko to Philadelphia for an open tryout, pitting the big men one-on-one at the block and running pick-and-roll drills. The Sixers offered Dedmon a 10-day deal by day's end.

Most D-League call-ups of that time offered little more than a salary increase. Many teams used those contracts to stash break-in-case-of-emergency point guards deep on their bench—as the Lakers had with Kendall Marshall. Brett Brown's rotation, however, offered plenty of opportunity. Dedmon played 14 minutes against Charlotte in his January 15 Sixers debut. He scored his first NBA bucket two nights later against Miami, before finishing with seven points in 20 minutes. "Evan Turner tossed me a lob and I smoked that joint," Dedmon says.

He signed for a second 10 days on January 24. Philly fell to Toronto that evening and dropped its next two contests against Oklahoma City and Phoenix's plucky playoff contender. The Sixers did return to the win column on January 29. They trailed at Boston, 94–93, with five seconds remaining, when Turner sized up Bayless, the Celtics' recently acquired point guard, and crossed the defender right-to-left at the top of the key. He surged into the paint and flipped a runner over Jared Sullinger as time expired. Turner sprinted down the parquet floor toward the visitor's bench, arms flexed at his sides, having stolen a rare victory for his 15–31 club.

The former No. 2 pick paced Philadelphia at 17.4 points per game. And with the February 20 trade deadline fast approaching, he found Brad Stevens in the TD Garden hallway connecting both postgame locker rooms. "It was after they put my jersey up for half off," Turner quips.

The pair had struck up a friendship back in 2009, when Stevens accompanied Butler stars Gordon Hayward and Shelvin Mack to Team USA's FIBA U19 training camp. In the busy cafeteria one afternoon, Turner, then a rising junior at Ohio State, saw the Bulldogs' boyish head man silently eating lunch. Turner's Buckeyes coach, Thad Matta, had preceded Stevens at Butler, so relying on that mutual connection, Turner unassumingly sat across from Boston's future play caller. They talked ball for over a half hour.

Four years later, Turner sought Stevens once more. "I knew I was on the trading block," Turner recalls. "I said, 'Hey, I'd love to play for you.'" He would repeat the message back in Philadelphia after Boston won 114–108 on February 5. "I was like, 'Yo,'" Turner says. "It's about to be over here."

His name lingered on the trading block all season, but the veteran began to fear February's deadline could pass without a change of scenery. Chicago had lost Derrick Rose once again in late November. After rehabbing a torn ACL during the entirety of 2012–13, a torn meniscus in his right knee prematurely ended Rose's 2013–14 campaign. But when the Bulls subsequently inquired about Turner's availability, Sam Hinkie demanded *two* 2014 first-round picks in any negotiation with Chicago. "In what was projected to be the best draft in a long time," Turner says. "It was getting to the point where you didn't know."

Teams lingering on the fringe of the postseason had already begun bolstering their rosters. Time—and roster space—was running out for Hinkie to find Turner a new home. Golden State already swung its January deal for Boston's two guards. Phoenix signed Leandro Barbosa on January 28. The speedy guard had thrived off the Suns' bench back during the Mike D'Antoni heydays. "He's always a spark," says forward Channing Frye.

With Barbosa, Phoenix topped the mighty Pacers in Indiana on January 30, its fourth victory in another five-game winning streak. The Suns also ran away with a 24-point rout when Indiana visited Arizona eight days earlier as well. "We could do nothing with them," says Pacers big man Ian Mahinmi. "That was kind of the beginning of a trend." Once starting the year 33–7, Indiana would finish 56–26. Acquiring Luis Scola from the Suns had indeed helped lift the Pacers to first in the East, yet opponents took note of how Phoenix's whirring offense dizzied Indiana.

Towering center Roy Hibbert couldn't keep pace with the Suns' tempo, and Phoenix's shooters traded three-pointers with David West's long twos. "It was a matchup problem for us," Mahinmi says. The contrast encapsulated the theological basketball debates dominating front office discussion around the NBA.

"They were very methodical and we kind of showed that if you run, you can run them out of the gym," Suns big man Channing Frye says.

When Frye and Miles Plumlee went to the bench, Hornacek subbed Marcus and Markieff Morris into the frontcourt, juicing the Suns with more speed despite facing a height disadvantage. The identical twin brothers, standing at 6-foot-9 with carbon copy tattoos, sped around opposing bigs like Hibbert and West. "They finish each other's sentences. They would wear the same clothes," says their college coach, Kansas' Bill Self. The twins' innate chemistry supported Phoenix's stingy second unit few foes could combat. Ryan McDonough's Suns, whom the general manager once cautioned not to be "too tanky," in Channing Frye's words, entered the All-Star break at 30–21.

Remnants of the Steve Nash era now seemed long in Phoenix's rearview. Head coach Jeff Hornacek's roster of misfits could taste the playoffs. Meanwhile, Nash wound up missing 39 games for the Lakers before finally returning on February 4 at Minnesota.

Lakers personnel began avoiding the topic of their uncanny injury misfortune. "You don't want to be next and jinx yourself," says Jodie Meeks. The shooter then sprained his right ankle in the first minute against the Timberwolves. An errant elbow to the head from teammate Chris Kaman next left forward Jordan Hill with a neck strain. Steve Blake appeared for the first time since sustaining an elbow injury on December 10, yet somewhere amid his 32 minutes at Minnesota, Blake somehow ruptured his eardrum.

Los Angeles arrived in Cleveland the following night with only eight available players for that February 5 contest. Like the beginning of the year, Nash sat the second night of a back-to-back. Bryant remained sidelined. A strained right groin had kept Pau Gasol inactive for some time. Then Nick Young injured his left knee before halftime.

When the Lakers regrouped at intermission, Nash pleaded with the coaching staff, hoping to play in the second half. "I'm going to do what I can to get out there," he declared, stretching and warming up his aching body. When Chris Kaman fouled out in the fourth quarter, leaving Los Angeles with just six players, Nash retreated to the locker room, stripped his street clothes, and rejoined the Lakers' bench wearing his No. 10 jersey. Sure enough, Jordan Farmar departed the final frame with leg cramps.

Only five players remained. Los Angeles was so depleted that Kaman splayed his entire 7-foot frame across the visitor's bench, mocking the absurdity of their situation with nearly half the roster undergoing treatment in the back. "We have nobody here!" he cracked. "It's crazy!" Television cameras spotted the giant stretched across several seats, sparking an evening of memes spiraling across social media. There was Kaman laying underneath a Muhammad Ali knockout punch and WWE's The Undertaker pinning the Lakers center for the 1-2-3.

"We always laugh," says forward Ryan Kelly. "He literally laid down on the bench for all of two seconds."

With 3:32 to play, center Robert Sacre then committed his sixth foul. The whistle should have disqualified Sacre from the game, like Kaman's sixth affront, yet league rules require teams to deploy five players on the court for the entirety of an NBA game. "We were all just looking around confused," Sacre says.

Mike D'Antoni's coaching staff huddled in bewilderment, unaware of how the Lakers could legally play a full lineup. "None of us had ever seen anything like it," says assistant Mark Madsen. After minutes of uncertainty, officials informed D'Antoni he could leave Sacre in the game, only each subsequent foul called against the center would also result in a technical and two free throws for the Cavaliers.

Nash's tenuous health eliminated any possibility he would have taken the court, although his physical woes clearly hadn't impacted his competitiveness. He wanted badly to play that night in Cleveland. When he did return two nights later, on his 40th birthday, Nash powered the wounded Lakers past the Sixers in Philadelphia. The oldest active player in the NBA finished with 19 points, five assists, and four rebounds, handing the Sixers' a fifth straight defeat.

There was no stopping Philly's streak. The Clippers' 45 point blowout over the Sixers in Philadelphia's next outing marked the other Los Angeles franchise's largest margin of victory in team history. "We literally beat the shit out of them," says sharpshooter J.J. Redick.

Midway through the second quarter, Blake Griffin thundered a windmill slam off Chris Paul's pass ricocheting from the backboard. The next Clippers possession presented another fast break. Griffin tossed the rock behind his back to Paul, who immediately lobbed another softball for Griffin to windmill atop the Sixers' retreating defense. "We were at the height of our play," says Clippers center DeAndre Jordan. "We were just trying to come out early and jump on teams."

Golden State then smacked Philadelphia by 43 the next evening in Oakland. "I felt like I was coming into each and every night bringing a knife to a gunfight," Sixers forward Thaddeus Young says. After a 105–100 loss at Utah on February 12, Philly, mercifully, reached the All-Star break. The midseason pause provided a necessary reprieve, with only their upcoming February 18 home game against Cleveland separating the Sixers' veterans from that Thursday afternoon's February 20 trade deadline.

Spencer Hawes and Evan Turner planned a vacation in the Dominican Republic, only inclement weather prevented their private jet from taking off in Philadelphia and meeting girlfriends awaiting their arrival in the Caribbean. As storms continued throughout the weekend, Hawes and Turner were stuck in the city they so desperately wanted out of. The teammates drowned their sorrows at Hawes' home. They finished his supply of alcohol before both would surely be dealt the next week.

Turner also exhausted Hawes' roll of toilet paper during one trip to the bathroom. Searching for a replacement, he found nothing but tissue with the current president's face printed on each square. A Republican, Hawes had received the gag gift over the holidays. And Turner, he of the media day hot microphone incident and the buzzer-beating jam against the Lakers, tweeted a picture suggesting Hawes used the product regularly. "That was one of those moments where you weren't thinking," Turner recalls. "But at the same time, who the fuck has Barack Obama toilet paper?"

Hawes hoped to flush his remaining time in Philadelphia without any other hitch or injury. The Spurs had shown strong interest in his shooting ability, and Hawes envisioned fleeing the league's tanking laughingstock for the reigning Western Conference champions. He coasted throughout the 20–33 Cavaliers' 114–85 dismantling of the Sixers in that February 18 contest, Philadelphia's ninth straight loss. The Sixers watched Kyrie Irving glide untouched to the rim. They allowed 20 fast break points while slogging back in transition. Tyler Zeller, Cleveland's unproven second-year center, abused Hawes on the interior. It appeared to many onlookers as though the Sixers center wasn't even trying. "I did not," Hawes confirms matter of factly.

Philadelphia was off the next day, that Wednesday. And having no plans to join Brett Brown's early practice before the 3:00 PM deadline on Thursday, Hawes prepared Keurig coffee at home that morning instead of schlepping toward PCOM. "I was just on my own, having breakfast, just all of a sudden with a free day," Hawes says.

He walked over to La Buca, an Italian restaurant in Center City where he ate before most home games. The bartender he'd befriended rushed over to Hawes in tears, wrapping the 7-footer in a bearhug and asking where he would be traded. They had their answer before noon.

While Hawes readied to join a championship contender like San Antonio, it was Cavaliers owner Dan Gilbert who dialed his cell. "Needless to say that when I got the call it was Cleveland, I was disappointed," Hawes says. The Cavs wanted him in Ohio that evening so their new acquisition could travel for Friday's game against the Raptors. They faced an uphill battle to reach the postseason, after all. And so Hawes returned home to pack a bag as Gilbert sent a private plane to fetch Cleveland's new starting center. "That was the last I ever saw of my apartment in Philadelphia," Hawes says. "That I'd been in for four years."

NINE

Greg Lawrence could hear it in Sam Hinkie's voice. The agent to both Spencer Hawes and Sixers point guard Tony Wroten, Lawrence maintained a steady dialogue with Philadelphia's president in the lead-up to the trade deadline. Whenever he reconvened with Hinkie over the phone, they'd compare intel from conversations with teams interested in adding Hawes' services.

Then the week before Thursday's 3:00 PM buzzer, Lawrence found Hinkie became frazzled by the amount of trade chatter he chose to engage. "I think he was almost communicating too much," Lawrence says. "It's almost like if you had a blindfold on and I was trying to tell you who was leading a horse race. You go, 'Okay, Phoenix is in the lead! Well, Toronto and Memphis are kind of gaining there.' And then you go, 'Oh! Detroit! Detroit's now winning!' It's a new team every time."

San Antonio, Phoenix, Portland, Houston, and the Clippers showed the most persistent interest in Hawes' size and shooting. When Lawrence called again the morning of the deadline, Hinkie told the agent he had a couple of discussions gaining steam, but he wasn't certain any would be completed by the afternoon cutoff. Cleveland was not one of the teams Hinkie mentioned.

While the executive had successfully swapped Jrue Holiday for Nerlens Noel and New Orleans' 2014 first-round pick back on draft night, Hinkie still represented an unfamiliar figure to many rivals in the trade market. "I didn't really start dealing with him in earnest until he was in Philly," says one longtime Eastern Conference executive. "I think everybody thought he was smart, I just don't think people knew him that much."

Hinkie mostly worked on trade calls during his Houston tenure when finalizing the details of draft pick protections. Front offices can stipulate specific scenarios in which the selection they deal doesn't convey to the other team. For example: the 2014 first-round pick Philadelphia acquired from New Orleans was top-five-protected, meaning if the Pelicans' choice landed between Nos. 1-5 in May's upcoming lottery, New Orleans would keep the selection. Oftentimes picks then roll over to the following year, where more protections still keep the draft choice in play for its original team.

That February, the trade value of first-round picks reached an all-time high. June's top prospects continued shining as March Madness fast approached. Andrew Wiggins, Jabari Parker, as well as Wiggins' Kansas teammate Joel Embiid, a gifted 7-foot center, all projected as franchise-saving talents. "It was those three guys," says Milwaukee general manager John Hammond. Other talents, and perhaps future All-Stars, would also be available later in the lottery.

And with that, Sam Hinkie found no team interested in parting with a 2014 first-rounder for any of Spencer Hawes, Evan Turner, or Thaddeus Young, or a combination of two players. The last 2014 first-round pick to change teams came back in October, when Phoenix took on Emeka Okafor's contract. Even then, Washington protected the pick for Nos. 1-12.

Like several analytics-minded front offices, the Sixers had developed their own metric to evaluate opponents' list of trade chips, spanning players and future draft choices. Hinkie's algorithmic model copied techniques from finance and sports organizations' valuation software and even included tools from political polling databases. "They had a metric, almost like a football coach with a big card on the sideline when it's third-and-whatever," says Bobby Marks, the longtime Brooklyn Nets assistant general manager. "When you're looking at that, if I am taking back $3 million in salary, what is the—is it cash, is it a second-round pick, is it multiple second-round picks?—that they had something they could look to, as almost like a guide, and that kind of gave them an idea." To move Hawes, Hinkie ultimately felt the big man was worth forward Earl Clark, center Henry Sims, and two 2014 second-round picks from the Cavaliers.

"It was like, 'Cleveland? What the fuck?'" recalled Hawes' representative Greg Lawrence. The agent knew Cavs executive David Griffin well, and he had never once asked Lawrence about Hawes. Trading for Hawes that February felt like a team that had drafted a player without a visit or having access to his physical. "Cleveland kind of came out of nowhere," Lawrence says.

Dan Gilbert's Cavaliers, still reeling from LeBron James' 2010 free agency decision, badly sought a postseason appearance. Cavs officials hoped Hawes could help space the floor for Cleveland's young backcourt, allowing Kyrie Irving and Dion Waiters to shimmy their way to the rim and into the playoffs.

The clock ticked toward the deadline. Golden State then upgraded for its own postseason push by sending young wings Kent Bazemore and MarShon Brooks to Los Angeles for Steve Blake. The veteran point guard had escaped the Lakers, excited about the Warriors' possible playoff appearance and better bill of health. General manager Mitch Kupchak welcomed Bazemore over the phone, promising an opportunity to play and play fast. "I hadn't played extended minutes other than the D-League at that time, so that was an important opportunity," Bazemore says.

Reality finally swept the 18–36 Lakers' front office, now ready to join the list of lottery-bound sellers. Los Angeles also hoped forward Jordan Hill could net a decent return before the deadline struck. Kupchak engaged with Phoenix chief Ryan McDonough on Hill. New Orleans and Brooklyn showed interest as well, but no deal would emerge. Despite many predicting a swirl of activity across the league that Thursday, only Steve Blake and Spencer Hawes marked significant contributors to change teams as noon struck on the East Coast.

Then a few minutes after 12:30 PM, as part of a three-team deal with Philadelphia, the Wizards agreed to send swingman Jan Veselý, point guard Eric Maynor, and two second-round picks to Denver for sage floor general Andre Miller. Washington lacked a backup for All-Star point guard John Wall, and Miller, the 15-year veteran, hadn't played since December 30—when his frustration amid the Nuggets' subpar season bore a verbal altercation with Denver coaches. Moving Miller not only extinguished that fire but helped shed salary. Jan Vesely's contract would expire by season's end, and a lesser-talented Nuggets team would surely slide a bit in the standings while clearing their deck for the off-season.

Denver hadn't tanked the 2013–14 season, but it now made quite a bit of sense to trim the 24–28 Nuggets' books for new lead executive Tim Connelly, hired back in June 2013 amid the modern wave that brought Hinkie, D'Alessandro, and McDonough into power. "We were struggling as a team and we were trying to find Andre [Miller] a home where he could play meaningful basketball," Connelly says. Denver's lead executive even morphed the deal into a three-team trade by sending those future second-rounders to Philadelphia to further offload Eric Maynor's contract.

Hinkie had been successful in moving Hawes and snuck his way into swiping two more future picks in the Denver-Washington swap, yet he made little traction toward trading Evan Turner or Thaddeus Young. Even as the deadline approached, Hinkie maintained his steep price for both former lottery picks.

Philadelphia had discussed Turner with Indiana throughout the weeks leading up to the deadline. "What they were asking for was a little bit too rich for us," says Pacers vice president Peter Dinwiddie. The morning before Thursday's cutoff, Sixers brass called once again, still seeking a first-rounder in exchange for their swingman, but Indiana's front office maintained its lower counter just the same. It wasn't worth the risk to move such a draft choice in such a talented 2014 class for Turner, whose contract would expire by season's end. Not to mention, his next deal would also bring a $13 million salary cap hold if Indiana hoped to extend Turner off his lucrative rookie deal as a former No. 2 pick. And Hinkie was clearly struggling to find a trade partner willing to pay his premium, or else Turner wouldn't still be available.

Deadline day had clearly emerged as a buyer's market. Milwaukee traded both Gary Neal and Luke Ridnour to Charlotte to aid the Bobcats' postseason push, yet only netted back veterans Ramon Sessions and Jeff Adrien to save $1.8 million off the Bucks' cap figure. General manager John Hammond once hoped Neal and Ridnour would aid Milwaukee's own playoff aspirations. "Preseason, people were saying, 'If Milwaukee's healthy...'" Hammond recalls.

Yet just like the Lakers' misfortune, injuries had long derailed any chance of a competitive Bucks unit, now just 10–43, and Hammond couldn't receive any draft capital in return for his two veterans. Milwaukee's other tenured players were still hoping to reach greener pastures as well, just like Evan Turner and Thaddeus Young. "It was one of the worst seasons I ever had," says forward Ersan İlyasova.

Other unsuccessful teams continued gauging the value of their veteran pieces. Orlando was open to parting with scoring guard Arron Afflalo—acquired back in the 2012 Dwight Howard blockbuster—yet the Magic ultimately retained his services with plans to resume discussing Afflalo trades before June's draft.

Sacramento looked to find a new home for Isaiah Thomas. DeMarcus Cousins' relationship with the punchy point guard had fully soured. As their disconnect became palpable throughout the Kings' facility, team owner Vivek Ranadivé, of course, sided with his big man. The Suns and Celtics expressed interest in Thomas, but their offers seemed to still value him as the former second-round pick he had been, not the dynamic starter he'd become. Sacramento general manager Pete D'Alessandro couldn't find a team interested in adding former lottery pick Jimmer Fredette, either—not even for a single second-round pick.

With just 10 minutes left before the deadline, Philadelphia phoned Indiana once more. The 76ers had come to terms with the reality of retaining Thaddeus Young past the 3:00 PM horn. "He was one of those guys that, for sure, the coaches didn't want to see him go," says Lance Pearson, the Philadelphia analytics staffer.

Hinkie, meanwhile, knew the Pacers still had serious interest in Evan Turner. Slated as the East's top seed, Indiana eyed final improvements for its destined clash with Miami in the Eastern Conference Finals. "We were looking to acquire talent," says Peter Dinwiddie, Indiana's vice president. The clock ticking, Philadelphia finally acquiesced and accepted the Pacers' 2015 second-round pick, plus Danny Granger, the former All-Star forward in the final year of his contract, in exchange for Turner and Sixers center Lavoy Allen. "That deal probably happened at 2:55 PM," Dinwiddie says.

Granger could only see the move as being banished to the league's lowliest, tanking franchise. "The first time any player is traded, it's difficult," Dinwiddie says. The No. 17 pick in 2005, Granger bloomed into an All-Star by his fourth season, scoring 25.8 points per game in 2008–09 and claiming the NBA's Most Improved Player award. Then in 2012–13, patellar tendinosis in his left knee limited Granger to only five appearances, while Paul George emerged as the Pacers' All-Star centerpiece in his place. Granger also missed the first 25 games of 2013–14 with a left calf strain, and when he finally returned, he never found his footing in Indiana's second unit. Offloading Granger for Turner made as much sense for Indiana as it did for Sam Hinkie's rebuild. The Pacers needed to capitalize on their apparent championship window while it remained ajar.

Turner had actually practiced in Philadelphia that morning. Head coach Brett Brown sensed a lull in his team's energy and organized three hours of intense live action, partly as punishment for the Sixers' dismal effort against Cleveland two days earlier. "At that point, we were losing, so a lot of people stopped caring," says Sixers center Lavoy Allen.

Depleted, Allen went to lunch at the California Pizza Kitchen down the street from Philly's PCOM facilities. He scrolled the Twitter feed on his phone in between bites. When news of Turner's move struck, Allen learned he was also headed to Indiana thanks to social media. Pacers lead executive Larry Bird called shortly after, welcoming the big man to his new franchise. "I almost shit myself," Allen says. "Larry fucking Legend is calling me." Bird said he envisioned minutes for Allen in the Pacers' playoff rotation. He would help fortify their defense, he was far more than a throw-in. "And then I went to the bathroom and changed my underwear," Allen says.

The Sixers sent a car to shuttle the young big man to the airport. Philadelphia arranged for another driver to chauffeur Turner. He packed enough belongings to endure a postseason run with the Pacers and hopped in the back row of the black Yukon Denali idling outside his Gladwyne home.

"What the fuck?" Turner said, cocking his head back as he slid into the truck.

Turner surprisingly found Sam Hinkie seated in the middle row of his ride. "Maybe he was just checking to make sure I got on the plane, who knows?" Turner smiles.

Philadelphia's president wanted to thank Turner for the leadership he'd shown the Sixers' young prospects, especially budding Rookie of the Year candidate Michael Carter-Williams. As their truck sped toward the airport, Hinkie recounted memories with Tracy McGrady during their time in Houston, suggesting Turner too could find greater success with a team that traded for his services. "I thought it was nice," Turner says. "I appreciated it." Hinkie's rebuilding plan didn't feature Turner's future, yet the veteran had come to understand the executive's ultimate goal. "He had the vision to turn it around," Turner says.

Granger had no interest in joining Philadelphia's process, and Hinkie knew full well waiving his contract would effectively keep his salary on the Sixers' cap sheet while Granger signed with a contender. Brett Brown, however, dreamed of the All-Star providing much-needed guidance for his struggling youngsters and necessary shooting on the Sixers' perimeter.

For several days, Philly coaches discussed how they could best integrate Granger into their offense. Would scheming isolations for the veteran stall Carter-Williams' development running pick-and-rolls, or prepare the point guard for deferring to a playmaking wing like Andrew Wiggins?

Granger, meanwhile, had eyes on joining San Antonio, Miami, or the Clippers. He did visit Philadelphia briefly after Brown convinced Granger to hear his pitch. "Danny came for a day," says Sixers guard Jason Richardson. Yet no projection of a Sixers offense starring Granger convinced the wing to join Brown's dilapidated, rebuilding roster.

With the veteran Sixer's tenure over, Hinkie phoned Dewayne Dedmon's agent, Mike Silverman. To maintain roster flexibility, Hinkie had asked Silverman not to negotiate with rival teams until after the trade deadline. And so Dedmon spent the past few weeks working out with his trainer, A.W. Canada, in Detroit. As he braced for his next taste of the NBA, only Dedmon understood his upcoming opportunity might not occur in Philadelphia.

Silverman expected Hinkie's negotiations to extend Dedmon past a second 10-day contract would hold true to the executive's early form, offering nothing more than a four-year, non-guaranteed minimum deal Hinkie first tendered Robert Covington on draft night. Agents had deemed this contract structure the "Hinkie Special."

"He was unwilling to move off of that," Mike Silverman says. When he rebuffed Hinkie's terms, Silverman could hear the executive stewing quietly on the other line. Brett Brown hoped to continue growing Dedmon in Philadelphia. While old for a rookie, the 24-year-old center hardly played organized basketball until late in high school. His early development pattern suggested Dedmon still had ways to improve before reaching an impressive ceiling.

After some time, Hinkie countered, offering Dedmon over $100,000 of guaranteed money to close 2013–14, while still leaving the next three seasons fully non-guaranteed, "to buy the remaining three years," Silverman recalls. The agent declined again. Any offer that included a fourth, team-controlled year would be a non-starter.

"As soon as we turned that one down, Orlando was knocking at the door," Dedmon says.

Magic general manager Rob Hennigan soon offered nearly $300,000 guaranteed in a multi-year contract. "That was a pretty dope feeling," Dedmon says. And while the center would start the final six games of Orlando's season, and later blossom into a starting-caliber NBA rim protector over the next few years, Sam Hinkie's rebuild could afford to pass on a long-term agreement with Dedmon if it wasn't on the executive's terms. He would continue auditioning a slew of other talented prospects.

"Sam didn't feel any of these guys were important enough to move off of their four-year deal," says Silverman. There would always be another young player on the league's doorstep eager for his opportunity.

"The more time goes by, I think what he was doing made sense," Silverman now concedes. "You establish a precedent from day one, you have a precedent. Just because other teams aren't doing it, it doesn't mean that you as an organization can't take certain stands. If people allow you to get over on them, then you keep going on it. That's what they were doing, they were holding their ground."

Longtime agent Bill Duffy, the representative for Steve Nash, signed his client Brandon Davies to Hinkie's four-year, non-guaranteed special before the 2013–14 season. An undrafted senior out of BYU, Davies was waived from the Clippers' training camp. And Duffy, having known Hinkie a bit from his Houston tenure, saw Philadelphia's rebuild as a proving ground for Davies, where minutes were available for all comers. "[Hinkie] just was evaluating players and I think he felt like the most information he could get on players, those types of players, there's probably 20 of them that he evaluated and just wanted to get a feel for," Duffy says.

After Dedmon's departure, Hinkie offered Jarvis Varnado a 10-day contract on March 1, and then inked the bouncy big to that four-year, non-guaranteed contract on March 12. He'd sign four more perimeter players to 10-day contracts along the way, including James Nunnally, the floor spacer Dionte Christmas had outdueled during Phoenix's training camp, and point guard Casper Ware.

Each new face, just like the Sixers' trade deadline acquisitions, lived in the Hilton adjacent to Philadelphia's facility at PCOM. "There were about six or seven of us at the same time,'" says point guard Eric Maynor. They'd convene in the hotel lobby each morning. "We would all hop cars with each other to get there," Maynor says.

Each addition harbored talent Hinkie hoped to examine up close, yet they lacked the polished skills to make a present-day impact on NBA games. And so the Sixers' losing streak that began before the All-Star break expectedly stretched deep into March, surpassing double digits. "We never knew who was our teammate because there were so many guys coming and going," says guard Jason Richardson.

When Indiana visited Philadelphia on March 14, ultimately dishing a 19th straight defeat, Evan Turner and Lavoy Allen found Thaddeus Young during warmups and hugged their former teammate. After learning they'd been traded to the Pacers, both called Young and apologized he was still stuck as a Sixer. The forward had prepared to land in either Houston or Phoenix, yet neither team offered the first-round pick Hinkie coveted. "Some kind of way, we got past the deadline, nobody talked to me, nobody called me," Young says. "So obviously I did walk in that day pissed off."

Young was Philadelphia's most valuable player, and his January West Coast demolition showcased a malleable talent helpful for any playoff contender. "I know you could have gotten something for me," Young says, "but you chose to hold me hostage and make me waste a year." He watched his teammates fumble one unthinkable loss after another. It was remarkable how quickly their close battles could spiral out of control. Young's jumper with 2:31 left brought Philly within three points of Indiana, for example, only the Pacers used a 7–0 run to escape victorious. The Sixers didn't score again until Young's layup with 15 seconds remaining. "I couldn't believe it would fall to pieces that fast," he says. "It was the 'You gotta be fucking kidding me' moments."

Philadelphia faltered in Memphis the following evening, suffering a 103–77 drubbing that tied the Sixers' franchise-worst of 20 straight losses. Former Magic head coach Stan Van Gundy lamented the Sixers as an embarrassment during the MIT Sloan Sports Analytics Conference on February 28. Commissioner Adam Silver coincidentally attended Philadelphia's game against Washington on March 1 the next evening, telling a local reporter, "I think what this organization is doing is absolutely the right thing. What they're doing is planning for the future and building an organization from the ground level up. And so, if you look at what's happened here over the last several years, it's badly needed. Somebody needs a plan. Somebody needs a vision to win here. And I think that's what's happening."

But each subsequent demise brought more national media scrutiny on Philadelphia. "You could feel the heightened attention in the locker room and the coaching room to a different level," says Lance Pearson, Philadelphia's analytics staffer. "It was just, like, desperation. 'Let's try not to set a new record for futility.'"

By March 27, the Sixers tied the 2010–11 Cavaliers for the longest losing streak in NBA history, dropping their 26th in a row. Cleveland first set the infamous mark squandering 26 straight while LeBron James found his footing in Miami.

Philadelphia, somehow, managed to avoid setting a new all-time mark. When Brett Brown's unit hosted Detroit two nights later, the Sixers raced past the Pistons 123–98 in front of a raucous crowd. The win marked their first victory since Evan Turner's buzzer-beater in Boston exactly two months earlier, on January 29. "We were going crazy that it was over," forward Brandon Davies says. Members of the coaching staff went out for rounds of drinks. Having the next day off, a handful even drove down to Atlantic City to celebrate.

Philadelphia still stood at 16–57 on the year. And without Turner or Spencer Hawes—or Danny Granger, after the veteran signed in Los Angeles to bolster the Clippers' title chase—the Sixers quickly found themselves right back in the losing column. Hawes' season outlook didn't appear much better in Cleveland, either.

Cavs owner Dan Gilbert had axed general manager Chris Grant two weeks before the trade deadline. Instead of aiding Cleveland's playoff hopes, Anthony Bennett hadn't yet found his NBA footing—marking just the latest in a string of unsatisfactory draft choices during Grant's tenure, although Cavs officials claim Gilbert was responsible for some of those personnel decisions, like drafting Dion Waiters No. 4 in 2012.

It hadn't helped that Cleveland coaches stuck their No. 1 pick on the bench, leaving Bennett just 12.8 minutes per game as a rookie. He was only able to produce 4.2 points and 3.0 rebounds. "How about that one? Mistake," says John Calipari, the Kentucky head coach. "Who knows what would have happened if [Nerlens Noel] had gone to Cleveland?"

With Chris Grant out, Dan Gilbert elevated assistant general manager David Griffin to the Cavs' lead executive. Adding Spencer Hawes at the deadline certainly aided Cleveland's playoff push, but Griffin's acquisition introduced another body to the Cavs' frontcourt logjam and further restricted Anthony Bennett's opportunity. "Man, I felt bad for him," Hawes says.

It's hard for any rookie to flourish in limited minutes. More first-year players have toiled on the bench than shown signs of development during fleeting playing time. "It's just, when you're the No. 1 pick, you don't have the benefit of getting to work shit out like that," Hawes says. And just nine games into Hawes' tenure, Bennett strained the patellar tendon in his left knee, effectively ending his troublesome first season.

Bennett never managed to find the conditioning and consistency to thrive in 2013–14. The Cavaliers felt so far away from college. At UNLV, Bennett had embraced the growing spotlight, signing each autograph request with an infectious smile. "He just has a way about him that he cares about other people," says former Rebels head coach Dave Rice. "And maybe he cared too much about what other people thought. It impacted him, and the pressure of him being the No. 1 pick in the draft was hard."

Making the postseason would prove just as challenging for the Cavaliers at large. Bennett's teammates flopped four of Cleveland's last six games. "We faded out," says point guard Matthew Dellavedova. Back-to-back losses to Atlanta and Charlotte, which claimed the eighth and seventh seeds in the East, respectively, ultimately ended another Cavs season short of the playoffs.

Cleveland was headed back to the lottery, where fortune had, oddly, tended to favor the wine and gold.

TEN

The Lakers missed the playoffs for the first time since 2004–05, Kobe Bryant's initial season without Shaquille O'Neal. That trip to the 2005 lottery marked one of only two during Jerry Buss' 34 years of Lakers ownership that Los Angeles failed to reach the playoffs. Now the Lakers were back in the lottery in the very first season since his passing.

Bryant's December injury had doomed the team before 2013–14 ever truly got off the ground. By March 12, the Lakers announced their superstar would miss the remainder of the season due to that ailing knee. And while Bryant appeared in just six contests during 2013–14, Steve Nash merely saw the court in 15 games himself—grinding his way back to availability only to rejoin such a battered roster.

Nash managed to play at Minnesota on March 28, although the Timberwolves did win, and by 36. With the Lakers not set to fly back to Los Angeles until the next morning, Nash felt no rush to retreat to the team hotel with a night ahead in Minneapolis. The 40-year-old lingered in the locker room postgame, soaking his worn body in ice as staff brought him a six-pack of Coors. With the rest of their teammates already en route to their suites for the evening, Nash invited 24-year-old Kent Bazemore to knock back a drink in their shared locker room. Acquired from Golden State before the deadline, Bazemore had grown up watching the Hall of Famer shine in Phoenix. "I had a beer with Steve Nash," Bazemore smiles. "It was cool."

The Lakers flew back west in the morning, with a day off before another date with Nash's old Suns on Sunday, March 30. Phoenix, Memphis, and Dallas were each on pace to challenge for 50 wins as they jockeyed for the final two playoff seeds out West.

The Suns had formed their own brotherhood, toasting wins in cities across the map. One veteran chose a restaurant for the evening's dinner and most of the team's traveling party would join, drinking and joking until the establishment closed its doors. "We weren't these Goody Two-Shoes guys that never went out and had a beer," says forward Channing Frye. "We're like, 'Dude, let's get after it after the game, but let's win first.'" The loudest members of those late-night gatherings often doubled as the first to arrive for morning shootaround.

Touching down in Los Angeles brought another chance for a stirring road trip. The Suns also had that Saturday night off before Sunday's matchup with the lowly Lakers. Then Phoenix would draw a free Monday morning in Hollywood before flying back home, where a Tuesday practice stood before that Wednesday night's clash with the juggernaut Clippers. As long as the Suns took care of business, as Frye reiterated, they could rage on Saturday, win Sunday night, and be back at the club shortly after beating the Lakers. "We really debated those two games," forward Markieff Morris says. "We wanted to go out." Phoenix, remember, had blasted Los Angeles 117–90 back on December 23 at US Airways Center.

And so the Suns kept partying as Saturday night bled late into Sunday. Sure enough, Phoenix shot just 22.2 percent from three later that evening. It was the Lakers who raced out to a 26–15 advantage and cruised to a 115–99 win. "I don't know if we had a single guy who came with the energy that they usually have," head coach Jeff Hornacek said postgame.

Players brushed off the loss. They simply hadn't taken the 24–48 Lakers seriously. A group still went out again on Sunday night. But then after a poor practice on Tuesday, the Suns squandered a 17-point third-quarter lead to the Clippers on Wednesday. "L.A. nightlife is undefeated and it's always going to be," Markieff Morris says. "It's always going to be."

Instead of standing alone in the West's No. 7 spot, the pair of losses dropped Phoenix into a three-way tie with Memphis and Dallas. Only seven games remained. The Suns quickly rallied to win three straight but dropped another tough battle in San Antonio, with Goran Dragić nursing a sprained left ankle.

Phoenix visited Dallas the following night. The Suns' postseason suddenly in jeopardy, Dragić started and played 40 minutes despite his lingering pain. "His ankle was like a freaking grapefruit," says forward P.J. Tucker. "He's battle-tested. He don't back down from anybody." Yet Dragić could only convert six of his 18 attempts, and a series of late-minute blunders cost Phoenix the pivotal contest 101–98, staging a win-and-in clash at home with Memphis two nights later to decide the West's final playoff berth.

The Grizzlies boasted a methodical scheme similar to that of the Pacers. Only unlike Phoenix's dominance of Indiana that season, Memphis cooled the Suns in each of their three previous 2013–14 encounters. "Zach Randolph was on a tear. A tear," Channing Frye says. "So I'm like, 'Gaaaahd daaamn! Anyone else! Anyone else!'"

A grueling fourth quarter saw 15 lead changes. Miles Plumlee's tip-in gave Phoenix a 91–90 lead with 1:27 left. Then, after Grizzlies point guard Mike Conley canned a triple and Goran Dragić turned the ball over, it was indeed Zach Randolph who scored the final pair of his game-high 32 points to give Memphis a 95–91 cushion and clinch the Grizzlies' postseason spot.

"I just couldn't believe we didn't make the playoffs that year; 48–34?" Markieff Morris says, referring to the Suns' record. "That's un-fucking-believable."

Ryan McDonough's organization landed back in NBA purgatory. One game short of the playoffs, Phoenix was clearly still far from championship contenders, and now would likely draw the 14th selection in May's lottery—rather than McDonough's expected poor campaign bringing more advantageous draft positioning. The Kings, for example, finishing 13th in the West at 28–54, also fell short of their playoff aspirations, but would still enter lottery night with the seventh-best odds at winning the No. 1 pick. Los Angeles, at 27–55, earned the sixth-highest chance at the top selection.

Even with the Lakers' poor health, Boston still finished two games below Los Angeles, handing Danny Ainge's Celtics the fifth-best lottery odds in May. Ainge held off trading Rajon Rondo and Jeff Green before the deadline, but Brad Stevens' roster still only featured so much talent. The Celtics, after all, were the only team Brett Brown's 76ers defeated three times in 2013–14. Philadelphia won at Boston again on April 4 and then at home on April 14.

Despite the widespread hand-wringing about Sam Hinkie's brazen bungling, Milwaukee actually out-tanked Philadelphia that spring. The Bucks' 15–67 mark landed Milwaukee a 25 percent chance at the No. 1 pick. "Nobody expected us to be the worst team in the league," Bucks general manager John Hammond says.

Meanwhile, if the Sixers, finishing 19–63 for a 19.9 percent chance at the first choice, weren't actively punting games, Hinkie's regime certainly kept limiting Philadelphia's roster until their final regular season affair.

Weeks before the Sixers' April 4 victory at TD Garden, Nerlens Noel had sent an ominous tweet, simply delivering "4-4-14" into the Internet ether. A native of Malden, Massachusetts, Noel knew Sixers staffers planned to rest their injured big man for the entirety of 2013–14, yet he dreamed of debuting in his hometown arena, just six days shy of his 20th birthday. "I was ready to go," Noel says.

"But they didn't want him playing," says Frank Catapano, one of Noel's early agents.

Philadelphia officials debated how to oversee their young roster throughout the trying season. In late January, a group of rookies returned from an evening out at 4:30 AM, mere hours before the Sixers' 2:00 Monday matinee in Washington, D.C. They proceeded to arrive late to the Sixers' morning meeting. Michael Carter-Williams later beamed about scoring 31 points that game, despite the Wizards winning 107–99. "They're acting like they own the whole arena," Thaddeus Young recalls.

"Coach didn't have to say anything because I lit into all of them," says Jason Richardson. The veteran guard reprimanded his teammates for over 15 minutes in the postgame locker room. "Just let them know that this is not how professionals act."

Richardson, himself spending all of 2013–14 rehabbing a knee injury, particularly grilled Noel, sidelined by his torn ACL. "There were a lot of times where I had to tell Nerlens, like, 'Man, you gotta be more professional. You gotta show up on time, you gotta come in and do your work.'"

Philadelphia often scheduled Noel to arrive at PCOM ahead of Sixers practices to undergo knee treatment, but the rookie consistently failed to report on time. After recurring tardiness, the team began fining Noel in conjunction with the NBA's player handbook. "I was a couple minutes late," Noel maintains. "Everyone goes through that."

Staffers decided to announce each penalty by leaving cuts of pink paper on the rookie's seat in front of his locker. A pile of salmon slips formed on Noel's chair, each denoting a fee $500 pricier than the last. Philly officials hoped punishment in front of his peers would incentivize Noel's punctuality. "It's a little bit embarrassing that you've got these fines now," says Lance Pearson, the analytics staffer.

Instead, Noel arrived one morning and swiftly brushed the stack of pink paper onto the floor. "Like they're nothing," forward Brandon Davies says.

Before numerous road trips, the Sixers' team charter idled in Philadelphia waiting only for Noel to report. "If it was me, I would have taken the plane and gone. I didn't like that we waited," says one Sixers assistant coach.

"That was my first babysitting experience," Spencer Hawes quips.

Sixers officials did actually discuss hiring full-time surveillance to keep tabs on Noel. "You can only do so much unless you put someone with him 24 hours a day," says Frank Catapano. Calls from Courtney Witte, the veteran personnel man, to Lance Williams, Philadelphia's director of security, pleaded for both Sam Hinkie and Brett Brown to employ an individual staffer for the injured rookie. Many pushed for a written agreement between Noel, his representatives, and the Sixers, outlining a detailed code of conduct.

While they feared possible long-term repercussions to the Sixers' culture, there was an equal argument for handling the franchise's future building blocks with kid gloves. A large reason Nerlens Noel billed as a future superstar was because he felt he *was* a future superstar, and in turn expected superstar treatment. Teams don't assign babysitters for future All-Stars.

"I understand why Brett didn't want to do that," says one Sixers voice. "But I thought Brett let too much go. He kind of kissed [Noel's] ass and wanted to try and do it through the buddy-buddy way."

Noel hadn't exhibited much tardiness at Kentucky. John Calipari barked at his players as loud as he sang their praises. Noel responded in kind. "He wanted to come out the first year, and he listened," Frank Catapano says. "I didn't know Nerlens had those issues until well into the first year at Philly."

Tod Lanter had watched Noel commit to Calipari's Wildcats in 2012 on television at an Applebee's not far from Rupp Arena. Noel choosing Kentucky convinced Lanter, a Lexington native, to transfer to his local program as a preferred walk-on. "Three weeks later I'm facing off against him in practice," Lanter says. He roomed with Noel during road trips, picking the brain of the presumptive No. 1 pick. "I got to know him really well and understood his fears," Lanter says.

Noel spoke often of the pressure to uphold his status as the nation's top prospect. He broke down on Kentucky's flight home from Florida following his injury, crying into Calipari's shoulder. The impending questions surrounding Noel's draft status were already battering inside his brain. "Is he ready? Can he heal?" Lanter says. "That's just a lot for any 18-year-old to think about."

Kentucky was also where Noel met Steven Dorn, who'd befriended several Wildcats players. When sophomore forward Terrence Jones turned pro in 2012, Dorn helped him organize lucrative autograph sessions. Come 2013, Dorn quickly emerged as Noel's manager, only he further clogged communication between the rookie, his agents, and the Sixers. Dorn moved into Noel's Philadelphia apartment. Apparently neither player nor manager felt the need to clean their home.

"Shit was in Nerlens' toilet for weeks at a time," says one former ASM staffer, the agency of Andy Miller, Noel's primary representative. "Hinkie should be given a fucking Nobel Peace Prize for dealing with him."

On multiple occasions, ASM staffers were forced to retrieve Noel from the apartment in order for their client to make a scheduled appearance. "It was that kind of hand-holding," the representative says. When ASM arranged an endorsement deal for Noel with Reebok, he starred in an October 2013 commercial, flushing a lob from Kings guard Isaiah Thomas during a pickup game at the park. Noel, however, nearly derailed his contract with the apparel company when it took several unresponsive days for him to sign their agreement. "People couldn't find him," the ASM source says. "He'd go missing."

When the Sixers had eyes on Noel, Philly officials even disagreed on the best approach to developing their prized prospect on the court. "He's a shot-blocker," John Calipari says. "Limited perimeter skills." Many NBA scouts had projected Noel as a fearsome rim-runner, setting a screen for his point guard before springing toward the basket. Several Sixers coaches wanted to mold Noel along those lines, mimicking what Tyson Chandler had done for the 2011 champion Mavericks. Brett Brown instead focused on tuning Noel's 15-foot shooting stroke, having seen how Tim Duncan's midrange jumpers kept foes honest during San Antonio's title runs.

Brown often isolated Noel on the foul line during practices, and the pair would hoist one-handed free throws during pregame warmups to better ingrain Noel's release. Coach and rookie spat junk in between heaves, turning their work into a playful competition. "He's one of the coaches that just always had your back," Noel says. "He'd keep it real with you and just tell you how it was."

Noel found respite in those intimate moments with Brown. "It was rough. He was in pain—a lot of pain—trying to get back," Tod Lanter says. The collegiate teammates spoke often during Noel's fraught season. "It's a lot of mental [struggle]," Lanter says. Many credit Brown's positivity for upholding Noel's spirits. He'd seemed to have won the babysitter debate, for the time being.

Brown's enthusiasm touched all Sixers players and staff, giving them a collective amnesia from their previous loss. Each practice quickly erased lingering frustrations from the night before. "You could see it really hurt him when we lost," says Vance Walberg, a Sixers assistant. "But it was so amazing. On the next day: 'Done. Over with. Let's get better.'"

"He'll walk in, it's raining hard as hell outside," Thaddeus Young says. "But he'll be like, 'It's a beautiful fucking day!'"

Brown especially took to both Noel and Michael Carter-Williams, sharing New England roots with his someday franchise saviors. Early in the season, Brown sat them down with 76ers legend Julius Erving to learn about being a franchise face in Philadelphia. "[We] just had a conversation and picked his brain and learned how he worked," Carter-Williams says.

Brown met privately with his young point guard throughout each week, hoping to meld their basketball minds as one. When the Sixers' 3–0 start ignited his unexpected Rookie of the Year campaign, ownership and team business executives eagerly marketed Carter-Williams' budding stardom. With Noel still sidelined, growing Carter-Williams became top of mind in Philadelphia.

Even dating back to Summer League, majority owner Joshua Harris had been especially invested in the former Syracuse floor general. After Khalif Wyatt scored 25 points in the Sixers' second July exhibition—compared to Carter-Williams' 13 on a dismal 4-for-19 shooting effort—a Philly official warned Wyatt's agent, Stephen Pina, his client needed to defer to their first-round point guard in their next outing. Harris was courtside lamenting how an undrafted Temple guard had outshined the Sixers' lottery selection. "I had to convey that information to Khalif," Pina says. "Let's scale back, be more of a point guard, and let Michael Carter-Williams score some more buckets."

Carter-Williams indeed stuffed the box score throughout 2013–14, finishing the year with nightly averages of 16.7 points, 6.2 rebounds, and 6.3 assists, numbers only all-time greats Oscar Robertson and Magic Johnson had eclipsed in their first professional seasons. But many NBA evaluators poked holes in Carter-Williams' production. He'd generated huge counting statistics in an up-tempo system while playing with zero pressure to win games. He outpaced Victor Oladipo, for example, by three minutes per contest while Brown's frenetic system also netted six more possessions for Philadelphia than Orlando on a nightly basis. "I checked [Oladipo's stats] all the time," Carter-Williams says.

Magic players would compare their most-recent 10-game samples, teasing Oladipo for motivation. "Man, MCW kinda had a crazy night!" Orlando center Kyle O'Quinn would shout. Any argument in favor of Orlando's rook fell flat when mentioning the Magic's superior record. Orlando finished just 23–59, earning the third-highest lottery odds. General manager Rob Hennigan would be picking yet again at the top of the draft, hopeful of adding another Rookie of the Year–caliber talent to his Magic rebuild, but

Oladipo earned just 16 first-place votes for the 2014 award, compared to Carter-Williams' 104.

"I was a pick away from going to Philly and probably being Rookie of the Year," says C.J. McCollum, whom Portland nabbed 10th before the Sixers took Carter-Williams at No. 11. Veteran players on contenders like the Trail Blazers scoffed at the award's outcome.

"I would never be a part of a tank," says Damian Lillard, Portland's All-NBA guard.

Many players and teams simply have no better alternative. While Milwaukee imagined developing Giannis Antetokounmpo mostly in the D-League his rookie season as the Bucks contended for the playoffs, poor health led Milwaukee to offload veterans and throw its youngsters into the fire. Antetokounmpo appeared in 77 games, playing 24.6 minutes per night. "It was just rebuilding. We knew they were going young," says Khris Middleton, then a second-year wing.

Another teenage phenom would soon join the Bucks' makeover as well. The May 20 draft lottery in New York City guaranteed Milwaukee no lower than the No. 4 pick in the most heralded class since LeBron James went No. 1 in 2003.

While the basketball world learns each lottery result on ESPN's annual television broadcast, the actual drawing occurs in a sequestered room backstage. It lasts no more than five minutes, but the closed-door proceedings begin nearly two hours before the outcome airs. Each lottery team sends one person to observe, typically brandishing a collection of lucky items. All involved must deposit their phones and other devices into sealed yellow envelopes.

Transparency and authenticity are of utmost importance. When former commissioner David Stern introduced the NBA Draft Lottery in 1985, auctioning the chance to draft Georgetown center Patrick Ewing No. 1, the league spun oversized envelopes inside a giant transparent orb. As an NBA official dropped in the envelopes—each containing a team's logo—the first three plopped directly to the bottom of the sphere. Yet the fourth clearly clanked off a metal bar running across the middle of the device, connected to the handle that would twirl its contents. Then just like the first bunch, the final three envelopes fell to the bottom without making any contact with the bar. Six revolutions later, Commissioner Stern unlatched the glass case. He pawed two envelopes, flipping both over, before ultimately retrieving what he revealed was New York's winning bid from the envelope that had—coincidentally—clanged against that metal bar.

Conspiracies abounded. Once a banner franchise claiming two titles in the early 1970s, the Knicks had failed to reach the conference finals since 1974. Landing a talent like Patrick Ewing in the nation's largest market conveniently benefited the NBA's overall marketability.

When Stern adapted the lottery for 1990, featuring a weighted system for the 11 non-playoff teams, the team with the worst record received 11 chances out of 66, the second-worst club had 10 chances, all the way down to the lottery team with the best record only holding one chance.

Come 1994, a new contraption burbled ping-pong balls, each printed with a bold number from 1 to 14. The team with the worst record entered the drawing with the highest chances to claim No. 1 and descending odds were awarded to clubs up the standings.

The new lottery machine, with a blue base bearing the NBA's logo and a simple on/off switch, was manufactured by Smartplay. The company claims it "preserves drawing integrity for lottery and gaming organizations in 85 countries." Smartplay's custom NBA device mixes the balls for 20 seconds before a league official selects the first number. The clock clicks 10 ticks before drawing the second, third, and fourth balls, creating a random four-digit combination out of 1,000 possible outcomes. Two more drawings decide the second and third selections. Through 2014, all remaining teams were then slotted Nos. 4-14 in reverse order, by record. That May drawing, Dallas held 250 potential four-number sequences that would have landed the No. 1 choice.

An error has yet to occur, but if the contraption malfunctions, a Smartplay troubleshooter and a backup machine are on site. Should the second device falter, they would dump the ping-pong numbers into a hallowed basketball and draw blind by hand. That would be quite the way to decide the NBA's draft order; the league's weighted lottery odds already sent team personnel and fans alike into a frenzy.

With the concept of tanking having captured as much attention as Miami's quest for a third straight title, thousands flocked to the website Tankathon.com to repeatedly simulate the lottery. Matt Hoover, a software engineer in Chicago, had coincidentally learned to code shortly after Sam Hinkie shipped Jrue Holiday to New Orleans. When the Bulls lost Derrick Rose once again to a season-ending knee injury in November, a dejected Hoover grew tired of checking the basement of the NBA standings. He wanted a cleaner status update, a way to keep tabs on the NBA's race to the bottom, even more so when the Bulls stumbled to 9–16 on December 19.

Hoover launched his URL after the calendar flipped. While Chicago rebounded into the postseason, Tankathon's traffic soared. "Over the year the buzz picked up about it more and more because of Hinkie and the Sixers," Hoover says. Fans and team executives alike logged on to refresh the reversed standings and mimic the upcoming May lottery. Daryl Morey followed Hoover on Twitter. "I know GMs visit the site," Hoover says.

The true 2014 lottery unfolded at Times Square Studios in New York. Smartplay's machine spit out the winning combination of 13-7-9-14 and the subsequent two four-digit sequences. A partner at the accounting firm Ernst & Young then stuffed large white envelopes, numbered 1 to 14 in bright red, with the matching team logos, before the NBA's vice president of security helped walk the stack onstage. Deputy commissioner Mark Tatum then revealed the picks during ESPN's broadcast. It was his first time presenting the draft order now that his predecessor, Adam Silver, had succeeded David Stern.

To Tatum's right, representatives from each lottery team—different from the personnel still being held backstage—lined a two-tiered, wood-paneled dais. Markieff Morris sat atop the second row for Phoenix. His pink suit and thick, black glasses weren't enough to luck one of the Suns' five possible combinations into the top three. Mark Tatum declared the 14th selection indeed went to Ryan McDonough's front office. Timberwolves general manager Milt Newton then smiled as Tatum announced Minnesota landed the 13th selection, also expected.

Fresh off his first year as Nuggets head coach, Brian Shaw knew only 15 four-digit combinations would have delivered the top choice to Denver. The Knicks marked the NBA's 12th-worst team yet exchanged their 2014 first-rounder as part of the package to acquire Carmelo Anthony back in 2011. If that pick, or Denver's own, somehow rose to No. 1, the Nuggets would improbably have their choice of talented phenoms. Yet if the Knicks' pick and their own selection held pat at No. 12 and No. 11, the Knicks' 12th choice would go to Orlando as part of Rob Hennigan's 2012 return for Dwight Howard. Sure enough, when Mark Tatum opened the next envelope, the Magic's logo appeared. Shaw promptly learned his Nuggets landed No. 11.

Pelicans general manager Dell Demps waited patiently. New Orleans entered the lottery with 11 possible outcomes to land in the top three. If not, as per the top-five protections agreed upon with Sam Hinkie, Philadelphia would land the Pelicans' pick as part of the Jrue Holiday trade. Yet much to Demps' chagrin, Tatum indeed proclaimed the 76ers would select 10th. Sixers fans rejoiced across the Delaware Valley.

Julius Erving represented Philadelphia on the dais in New York. Having helped the Sixers to their last championship in 1983, Philly faithful hoped Dr. J's presence would deliver the No. 1 pick and make a dreadful season worthwhile. Erving, too, was focused on the top of the lottery. When the broadcast panned to the 76ers legend after Tatum announced Philadelphia secured the No. 10 pick, Erving scrunched his face. "He kind of turned and said to me, 'What's going on? What happened?'" says Pat Williams, Orlando's lottery representative.

While Erving held an official title of special advisor in Philadelphia, the Sixers never informed their delegate about the likelihood of drawing an *additional* selection toward the back of the lottery. "It was like a 'What the fuck?' moment," Erving says. "I didn't come here to get No. 10."

Philadelphia's first result surprised few others; so far the lottery's outcome had unfolded in its most likely order.

Cleveland, unlikely winners of the previous year's drawing, entered the 2014 lottery with the ninth-worst record and just a 2.4 percent chance at drawing a top-three selection. The Pistons, four games worse than the Cavs, only had a 3.9 percent chance to jump in the lottery, but Detroit merely needed the order to hold as expected to keep its top-eight-protected choice from conveying to Charlotte. So when Mark Tatum opened the ninth envelope and the Hornets' new modernized logo emerged, Pistons swingman Kyle Singler restrained his disappointed reaction on the dais. And for the third time in four years, the Cavaliers improbably soared into the top three.

David Griffin, Cleveland's new general manager, jittered in his seat onstage. He bowed his head bashfully, touching his grandmother's gold pin fastened to his left lapel. One of Andrew Wiggins, Jabari Parker, or Joel Embiid was now likely to become a Cavalier. Plus, with Cleveland's jump, each remaining team that didn't also luck into a top selection now slid down one position. Sacramento thus fell to eighth. If the order held firm, Los Angeles would draw No. 7.

An internal battle had continued waging within the Lakers franchise. After the regular season mercifully concluded, head coach Mike D'Antoni met with Mitch Kupchak. "I think Mike kinda knew that this was probably gonna be it," says Johnny Davis, the assistant coach. Kupchak could have exercised the team option on the final year of D'Antoni's contract, yet former players and fans clamored for another change on the bench.

"The Lakers have not historically been very coach friendly, in terms of how they've compensated and taken care of people," says Clay Moser, the former analytics staffer. While Kupchak was open to retaining D'Antoni, the head coach's agent, Warren LeGarie, refused to prolong his client's Los Angeles tenure without inking an additional extension beyond the upcoming 2014–15 season.

"There was too much politics going on," says Dan D'Antoni, the head man's brother and former Lakers assistant. "You can't expect a team that was kind of put together, that doesn't have the real talent to be at the level they all wanted, and have the politics go wrong too."

After meeting with Kupchak, D'Antoni told his staff 2013–14 would be his last with the franchise. The sides ultimately agreed to part ways, paying their former head coach more than half of the $4 million remaining on his deal.

"Happy days are here again!" Magic Johnson tweeted following the team's April 30 announcement. "Mike D'Antoni resigns as the Lakers coach. I couldn't be happier!"

The Lakers great, along with other critics, had railed against D'Antoni all season, ignoring Los Angeles' dismal bill of health and lambasting his up-tempo scheme that left their depleted roster susceptible defensively. "Everyone knew he was a good coach," says swingman Xavier Henry, "it was just the narrative they started pushing."

With D'Antoni out, the Lakers proceeded with their Hollywood off-season strategy nonetheless. They'd maintained enough cap space to lure a max-level free agent to join a hopefully healthy Kobe Bryant, a hopefully healthy Steve Nash, and June's on-the-horizon lottery pick.

Los Angeles' lottery representative, Hall of Fame swingman James Worthy, plopped bobbleheads of longtime Lakers announcer Chick Hearn and Dr. Jerry Buss onto his podium on the Time Square Studios dais. The figurines, though, brought no good fortune. Mark Tatum opened the envelope to announce the No. 7 selection and out popped Los Angeles' storied logo.

Celtics co-owner Stephen Pagliuca wore a navy tie gifted by fabled head coach Red Auerbach the day Pagliuca and Wyc Grousbeck assumed control of the franchise. But Boston's leprechaun logo appeared out of the envelope introducing the No. 6 selection. Utah had no luck as well, landing at No. 5 to leave two slots in the top three for Orlando, Philadelphia, and Milwaukee to join the charmed Cavaliers.

Pat Williams braced for a stroke of fate. Over the years, Orlando's senior vice president stuffed rabbits' feet and wads of four-leaf clovers into his pockets. One lottery appearance, the Magic called for fans to bring their luckiest personal items to Orlando's facilities. "I don't think they ever got them back," Williams chuckles. In 1991, he slung a sack of Magic-branded ping-pong balls over one shoulder and carried boxes of Lucky Charms cereal underneath his other. "Finally, I just gave up," he says.

Bringing nothing but Orlando's futile record to 1992's event, the Magic at last struck gold and landed the No. 1 pick to select Shaquille O'Neal. In the following spring, Williams returned to the lottery with the Magic's 41–41 record and the lowest odds for the top choice, and still emerged with the No. 1 selection that led to acquiring Penny Hardaway. Orlando lucked into the top pick again in 2004 in order to draft Dwight Howard. Williams' fortune, however, seemed to run out in 2013. Orlando slipped from the first slot to No. 2, which led to Victor Oladipo. And the Magic's second season since trading Howard to Los Angeles only brought the No. 4 pick in 2014's lottery, one slot below a chance at adding Wiggins, Parker, or Embiid.

As ESPN's broadcast cut to commercial, David Griffin, Julius Erving, and Mallory Edens, the daughter of Bucks co-owner Wes Edens, walked anxiously to the right of the giant dais. Each franchise was all but guaranteed one of the draft's three elite prospects, but when the program returned to air, deputy commissioner Mark Tatum announced the Sixers had drawn the third selection. Philadelphia's porous year hadn't delivered the top choice.

And while the Bucks entered the evening with 233 more four-digit combinations than the Cavaliers, it was David Griffin who emphatically clapped his hands as Tatum then announced Milwaukee would pick second. Cleveland's remarkable string of lottery fortune, first in 2011 and then 2013, somehow continued in 2014—atop this celebrated class, no less. "I think it's just a really defining moment for us," Griffin told ESPN onstage in New York.

The network's telecast soon shifted to Indianapolis for Game 2 of the Eastern Conference Finals, while Cavs officials kept celebrating their incredible coup. The lottery, after all, is meant to disperse young talent to help poor teams morph into future contenders like the Miami Heat and Indiana Pacers.

Indiana expected its fortified second unit, now featuring Luis Scola and Evan Turner, could push the Pacers past the Heat once and for all. "We had everything we needed to beat them," says Indiana center Ian Mahinmi. Except Turner's arrival hardly boosted the reserve group as they'd hoped.

The efficiency and overall production he'd showcased in Philadelphia tumbled in Indianapolis. In response, head coach Frank Vogel spent the last weeks of the regular season filtering in little-used bench wings, experimenting a slew of rotation changes in case Turner's woes continued throughout the postseason. After starring over 34.5 minutes per game with the Sixers, Turner indeed saw just 12.4 minutes each night in the playoffs while scoring only 3.3 points per game. "Stuff had hit the fan with Indy," Turner recalls.

He missed Game 1 against Miami with strep throat. He never left the Pacers' bench as the Heat evened the series two nights later. Frank Vogel only offered Turner 3:34 of playing time during Game 3 in South Beach. Turner looked sluggish defensively and couldn't dribble past Heat defenders. His shooting struggles were obvious within the half court.

Miami took a commanding 3–1 series lead in Game 4. And while Indiana staved off elimination back home in Game 5, Turner didn't play a second. He'd sit the entire decisive Game 6 as well, watching Miami build a 25-point victory to book a fourth straight ticket to the NBA Finals. "We fought hard," Ian Mahinmi says. "We gave it everything we had."

The Eastern Conference simply belonged to LeBron James, Dwyane Wade, and Chris Bosh's Heat, further justifying the rival franchises that had decided to prioritize building through the 2014 draft. Why fight a losing battle with Miami's starry triumvirate when you could add the next wave of championship-caliber superstars, patiently develop their elite skill sets, and contend once the Heat's stronghold on the East withered?

Miami's long-term reign stood on even shakier ground than most truly understood.

ELEVEN

While every NBA draft scatters prospects across the league, each pick also starts the clock on that team's long-term efforts to retain that player. Teams can control a first-round pick's rookie contract for four seasons before they reach restricted free agency, where clubs still have the right to match any rival's offer. Stars typically take at least a three-year deal for their second contract. So after seven years, when a 19-year-old draft pick emerges as a 26-year-old All-Star, if his franchise hasn't done enough to impress that player, he'll likely signal the end of their marriage before their final season even begins.

Cleveland ultimately ran out of time with LeBron James, as with Orlando and Dwight Howard, not to mention Denver losing Carmelo Anthony and New Orleans Chris Paul. Now Timberwolves forward Kevin Love marked the latest marquee player to request a trade from the only NBA team he'd ever known.

Love broke the news to Timberwolves executives days before May's draft lottery: he intended to reach free agency in 2015 if Minnesota didn't move him sooner.

Love made three All-Star teams since the Wolves acquired him in the 2008 NBA Draft. His 26.1 points, 12.5 rebounds, and 4.4 assists per game during 2013–14 vaulted him into MVP discussions, yet Minnesota's 40–42 campaign left the Timberwolves outside of the postseason once again. Phoenix, after all, was kept out of the playoffs with 48 wins.

Minnesota hadn't reached the postseason since Kevin Garnett carried the Timberwolves to the 2004 Western Conference Finals. And like KG before him, Love finally determined his best chance at capturing an elusive championship resided in a different city than Minneapolis.

Team president Flip Saunders had rebuffed all offers for Love before the February trade deadline. Only now, with Love's free agency less than 14 months on the horizon, Saunders finally realized Minnesota's grim reality. "He understood," Love says. "But we had come so close, it was tough for me to let that relationship, to have to kind of push that aside to get to a different team and win."

Surveying the league, Love initially viewed Golden State and Chicago as attractive destinations. Before Los Angeles fell to No. 7, the Lakers hoped lottery luck would bring a top selection that could entice Minnesota. Phoenix and Boston boasted a trove of future draft capital that surely interested Saunders, except neither team presented the immediate contending situation Love desired, and no rival franchise would acquire the skilled big man without assurances Love would re-sign the following July in free agency.

The last Friday night of May, Celtics fans conveniently ignored that context when Love entered a bar near TD Garden with a gaggle of friends. Photos of the All-Star strolling down Boylston Street flooded social media. Over the coming days, Love's group was spotted eating in the Seaport District, lunching at a sports bar outside of Fenway Park, and partying on a hotel rooftop near Boston Common. "Somehow somebody leaked most of our schedule, what we were gonna do for the rest of the weekend, and then it became chaos," Love says.

"Listen, I ain't no dummy. If you told me I could trade Jared Sullinger and get Kevin Love, I'd do that shit in a heartbeat," says Sullinger himself.

The pandemonium reached a crescendo Sunday afternoon when cameras captured his crew watching the Red Sox's 4–0 victory over Tampa Bay from a suite. A photo of Love shaking hands with Celtics point guard Rajon Rondo in the ballpark's Champions Club erupted Boston sports social media once more. Patriots tight end Rob Gronkowski soon joined Love. And David Ortiz, the Red Sox's powerful designated hitter, later tweeted at the All-Star, "If you need any advice on moving from Minnesota to Boston just let me know." The slugger, too, spent his first six professional seasons in the Twin Cities before signing as a free agent with the Red Sox in 2003.

"I was like, 'Man, this is getting out of hand,'" Love says.

In reality, Love maintains the trip merely brought the All-Star to Boston for a vacation with friends and his agent, Jeff Schwartz, a longtime Red Sox fan. Living in New York for part of the off-season, Love scooped up a buddy in Rhode Island on the drive to Massachusetts. His skills trainer, Rob McClanaghan, also joined the weekend of festivities.

Love insists his interaction with Rondo was plain happenstance. The point guard strolled from his luxury seat to Love's accommodations simply to say hello. "We were just chilling, having a beer, eating food," Love says. No sales pitch occurred. By the time Love's group boarded a private plane to Los Angeles on Monday morning, news of his noisy Boston getaway headlined studio show after studio show. "Everybody was talking about this trip," Love recalls. "It was out of control." What became known as the "Summer of Love" only quieted momentarily when the NBA Finals took center stage on June 5.

San Antonio hoped to avenge its devastating 2013 championship defeat to Miami.

"That was, personally, probably the toughest time in my career," says Spurs guard Manu Ginóbili. "It was very hard to digest, to swallow."

San Antonio rebounded in 2013–14 nonetheless, winning 62 games to claim the West's No. 1 seed and holding serve throughout the conference playoffs for its first back-to-back NBA Finals appearances in franchise history.

Gregg Popovich's team promptly took Game 1. After LeBron James responded in Game 2 with 35 points and 10 rebounds to even the series, the Spurs dispatched the two-time defending champion Heat by a combined 57 points over the next three contests, clinching San Antonio's fifth title since 1999. Their offensive demolition rendered Miami's trapping defense useless, while a sense of fatigue seemed to blanket Heat players, coaches, and executives alike.

Four consecutive Finals appearances requires abnormal stamina and fortitude. Had the Heat wrestled another banner from the Spurs' clutches, they'd have completed another storied three-peat of championships in NBA history, and James would have, in all likelihood, remained in Florida. Only now the Heat's collective emotional tank sputtered on empty. And when James opted to test free agency on June 24—as the Lakers had long hoped—two days before James' hometown Cavs selected No. 1 in the draft, the spotlight burned its brightest on South Beach since the superstar first chose Miami in free agency four years earlier.

James had followed Cleveland's tinkering under new general manager David Griffin. The executive cut his teeth in Phoenix's front office as Steve Nash and Mike D'Antoni blitzed the NBA. Griffin was the only analytics-leaning Suns executive. He coded the team's scouting software himself. Now in Cleveland, the Cavs boasted an expansive analytics department with a powerful database. Cleveland had also recently constructed a glimmering practice facility. "Dan Gilbert was willing to spend so much money on process," Griffin says. But the owner's fractured relationship with James, having penned that scathing open letter back in 2010, loomed as the largest obstacle in The King's potential return to Ohio in 2014 free agency.

Pragmatism still forced Griffin's front office to consider their possibility of signing James while making their first pick of June 26's draft. After so many rival teams emphasized building through young picks and waiting out James' dominance in Miami, Cleveland now faced the inconceivable combination of adding their choice of Andrew Wiggins, Jabari Parker, or Joel Embiid *and* James in one fell swoop.

One hiccup: the trio of top prospects all skipped the draft combine in May, meaning each phenom's agent could determine which teams would receive their clients' medical records. Obtaining that information would be particularly crucial for teams evaluating Embiid.

While Wiggins and Parker entered the campaign as a dynamic wing duo, appearing on numerous magazine covers together, it was Kansas' center who actually emerged as the prospect projecting the highest ceiling of any in the

2014 class. If healthy, Embiid was trending toward No. 1 on Cleveland's big board over his Jayhawks teammate. "That was probably the best recruiting class we've ever had," Kansas coach Bill Self says.

Self first scouted Embiid as a senior at The Rock School in Gainesville. "I told our staff he was going to be the best player, maybe the most talented kid, we've ever coached," Self says. The enormous, skilled teenager looked over 7-feet tall. And he was still growing into his frame while just beginning to learn the game.

Born in Yaoundé, Cameroon, Embiid found basketball at age 15, after first dreaming of playing professional volleyball. "Watching the [2010] Finals, Lakers against Celtics, that was the turning point of my life," Embiid says. He mimicked Kobe Bryant's head fakes and fadeaways. He studied film of Hakeem Olajuwon's shimmies and interior ballet. When NBA forward and fellow Cameroonian Luc Mbah a Moute discovered Embiid at his local basketball camp in 2011, he quickly fast-tracked the 16-year-old to Florida for high school, one stop of several en route to the NBA. "I finally got the chance to start playing," Embiid says.

Even when he reached Kansas, the young giant still felt like an enormous Bambi on hardwood. Embiid jokes frequently, "I sucked," before the Jayhawks' preseason. After his first Kansas practice, Embiid slumped into Self's office, confessing he wasn't good enough to play that season and wanted to redshirt.

"Jo, I hate to say this," Self replied. "But you're not redshirting and you're going to be the No. 1 pick in the draft."

Embiid made instinctual defensive reads that made Self stop the scrimmage and teach the rest of his more-experienced teammates. "You would see it in practice daily," Self says, "From an intellect, from a competitive standpoint, from a skills standpoint, that you just don't see with guys that only played basketball for two years."

When Kansas and Duke clashed in November at the Champions Classic, Wiggins and Parker's perimeter duel stole headlines, but Embiid quietly dished five assists and gobbled seven rebounds in 20 minutes. He stalked the backline of the Jayhawks defense like a seasoned veteran. "Just the stuff he was doing at his height, the passes he was making, the moves he was making, you could tell," Wiggins says.

Embiid developed rapidly following that 94–83 victory over Duke. "You could see it," Wiggins says. "His size, the talent, the ability to keep getting better. His work ethic was very, very good." Embiid scored 16 points in Kansas' January 13 victory at Iowa State, adding nine rebounds, five blocks, and two steals. Cyclones head coach Fred Hoiberg believed he'd just watched college basketball's best player.

Iowa State schemed to double team Embiid the moment he gained possession on the block. Only he'd retreat with a quick, hard dribble, peer over the trap, and find his open teammate. The Cyclones rostered no player who could battle Embiid one-on-one. After one vicious swat, he sprinted down the floor and embarrassed a defender with a spin to the rim. "You could tell that game he was going to be special," Hoiberg says.

Back in Lawrence, the Jayhawks watched Embiid in wonder every morning. Remarkably, he could examine a highlight of Olajuwon one time, grab a ball, and master the mechanics of that move within a few minutes of attempting it. "You could see things Joel would do daily that would just make your jaw drop," Self says. The more NBA scouts that flocked to Kansas' practices, the more Self showcased his center. He'd call for Embiid to squat in the post, and bark for the freshman to flash a shoulder shimmy into a hook shot. An assistant tossed lobs far too high above the rim, yet Embiid still hammered leather through iron. "Just to tease those NBA guys," Self says. "They're like, 'Oh my god. It looks like Hakeem!' Of course, that's who he tried to emulate his game after!"

Embiid's sense of humor impressed as much as his prolific game. He repeatedly recounted a suspicious story from his childhood in Africa, claiming he was required to kill a lion in combat as part of a tribal initiation. Most laughed off the tale, but several players quietly approached Self. "And then they'd say, 'Is he being serious or sarcastic?'" Self recalls.

Embiid would squeal with joy every time a server delivered his Shirley Temple to the table, and the high-pitched sound emanating from such a towering frame only made the moment funnier. "His personality is out of this world," Wiggins says.

Embiid, though, would soon be out of Kansas' rotation. He tweaked his hulking back during a March 1 game against Oklahoma State. After Embiid saw a specialist in Los Angeles, Self announced he'd suffered a stress fracture with an indefinite recovery timetable. The OSU contest ultimately marked his last college appearance. After Kansas fell in the round of 32 without its giant, both Embiid and Wiggins declared for June's NBA draft. Neither decision required much deliberation.

Scouts had filtered through campus all season, fully confident teams would need lottery luck to land either phenom in the first three picks. David Griffin, Cleveland's general manager now armed with the No. 1 pick, had spent so much time at Kansas, he even offered the Cavs' head coaching job to Self.

Griffin joined a May 23 flock of team personnel descending upon Santa Monica High School for the Wasserman agency's pro day. In such an event, agencies can showcase each of their draft clients in a controlled environment. And team personnel in attendance were certainly eager spectators. For 2014, Wasserman represented Embiid, Jabari Parker, and another top-10 prospect, Oklahoma State sophomore Marcus Smart.

For weeks, Embiid had regained strength in his back and legs, ramping up toward regular availability. He enamored Wasserman onlookers just as he'd done at Kansas. "When he wanted to turn it on, it was—in a class that we had Jabari and Smart—if you came and sat in and knew nothing about basketball and just watched them play a pickup game, within 20 seconds, you would have said that's the guy, and it's not even close," says Greg Lawrence, the Wasserman agent who represented Spencer Hawes. The agency believed their showcase that Friday morning would end any discussion over who should be the No. 1 pick. "Because if you saw him work out," Lawrence says, "you were gonna want him."

Embiid didn't disappoint. He flashed the low-post brilliance from college. He drained triples with ease. He needed just one dribble from the three-point line to tear down on the rim. His powerful slams looked like they might topple the entire basket. "It was hilarious, just because that's when he had the whole injury thing going on and he really wasn't supposed to be doing too much," Marcus Smart says.

Bucks general manager John Hammond watched agape. He foresaw an impossible defensive front of Joel Embiid and Giannis Antetokounmpo, two youngsters with unthinkable athleticism and titanic length. If healthy, though, Embiid wouldn't be available when Milwaukee selected No. 2. "When a guy like Bill Self says to you, 'He might be the best player I've ever coached at Kansas,' that gets your attention," Hammond says. "That's *Kansas*."

The Bucks' front office still managed to meet with Embiid in Los Angeles for dinner. Luc Mbah a Moute, the fellow Cameroonian, spent the first five years of his career in Milwaukee, and helped his former franchise get extended access to the coveted prospect. "We had as much time with Joel as any other team," Hammond says.

Embiid's conversational nature impressed Bucks officials. They were drawn to his charisma and fun-loving giggle. He exuded such confidence for someone so young and so far from home. "Man, what a guy," Hammond recalls. Milwaukee brass had seen Embiid at Kansas and even closer at Santa Monica High, yet sharing a meal brought an entirely different perspective. Embiid barely folded under the table. "When you saw how big he was, it really blew you away," Hammond says.

Alas, Embiid appeared destined for Northeast Ohio. His agent, Arn Tellem, informed both Milwaukee and Philadelphia he wouldn't work out for either organization until he first visited the Cavaliers. Without any surprises, the Bucks would be choosing between Andrew Wiggins and Jabari Parker.

Parker had also shown out at Wasserman's pro day. His solo session utilized the full court and captivated the entire gym. "It was one of the most impressive workouts I've ever seen," John Hammond says. Parker whipped a quicker dribble than he had at Duke and canned step-back triples with ease. He exploded into the paint to hammer dunks with impressive bounce.

Drenched in sweat, Parker sat to the side to watch Wasserman's next group. Only a month separated the phenom from an early selection and millions of guaranteed dollars, yet when the cast of second-round prospects were whistled for a break, Parker jumped over to the water cooler and started filling cups. "When I watched him do that, I was like, 'Wow, who is this guy?'" Hammond says.

Parker was one of the most decorated players in the history of Chicago high school basketball. He also grew up a member of the Church of Jesus Christ of Latter-day Saints and regularly attended its meetings. And so months before he officially entered the draft, Parker deliberated delaying an NBA career to serve his Mormon mission, the same service that visited the island nation of Tonga and first converted Parker's great-grandfather. "The spiritual is the most important thing for me," he says. "That's what helps me become sane. I just wanted to consider it." He brought his brother, Christian, who served a mission in Atlanta, to Durham for counsel. Parker also confided in his bishop. He then penned an open letter declaring pro. "From the answers that I sought out, it meant that my mission was to play this game," Parker says now.

While Kansas topped Duke in that November clash, it was Parker who led all scorers with 27 points. His rampage to start the winter looked like a bouncier Carmelo Anthony. Duke's phenom would eclipse 20 points in each of his first seven games, the longest debut streak of any freshman in school history. Parker climbed to the top of many NBA scouts' draft boards. "At the time, a legit chance at going No. 1," says a Duke staffer.

The Bucks were more than sold on Parker. Word even suggested Parker preferred to play in Milwaukee, a short drive from his hometown Chicago. The Bucks, though, still hoped Joel Embiid would visit for a workout. Co-owner Marc Lasry lobbied the prized center for 15 minutes by phone. Embiid had continued progressing in Santa Monica, saying his back was completely healed. But Embiid wouldn't work out for any other team until after his visit to Cleveland.

Cavs officials thus welcomed Kansas' giant on June 10. Embiid began sparring against 6-foot-10 assistant Vitaly Potapenko and easily bulldozed Cleveland's coach into the padding behind the basket. He drained triple after triple, connecting on 12 straight attempts from the corner. "His touch and everything, you could tell that was easy for him," says Jordi Fernández, another Cavs assistant. With each make, Embiid hollered to David Griffin, shouting that Cleveland's general manager had no other choice at No. 1. "He was not shy," says Fernández, a native of Barcelona. "For foreigners like myself, it's hard to speak and learn the league *and* show your personality. But he didn't have any problems with that."

Griffin beamed. How could he disagree with Embiid? The executive just watched, far and away, the greatest pre-draft workout he'd ever imagined. If Embiid's medical evaluation came back clean, Cleveland had its man, visualizing a lethal pick-and-roll combination with...LeBron James?

Embiid further charmed Cavs brass over dinner. "He ate everything," says one Cleveland executive. Word of Embiid's affinity for Shirley Temples preceded him. "We knew that coming in he had a sweet tooth." Rumors thus filtered throughout Cleveland's front office. Embiid had eaten as many as four enormous slices of chocolate lava cake during dessert.

Come morning, though, the momentum pushing prospect and franchise toward a long marriage vanished. Embiid limped into Cleveland's facilities for his physical. An X-ray soon detected a fracture within his size-17 foot. Cavs executives believe Embiid sustained the injury during his workout.

Arn Tellem, Embiid's agent, whisked his client back to Los Angeles for further evaluation. Word remained hushed. "There was always a change of course as to what was wrong," says Greg Lawrence, the fellow Wasserman representative. "You'd always hear, 'Oh, Joel's not working out today, he's going to see a doctor.'" When Wasserman staffers asked if they were still evaluating Embiid's foot, Tellem demurred. He had scheduled the center's workout in Milwaukee but cancelled the trip providing no clearer explanation. "There was always something," Lawrence says.

The Bucks continued their evaluation process nonetheless, filing into Westmont College's main gym in Santa Barbara on June 13 to watch Andrew Wiggins work out with his trainer Drew Hanlen. Wiggins had stolen predraft headlines when a photo of the Jayhawk registering a 48-inch vertical took the Internet like wildfire. "It looked like Andrew was jumping into outer space," Hanlen says.

Most mock drafts, though, projected Wiggins falling past Milwaukee at No. 2. "Everyone was basically having Andrew at third," Hanlen says. Despite his athletic profile, some scouts questioned if Wiggins' offense would translate to the next level. Hanlen thought the Bucks in particular doubted Wiggins could outshine Parker, so he exhibited Wiggins' tighter ball handling within a series of mid-post drills. The phenom unfurled gorgeous fadeaway, step-back and side-step jumpers. "They were like, 'Holy shit. This dude. This kid can be special,'" Hanlen says.

Hammond left more than impressed. "Now you're in a can't-miss," he thought, exiting the gym.

Milwaukee still favored Parker, though, prompting Wiggins to visit Philadelphia on June 16. The 76ers hurried him into their PCOM facilities under cloak and dagger. While many teams announce their pre-draft workouts—some even post videos with each prospect on their official website—Sixers president Sam Hinkie opted for the opposite approach. From the beginning of his tenure a year earlier, Hinkie sought to host as many players and leak as few names as possible. "We worked out...Jesus, 100, 120 people?" says Vance Walberg, the Sixers assistant coach. That total more than doubles some teams' annual average.

Hinkie especially applied his mum approach for elite prospects like Andrew Wiggins. The executive believed that tipping any morsel of information to rival organizations would inherently sacrifice leverage in his franchise's decision-making. That's why the media wasn't permitted to watch Wiggins work out.

A smattering of reporters formed outside the practice facility anyway, hoping to interview Wiggins upon his exit. PCOM campus security demanded the group disperse. A Philadelphia police officer then banished them from the sidewalk to the pavement across the street. They merely caught a glimpse of Wiggins entering a black Chevy Suburban with Sixers center Nerlens Noel and vice president Brandon Williams at 12:51 PM. "The team was clearly trying not to advertise who they had in," says one Philadelphia staffer.

Public relations director Michael Preston later emerged to apologize for the mishap. He dubiously claimed the Sixers were not responsible for security's behavior. Many of the reporters felt an innocent party wouldn't have brought the box of donuts Preston offered for their inconvenience.

Philadelphia, after all, had coveted Wiggins all season, and the stars were seeming to align for head coach Brett Brown. He has frequently said he spent the spring planning how to incorporate Wiggins and Michigan guard Nik Stauskas, a possible selection at the Sixers' additional pick at No. 10. Having yet learned of Embiid's precarious foot injury, it was assumed the center was still a lock for Cleveland.

Then at No. 2, Milwaukee was said to prefer Parker over Wiggins. While Wiggins harbored greater athleticism and upside, his offensive game was far from Parker's polished product. And Giannis Antetokounmpo already marked Milwaukee's developmental project. "Our view was, we want to win, and we want to do it now," says Marc Lasry, the Bucks co-owner. "We're gonna do what's best for the organization."

Wiggins indeed seemed destined for Philly at No. 3, potentially adding a generational wing prospect to lead an attack bookended by Michael Carter-Williams and Nerlens Noel. He wasn't Embiid, but Sixers brass cheered the possibility of landing Wiggins, their No. 2 prospect, with the third pick. "People thought it was going to turn around," says a Sixers staffer. "And if you just got Andrew Wiggins and you had these other two guys, you were set."

With Embiid, Parker, and Wiggins seeming to slot in at Nos. 1, 2, and 3, Cavs officials believe Parker even tanked his workout in Cleveland on June 20, just as the team had once tanked to position itself to select Kyrie Irving back in 2011. While scouts across the league debated whether Parker had the foot speed to guard NBA wings, his athleticism could still pop off the screen in college. He was listed at 235 pounds then, but Parker weighed in at 255 in Ohio. He missed shots. His drives sputtered in mud, apparently in an effort to cement Milwaukee as his destination. "That was false," Parker maintains. "I would never do anything like that, waste people's time and waste my time." A Duke staffer confirms, "I don't think he'd do something like that."

Regardless, Cleveland's doctors red-flagged Parker's foot injuries that had disrupted the end of his high school career. It seemed medical evaluations would ultimately determine the Cavs' choice atop such a decorated draft; the same morning as Parker's offbeat workout, Arn Tellem, Embiid's agent, announced the big man underwent surgery at Southern California Orthopedic Institute, inserting two screws into the navicular bone in his right foot.

Embiid's rehab would last four to six months, meaning he'd be unable to attend the NBA's draft the following week, forbidden from flying so soon post-surgery. The Cavaliers would have to think long and hard about drafting a 7-footer with such an unpredictable bill of health.

So Cleveland hosted Wiggins for a last-minute workout before he flew to New York for the draft. Wiggins went through drills with Cavs assistant coach Phil Handy, at one point shedding his shirt to reveal a sculpted frame primed to pack on more muscle. "When you see someone who's NBA ready, you can tell," says Jordi Fernández, the Cavs assistant.

Wiggins spun and finished high-flying dunks. He lofted pretty jumpers through the net. Wiggins was, after all, once billed as 2014's glitziest prospect. His high school mixtape garnered millions of views on YouTube and comparisons to LeBron James himself. Wiggins had covered the college preview issue of *Sports Illustrated*, figuratively accepting the Kansas torch from none other than Wilt Chamberlain. And he highlighted an as-advertised freshman season with a breathtaking 41 points at West Virginia.

"I knew I was going to be a high draft pick, either 1, 2, or 3," Wiggins says.

No skeptic could criticize Cleveland if they grabbed Wiggins first. Even with Joel Embiid having enamored David Griffin, his broken foot simply left the Cavs' general manager with no choice. Wiggins also currently boasted the most trade value among the draft's top prospects.

The NBA, at day's end, is a business first. If LeBron James indeed returned to Cleveland, the Cavs would face a very short window to support him with a championship roster. Remember: Cleveland finished 2013–14 just 33–49. One quick method to supplement its prodigal son would be dealing the No. 1 pick for an established star. And general manager David Griffin knew the Timberwolves preferred Wiggins amongst the draft's elite crop.

Like Phoenix and Boston, Cleveland had inquired about Kevin Love following the All-NBA forward's trade request, but Griffin hadn't received assurances Love would re-sign with the Cavs following a trade. Then once Golden State's talks with Minnesota slowed—they nearly swapped sharp-shooter Klay Thompson for Love that June—Griffin's front office believed that Love would still be available should Cleveland indeed triumph in LeBron James' upcoming July free agency.

The Cavs also continued listening to offers for their No. 1 pick, even as commissioner Adam Silver declared Cleveland on the clock from Barclays Center in Brooklyn. One year removed from the same position, Cleveland saw far greater interest than it had in 2013. Philadelphia once pitched Thaddeus Young and the No. 3 pick, hoping for a chance to land Embiid, but now believed he would be available at their third selection if president Sam Hinkie wanted to draft another sidelined center. Orlando offered an intriguing package of veteran guard Arron Afflalo plus the No. 4 and No. 12 picks. Utah suggested forward Derrick Favors and its fifth selection.

The Jazz also discussed swapping the No. 5 choice and their No. 23 pick for Philly's third. The Sixers believed Embiid could still be available at the fifth pick. His agent, Arn Tellem, had withheld the prospect's crucial medical records from the Magic and Jazz. "We did not think either of them were going to pick him," agrees Celtics assistant general Mike Zarren.

No sensible owner would approve drafting a 7-footer who'd suffered from the same injury that ended Yao Ming's career without access to Embiid's information. Rumor even suggested Orlando offered to purchase the results of Embiid's X-rays. "Every single year there's a team that will call some other teams looking for some guy's medical records," says one longtime Eastern Conference executive. Tellem did provide Boston and Los Angeles with Embiid's info. So as long as Philadelphia drafted above the Celtics and Lakers, Hinkie would likely have his chance to pick Embiid.

Back in Barclays Center, commissioner Adam Silver indeed announced Andrew Wiggins as the No. 1 pick. Cleveland officially added an impressive young focal point, who could either flank LeBron James should the Cavs sign the superstar in free agency or net an established star running mate for James instead.

ELEVEN

Milwaukee came on the clock. "You know, it was between Jabari and Embiid," says Marc Lasry, the Bucks co-owner. They'd never managed to get the Cameroonian to Wisconsin, even with their Luc Mbah a Moute cheat code. Embiid's ailing foot simply presented a size-17 question mark. And Milwaukee's new ownership, having purchased the franchise in May, were allured by the postseason. "I don't think it's fun losing," Lasry says. "And also we thought Jabari was a great player."

Silver expectedly announced Parker at No. 2. After months of gossip and fanfare, Joel Embiid finally remained on the board as the clock began Philadelphia's third choice.

TWELVE

Some rivals prepared for Sam Hinkie to select Joel Embiid with the No. 3 pick, just as he'd drafted the injured Nerlens Noel a year prior. Over a year into Hinkie's tenure, he was obviously under no time crunch in Philadelphia. When the Kings called Philadelphia vying for the chance to swipe Embiid for themselves, the Sixers quickly rebuffed.

Word had circulated, though, that Embiid might prefer to play in Los Angeles. He hadn't visited the Lakers throughout the pre-draft process but spent the previous six weeks living in his agent's sprawling L.A. home. The possibility of taking the keys from Kobe Bryant was nothing short of a dream. "Kobe was the idol," Embiid says.

Another large portion of NBA observers believed the Sixers would instead choose Dante Exum, an Australian point guard dubbed 2014's international basketball prospect of mystery. After averaging 18.2 points per game at the 2013 FIBA U19 World Championship, Exum measured 6-foot-6 in shoes with a 6-foot-9.5 wingspan at the draft combine and wouldn't turn 19 until mid-July. The teenager, though, didn't compete in drills, and no significant tape existed of Exum battling against the talent level other prospects had faced in college. Questions still remained about his outside jumper after he spent four months training in Anaheim.

Brett Brown was more than familiar with Exum—he'd coached Exum's father, Cecil, with the 1990 Melbourne Tigers. "There was definitely pressure to draft Dante," says Lance Pearson, the Sixers staffer. While Philadelphia already rostered Rookie of the Year point guard Michael Carter-Williams, the idea of pairing two interchangeable ball handlers in the backcourt appealed to several Sixers evaluators. That is, until Exum visited Philadelphia.

"High-level picks usually won't play one-on-one," Pearson says. Sam Hinkie, however, pushed Exum's camp to allow him to secretly work out alongside another prospect. Philadelphia gave his agent, Rob Pelinka, a list of lower-rated players they'd already evaluated. If Pelinka, who famously represented Kobe Bryant, allowed Exum to go against one of Philadelphia's prepared names, the other guard would serve as a greater talent barometer no other NBA team had. Pelinka ultimately chose Penn State point guard Tim Frazier. He expected Exum would overpower the 6-foot fringe prospect in any head to head format.

Philly's previous regime pulled a similar move just days before the 2010 NBA Draft, when Sixers brass convinced DeMarcus Cousins and Derrick Favors to work out together in secret on their way to New York. The Sixers promised only 60 minutes of on-court drills, with the two freshmen bigs merely taking turns during skill work. Training staffers first put the towering teenagers through physical measurements and agility testing. When they jogged over to the water cooler for a brief rest, Favors filled his cup, sat down, and sipped. "And [Cousins], as I walked into the gym, was standing over him and basically challenging his manhood," says a former Sixers executive.

Cousins grunted and puffed his chest. With such a competitive spirit brewing inside the PCOM facility, Philadelphia coaches scrapped any designs of a breezy round of jumpers. They coaxed Cousins and Favors into playing one-on-one, virtually unheard of between two elite prospects during a pre-draft workout.

Cousins had also battled Hassan Whiteside in Sacramento, when the Kings invited Whiteside back for a second visit to serve as competition for the Kentucky talent. Whiteside's agent happened to be Andre Buck, who now represented Tim Frazier. And after seeing Sacramento select Whiteside at No. 33 in 2010, Frazier's second pre-draft opportunity in Philadelphia seemed like a no-brainer in 2014. "Competing against an Exum, you can show yourself against a guy who's projected much higher," Buck says.

Frazier had already demonstrated enough to earn the additional look, but he returned to Philly eager to improve upon what he considered a poor first impression. "I was hungry," Frazier says.

The Sunday before draft night, both guards laced their sneakers inside PCOM. Sixers officials knew Frazier would battle, but most staffers truly anticipated little competition. They were proved correct, except it was Frazier who unexpectedly dominated Australia's top phenom. "Tim came in and just put it to Dante," Lance Pearson says. Frazier boasted a far cleaner shooting stroke. He countered Exum's superior length with dexterous change-of-pace dribbles, slipping to the basket unencumbered. Frazier played like a 23-year-old, four-year college starter simply picking on an unassuming freshman.

"Shit, I loved Tim," says Vance Walberg, the Sixers assistant coach. "He was just older, smarter, knew how to play, could do a lot of little things." It wasn't long before the Sixers phoned Buck with a positive recap. Philadelphia's scouting department had quickly amended its big boards.

"That ended any discussion that we were gonna draft Dante," Pearson says.

Even so, when the commissioner strolled onstage to announce the Sixers' selection at No. 3, several rival teams still expected Hinkie would nab Exum for his Bostralian head coach Brett Brown to develop. Unlike the first two selections, news of Philadelphia's pick had yet to leak on Twitter. "It was noticeable nobody heard anything until Adam Silver came up to the podium," Pearson says.

When the commissioner finally declared the selection, it was indeed Joel Embiid who was headed to Philadelphia. The Sixers' scouts assembled in PCOM's conference room could hear cheering inside Sam Hinkie's sequestered office. But when ESPN's broadcast panned to Embiid watching the draft from L.A., cameras captured the 7-footer brooding on a couch. A large segment of Philadelphia social media erupted in dismay. Having first suffered through a lost year of Andrew Bynum, then a 26-game losing streak as Nerlens Noel sat sidelined with a torn ACL, the Sixers drafted *another* injured big man doomed to miss the entire 2014–15 season? "Sam didn't feel the need to mask tanking," says one longtime NBA executive.

In actuality, Embiid's televised reaction was merely a broadcast mishap—his screen experienced a 30-second delay from the live action. What was first viewed a disgruntled response was actually a nervous Embiid hoping to hear his name called. ESPN soon rolled the clip of Embiid pumping his giant fists. Despite his interest in Los Angeles, his agents had sold the center on Philadelphia and Brett Brown's surplus of playing time.

The Sixers' public relations wound had still been opened. The antsy portion of Philadelphia's fan base scoffed at drafting another rehabilitation project. Although for Hinkie's staunchest supporters, drafting Embiid marked another pragmatic decision to acquire the draft's greatest value at a discounted cost. "It was a lesson on prioritizing the long term and being patient," says Michael Levin, co-host of *The Rights to Ricky Sanchez* podcast.

Dante Exum would have also marked a selection for the future. "Dante was very raw and new to that process," says one international NBA scout. The Australian bombed his workout with Orlando in addition to Philadelphia. "It was a bit of an eye-opener for him. He was an 18-year-old kid that basically never played anywhere," the scout says. Orlando selected Arizona freshman Aaron Gordon instead.

Magic executive Scott Perry convinced his colleagues Gordon could become an NBA small forward. "We saw this potential for multi-position defense," says an Orlando official. Gordon became just the latest athlete to join general manager Rob Hennigan's youth movement, alongside Victor Oladipo and Tobias Harris.

Adam Silver declared Utah's fifth selection was on the clock. Rob Pelinka had called the Jazz a few days before the draft. He'd only scheduled Exum to work out for the top four teams, but after his subpar displays for the Sixers and Magic, Pelinka informed Utah his client would likely be available at No. 5. Jazz officials soon Skyped with Exum from New York as he prepared for Thursday at Barclays Center.

Utah understood Exum would face an adjustment period. "Not many rookies are very good their rookie year," says one Jazz exec. Utah had finished 2013–14 just 25–57 while pivoting into a new era led by 2010 first-rounder Gordon Hayward. This pick marked the Jazz's reward for a steady, one-year fall to the league's bottom. Utah believed Exum's family and background proved he was smart and willing to learn, the type of prospect worth a season full of losses. Commissioner Adam Silver thereby announced the draft's youngest prospect was on his way to Salt Lake City.

Coming up at No. 6, Boston's front office once thought Joel Embiid could fall to their selection. They were quite impressed by Aaron Gordon; a photo of him falling asleep on the T, after a day training near his sister's apartment off Harvard's campus, sparked a round of Twitter intrigue. Even still, Danny Ainge happily took Oklahoma State sophomore Marcus Smart with the sixth pick. "Everyone on our staff just loved his tenacity," says assistant GM Mike Zarren. "And that hasn't changed one bit."

Smart's inconsistent outside stroke brought concern to teams drafting in the top five but he caught fire during his Wasserman pro day. "I didn't miss a shot," Smart says. "I was damn near perfect." Only he could hardly buy a bucket during his first Celtics workout. Boston even called Smart back to Massachusetts for a second visit. He converted enough to quell any major skeptics in Boston's scouting department.

Celtics staffers knew Smart's work ethic matched his in-game intensity. No matter what, Smart would bring an unwavering motor to Boston's rebuild. He could spearhead their attack on opposing guards. "His defensive instincts were as good as anyone we've ever seen in the draft," Zarren says.

Assistant coach Walter McCarty played with OSU head coach Travis Ford at Kentucky in the early 1990s. "[Smart] loves to win and is a winner, was gonna do anything on the court possible for his teammates to win," McCarty says. "You see that with the way he worked out."

Smart had wanted to compete for a national title so badly, he shockingly deferred a likely lottery selection in 2013 to return for a second season at Oklahoma State, despite the rapid trend of one-and-done freshmen fleeing for the NBA.

Kentucky, for example, danced all the way to the 2014 NCAA championship game starting four first-years before freshmen Julius Randle and James Young declared pro. Randle averaged nearly a double-double through Kentucky's first five tournament bouts, although scouts still worried his broken right foot, suffered in the second game of his senior high school season, hadn't fully healed. If Los Angeles' doctors cleared Randle, he seemed like a strong possibility for the seventh pick.

When the Lakers hosted Kentucky's forward pre-draft, they were impressed by his work ethic yet disappointed by his conditioning. "He was in incredibly not good shape," says Clay Moser, the Los Angeles director of basketball strategy.

Randle also wowed Sixers evaluators with his speed at such size, only they couldn't help but notice his status afterward. "The guy was gassed," says Lance Pearson, Philly's analytics staffer.

Los Angeles had no room for error at No. 7. Kobe Bryant tracked for a healthy 2014–15 return. And with his hefty two-year contract on the books, their seventh selection would play a key role alongside The Mamba and the Lakers' hopeful max-level free agent acquisition. Perhaps LeBron James?

General manager Mitch Kupchak ultimately swallowed any concerns, and Adam Silver proclaimed Randle as Los Angeles' No. 7 choice. He was simply the best phenom still available. "Julius was always going to be a pretty high prospect," says Tod Lanter, Kentucky's walk-on who'd roomed with Nerlens Noel. "He's just an unbelievable talent with an incredible skill set."

The Kings came on the clock at No. 8. While it trailed many rival organizations quickly bolstering their analytics departments, Sacramento had launched "Draft 3.0" back in May, an online challenge that crowdsourced Internet basketball number-crunchers to submit their 2014 positional rankings, research, and analysis. General manager Pete D'Alessandro then selected the best entries to join his Draft Advisory Council that included Hall of Famers Mitch Richmond and Chris Mullin. Sacramento's old-school scouting department had already determined its top targets; they just wanted to confer with the numbers.

Kings brass treated Creighton shooter Doug McDermott to dinner one evening during the draft combine. "I had a good connection with them," McDermott says, "but I also knew they liked [Nik] Stauskas a lot."

McDermott and Michigan guard Nik Stauskas spent pre-draft training together in Chicago, both clients of noted agent Mark Bartelstein. Each marksman drilled over 44 percent of their triples in college, yet skeptics considered them athletic question marks. So when Kings officials visited several of their sessions, McDermott and Stauskas finished most drills above the rim. "We were throwing down dunks and stuff in all the workouts to show that 'sneaky bounce,'" McDermott says.

After one morning where Stauskas particularly caught fire, Pete D'Alessandro's group took him to lunch. The affable Canadian impressed with his sense of humor. When interviewing with the Magic, Stauskas was asked if he'd prefer to win Rookie of the Year or party with countryman Justin Bieber. "If I win Rookie of the Year," Stauskas smiled, "I'll probably be able to party with Justin Bieber whenever I want, and he'll want to party with me."

Stauskas knew Sacramento presented his ceiling. Boston officials transparently told him following his workout the Celtics were not drafting him. Stauskas then sensed a similar vibe with Lakers executives, while the Kings were already conjuring schemes to feature him as a versatile point guard. Sacramento owner Vivek Ranadivé believed Stauskas would open up Sacramento's offense around the mercurial DeMarcus Cousins. Ranadivé was mesmerized that Stauskas claimed to regularly sink 91 out of 100 free throws.

Kings evaluators were also considering Elfrid Payton, a junior guard out of Louisiana-Lafayette. Payton was no shooter, but the gangly point guard hounded any foe in sight. He looked to score only when necessary, a perfect match for Cousins in pick-and-roll dances. Sacramento even pitted Payton against Marcus Smart one-on-one during a pre-draft workout, equally as rare as Philly's Exum-Frazier showdown. Smart characteristically welcomed the competition, and Kings brass were impressed by Payton's toughness against the famously fiery Oklahoma State sophomore. Sacramento's Draft 3.0 group of finalists also valued Payton's advanced numbers.

D'Alessandro selected five men eager for their chance at NBA decision-making. A few days before the draft, the volunteer analytics team entered Sacramento's war room to mix their numerical ice with the old scouts' fire. They agreed Nik Stauskas presented an intriguing offensive weapon, however analysis suggested Sacramento had experienced greater defensive woes than scoring issues in 2013–14. For that reasoning, Draft 3.0 favored the Kings choosing Elfrid Payton.

Sacramento's coaches nodded in approval. Since the beginning of Mike Malone's tenure, he'd preached solidifying the Kings' defense before getting cute on their attack. "You have a greater chance if you're in the top 10 of defensive statistical categories in the NBA," says Chris Jent, the Kings assistant coach.

But that spring, Ranadivé suggested a different priority when Kings management met with Malone and his staff. Sacramento's owner believed the whirring Warriors were the future champions of the NBA, and the team that had slayed Golden State that 2014 postseason was the Clippers. Doc Rivers' scheme generated 112 points per 100 possessions, to lead the NBA. Ranadivé was clear: he wanted Malone's staff to prepare a playbook hinged on Rudy Gay and DeMarcus Cousins, capable of that 112 offensive rating, to defeat the Warriors. That would require playing at a far greater pace—which would naturally leave the Kings equally susceptible in transition defense.

"We needed better shooting, more aggressive play, and we gotta have 'Cuz' be used more like a guard out on the floor, rebound, start our break." Jent says. "It just…" he pauses to sigh, "if you don't play defense, if you don't pride yourself on defense, you're just not gonna win."

And with Ranadivé's mandate, the front office shifted their thinking on No. 8 toward Nik Stauskas. Their analytics crew had confirmed Kings scouts' projection of Stauskas' potential creating ability. The data suggested Michigan's shooter was also proficient when pulling up off the bounce. When the Draft 3.0 winners finished their presentation, Sacramento's front office burst into applause.

"I'll tell you what," general manager Pete D'Alessandro said. "You guys did a great job."

"You guys cleared it up for us," assistant GM Mike Bratz said. "You guys were pretty right on, too. I mean, very, very good."

"Either that or we're all wrong," D'Alessandro laughed. "We'll know that in two years."

Come Thursday night, Stauskas became a reality at No. 8. After failing to trade with Philadelphia at No. 3, picks Nos. 4-7 unfolded exactly as

Sacramento hoped. Ranadivé and D'Alessandro shouted as Marcus Smart went to Boston and Julius Randle went to Los Angeles.

Then as the clock started on their selection, Sam Hinkie called D'Alessandro back. He'd declined the Kings' earlier trade, but now Philadelphia's savvy president offered his upcoming No. 10 selection and two second-round picks for the right to draft eighth. Many Sixers evaluators maintained their interest in Stauskas. The coaching staff longed for a bona fide outside threat. Brett Brown fawned over Stauskas' skill set, closing his eyes and imagining a young Manu Ginóbili in 76ers blue. D'Alessandro, however, dismissed Hinkie's attempt.

Kings officials went around the room one last time. Their vote was unanimous. Stauskas was the pick. "We knew he was gonna be somewhere in that range, but all the way up to eight?" says Michigan coach John Beilein. "That was cool."

D'Alessandro grabbed his cell phone and dialed Stauskas in Brooklyn's green room. "Didn't we tell you you were coming to Sacramento!" the general manager cheered. "Congratulations, man. We're really excited about this. You've got a whole table full of people here with smiles on their faces."

The executive handed off to Ranadivé, who requested the call be placed on speaker. "We just want to give you a California welcome!" Ranadivé sang. The Kings owner instructed his front office to collectively shout a specific cheer.

"And he was like, '1...2...3,'" Stauskas recalls, chuckling.

"Nik rocks!" the group bellowed.

Stauskas, wearing a navy-checkered suit, could only giggle an uncomfortable laugh. "That whole thing caught me off guard because I didn't really know what to say back," he says now. "At the time I was obviously so excited they drafted me, but it was so awkward. I was sitting at my draft table and I was like, 'Thaaaaanks, guys! Appreciate it!'"

Stauskas' workout partner, Doug McDermott, thought he could land next at Charlotte's No. 9. Hornets head coach Steve Clifford had raved about McDermott's workout, but the front office selected Indiana forward Noah Vonleh instead. He offered a sweet shooting touch and perimeter handles as a 6-foot-10 power forward. Some scouts believed he had the potential to guard three positions and double as a small-ball, outside-shooting center. Philadelphia had envisioned Vonleh as an ideal complement to Nerlens Noel. He'd visited the Sixers en route to New York City. Vonleh hadn't worked out for teams due to a foot injury, but Brett Brown chatted Indiana's freshman on the PCOM court while they hoisted shots like old friends in the backyard.

With Stauskas and now Vonleh off the board, Sam Hinkie reevaluated his options. The Sixers' staff featured many fans of Croatian forward Dario Šarić. He was a decorated European player, and Hinkie saw flashes of Spurs playmaker Boris Diaw, the skilled forward who unlocked San Antonio's scoring and helped pester LeBron James on defense during the 2014 NBA Finals.

Bosnian brute Jusuf Nurkić also intrigued Philadelphia's staff. "He's just like a big dancing bear on the tape," says Lance Pearson. The hulking 7-footer rumbled through the Sixers offices during his visit, shaking hands with every lower-level employee. Nurkić's paws enveloped theirs as he cracked a wry smile, winking with each exchange.

The clock ticked on Philadelphia's pick. And instead of drafting one of their preferred prospects, one of the prepared outcomes Hinkie had kept quiet actually called for selecting Elfrid Payton. When Adam Silver thus announced Payton as Hinkie's choice, the news stunned Sixers fans and rival teams. Michael Carter-Williams had just won Rookie of the Year, despite his shooting struggles. Why add another big ball handler with a questionable jumper?

A smattering of fans up from Philadelphia rained boos down from the Barclays Center crowd. ESPN's draft broadcast even panned to Carter-Williams. He was milling about Brooklyn's green room in a powder blue suit, available as an interviewee for the network's on-air reporters. And like Joel Embiid's delayed expression at No. 3, Carter-Williams' live reaction now beamed onto televisions across the country. The point guard incredulously peered up at the jumbotron, then immediately dropped his head.

Hinkie often told Carter-Williams he was Philly's first building block. Suddenly, Carter-Williams now understood what it was like to hear your name gossiped on the trading block. "I had no idea what was gonna happen," Carter-Williams says.

After Payton shook Adam Silver's hand on stage, photographers funneled the two point guards together to snap a picture. Payton beamed while Carter-Williams pursed his lips. "I was just excited to be drafted," Payton recalls. "I didn't even think about what was going on with him."

The selection left Dario Šarić stranded at his table, equally as befuddled as the Sixers' sophomore floor general. "I was like, 'What's going on?'" Šarić recalls. "It was crazy." Two days before the draft, he'd met with Philadelphia officials in New York. Sixers international scout Marin Sedlaček, a veteran Serbian coach and talent evaluator, had seen Šarić in person play over 30 times. Philly's scouts listed him seventh on their consensus big board. And after Sacramento denied their move for No. 8, the Sixers even phoned Šarić's agent, Miško Ražnatović, committing to draft the Croatian.

Seated in the conference area adjoining Hinkie's office war room, Sedlaček stewed upon hearing Silver alternatively announce Payton. "It was just on his face," Lance Pearson says. The analytics staffer turned to his colleague. "It's a long draft," Pearson reassured the Serbian scout. "You never know what's going to happen."

Meanwhile, Denver took center stage at No. 11. After speaking with Minnesota all day, inquiring about Kevin Love, general manager Tim Connelly ultimately swung a different trade, swapping the 11th choice to Chicago for pick Nos. 16 and 19. The Bulls desired Doug McDermott's shooting, and moving off two first-round picks also trimmed Chicago's expensive payroll for their efforts to chase Carmelo Anthony in July.

If he fell in the lottery, McDermott long hoped to join the Bulls' contender. He rooted for Chicago and fellow Iowan Kirk Hinrich throughout childhood. Now his dream quickly became reality. "But it took more than two hours for the trade to go through," McDermott says. "It was just a lot of sitting around."

NBA officials ushered McDermott into a holding room, just as Nerlens Noel was sequestered a year earlier. He briefly sat alone watching the broadcast until a fellow draftee joined the private quarters.

Elfrid Payton was fielding questions in the Barclays Center interview room, answering queries about playing with Joel Embiid and his fit alongside Carter-Williams. "And then somebody said, 'Well it doesn't matter, 'cause you just got traded to the Magic,'" Payton remembers. After struggling to first fit his tangled mass of hair inside the blue 76ers draft hat, Payton was ordered to return his cap before being swept alongside McDermott.

At No. 12, Orlando originally hoped to select Latvian big man Kristaps Porziņģis. Enamored by his natural talent, Magic officials obtained Porziņģis' physical and promised, if Porziņģis remained in the 2014 pool, Orlando would select him. Only to Rob Hennigan's disappointment, the youngster preferred to play another season in the Spanish ACB League. "I trusted that I was gonna have a good year and be higher in the next year's draft," Porziņģis says now. He officially withdrew on June 15, allowing Orlando's front office more than a week to regroup.

With Porziņģis is unavailable, Magic evaluators entered draft night coveting Elfrid Payton, despite already attempting to mold Victor Oladipo into a lead ball handler. "We had kind of committed to this athleticism and building with defense," says a Magic executive. "We felt he kind of embodies that."

Selecting Aaron Gordon, of course, echoed that sentiment at No. 4, and also confirmed Sam Hinkie's suspicion that Orlando was targeting Payton at No. 12. While Philadelphia valued Payton's profile and potential, Hinkie drafted the point guard with sole intention of dangling him in front of the Magic. "It was a gamble," says Lance Pearson.

Several Sixers staffers believe Hinkie had direct information from a Magic personnel man as he phoned Orlando's war room, soon after stealing Payton. "They did it just to get an advantage on us," says Pat Williams, Orlando's senior vice president. Hinkie not only held the Magic's playbook, but Orlando also owned Philadelphia's 2018 first-round pick dating back to the 2012 Dwight Howard trade that rerouted Andrew Bynum to the Sixers.

Hinkie once again checked Thaddeus Young's value, although Orlando had no significant interest. If Hinkie failed to strike a deal, Philadelphia looked forward to incorporating Payton, awkward fit and all. "It was never a draft based on need. That wasn't part of the equation," Lance Pearson says.

"It was, 'We'll make it work,' even with the coaches. We'll make it work as long as it's guys that have talent."

Yet before time expired on Orlando's 12th selection, Hennigan finally agreed to draft Dario Šarić for the 76ers, attach a 2015 second-round pick, and return Philadelphia's future first in exchange for Payton.

Sam Hinkie supporters applauded the executive's brazen bullying. "It was fun to see how many picks we had in the future and imagine the hope of what all these could become," says Michael Levin, the Sixers podcast host. They jeered Orlando's front office. Hinkie, in one view, had won yet another trade.

Magic officials, however, believe they'd landed their preferred prospect at the low cost of next year's second-rounder. More losing seasons surely awaited Philadelphia. Orlando predicted that 2018 first-round pick may never have even conveyed to the Magic. "It was protected, and it wasn't gonna manifest into a first-round pick," an Orlando executive argues.

Joel Embiid would likely sit the entire 2014–15 campaign, like Nerlens Noel before him. Dario Šarić intended to play the next two seasons with Anadolu Efes in Turkey before he planned to decline the third-year option in his contract and join the NBA for 2016–17.

"I do think that night was a real test of belief," says Spike Eskin, Philly's radio czar and Levin's podcast co-host. After compiling a historic losing streak larger than the team's win total, Philadelphia's two 2014 lottery picks netted no immediate contributors. Eskin quickly compartmentalized his own frustration. Before recording that night's episode of *The Rights to Ricky Sanchez*, he felt responsible for maintaining the podcast's ardent pro-Hinkie tone. "There was the reality that, 'Man, we're really going to throw away a second season,'" Eskin says. "'That's how this is gonna go. We're all gonna have to buy into this.'"

Hinkie's outcome dawned on the rest of the NBA. "The thing that was unique about Philly was the extremeness of it," says a rival team executive. "Once it became clear it was a multi-year endeavor and not a one-year attempt at a high pick, once it was established as a long-term plan, it created some of the narrative."

If there were any remaining questions, tanking had fully swept the NBA.

Once the draft concluded, Hinkie, characteristically tight-lipped, warned several staffers he was worried about Brett Brown. The coach was hired for his unflinching optimism as much as his acclaimed development ability, yet losing out on Andrew Wiggins and Nik Stauskas pained Brown deeply. He did understand Hinkie's decisions. Embiid might be Hakeem Olajuwon reincarnate. Šarić projected as a perfect complement and character for their budding program. "Anyone that watched the video, he was exactly 'Brett Brown, blood on the floor, 100 percent effort at all times, loved the game.' Coach's dream," Lance Pearson says. "From a culture standpoint, everyone loved him. It was always just a question of if he was athletic enough or was he gonna come over."

Pearson had analyzed Philadelphia's potential season outlooks depending on which prospects they ultimately added, weighing expected win totals along with offensive and defensive production. His study also measured the Sixers' likely success depending on different dates for Embiid's return from injury, whenever Šarić finally came over from Turkey, and if the Sixers indeed drafted both. Brown knew Pearson ran his model to calculate myriad possibilities, including a worst-case scenario where both Embiid and Šarić didn't play until the 2016–17 season. Sure enough, the coach called Pearson into his office late that evening.

"What does it look like?" Brown sighed, masochistically requesting their new 2014–15 prediction.

"We're gonna lose a lot of games," said Pearson.

THIRTEEN

Adam Silver returned to the Barclays Center podium to announce Minnesota's No. 13 selection. With Kevin Love's departure seeming imminent, the Timberwolves were likely to launch another rebuild in Minnesota, and so team president Flip Saunders picked Zach LaVine, the springy freshman guard out of UCLA. Having also named himself head coach on June 6, Saunders' staff would have ample time to shape LaVine's athletic ball of clay once the Wolves joined the NBA's 2014–15 race to the bottom.

When Phoenix next came on the clock at No. 14, the Suns chose N.C. State scorer T.J. Warren. General manager Ryan McDonough hoped this would be his last lottery pick for years to come, where adding Warren to Phoenix's already-potent second unit would help boost the Suns into the postseason.

The 2014 NBA Draft ticked onward, soon bringing Boston up again at No. 17—the Celtics' first pick to convey from the previous summer's epic Nets trade that sent Kevin Garnett and Paul Pierce to Brooklyn and commenced Danny Ainge's rebuilding effort.

Kentucky freshman guard James Young made perfect sense here for the Celtics. With Brad Stevens and No. 6 pick Marcus Smart cemented as the first foundational blocks of Boston's new era, they would inevitably need scorers and shooters to flank the wings, and Young had flourished in that exact role with the Wildcats. "James was a little bit protected in the offense we ran," says Tod Lanter, Kentucky's trusted walk-on, "because we were able to leave him on that one side so he didn't have to use his off hand much, which was his biggest weakness."

John Calipari often positioned the lefty on the right wing. Young lacked the shake to honestly beat defenders in isolation, but off the catch, he boasted the length to fire over smaller foes and the quick first step to burst into the middle with his strong hand. Like when, midway through the second half of April's NCAA title match, Connecticut leading by nine with 10:44 to play, Young sliced down the heart of the paint.

"Our last-ditch effort to make it a ballgame," Tod Lanter says. Young only needed two dribbles from a step beyond the three-point line to gather and rise into the chest of 7-foot Huskies center Amida Brimah. No matter, Young cracked his left arm on the giant's head, flushing a dunk that sent Lanter, Kentucky's entire bench, and much of the enormous AT&T Stadium crowd to their feet. "The tournament kind of opened the door for him to shine," Lanter says.

With a little guidance from the Celtics' coaching staff, Ainge's front office hoped Young's star could truly turn in Boston. He did lead Kentucky with 20 points that evening despite UConn ultimately prevailing for the national championship. Huskies point guard Shabazz Napier just proved too much for Calipari's Wildcats.

Napier carried seventh-seeded UConn to the championship almost by himself, averaging 21.2 points per game while draining 46.5 percent from deep. He controlled the entire ebb and flow of the title bout, raining triples over Kentucky's perimeter defenders too afraid of his slippery handle.

After confetti fell that evening, none other than LeBron James joined the Twitter discussion dissecting the Huskies' championship. "No way u take another PG in the lottery before Napier," James tweeted. Napier, though, had yet to join the social media platform. "I didn't see it until my teammates told me," he recalls. "I didn't think nothing of it. I think everybody kind of blew that out of proportion."

Flash forward to June 26 in Brooklyn. Despite James' analysis, Napier still remained on the board, and waiting in the green room, well after the lottery range had concluded. While he was clearly talented, two weeks separated Napier from his 23rd birthday. Most teams in the lottery are there for a reason, after all, and it benefits those crummy clubs to swing on a lesser-finished and younger prospect, banking their coaches will grow him far beyond Napier's abilities after four NBA years—when that prospect first turns 23 years old.

Miami, however, holding pick No. 26, needed immediate help to maintain its championship window. The Heat could only take James opting for free agency as a message; he hadn't *yet* walked out of South Beach. If Miami supplied its King with the best supporting firepower of any team, perhaps James would still chase a fifth straight Finals appearance where he'd reached the previous four. Adding Napier in the back of the first round, already stamped with James' approval, marked nothing short of a coup for Pat Riley's front office.

Miami first tried to get No. 23 from Utah, but eventually moved up just two spots to ensure it could select Napier. In addition to sending the No. 26 choice to Charlotte, Miami also delivered the 55th pick, plus a 2019 second-rounder and cash.

The Heat had made their intentions clear. And when the trade was finalized, James once again reacted online. "My favorite player in the draft! #Napier," he tweeted. Cavs officials bristled at the post. Was James signaling Miami was in the lead for his services?

Soon enough, Cleveland and other James suitors had more clarity on his evolving free agency. By end of day on July 1, James' agent, Rich Paul, informed the Mavericks, Lakers, Suns, Bulls, Heat, and indeed the Cavaliers that James would grant them an audience for a free agency pitch. Los Angeles would finally get its chance at courting James to join Kobe Bryant in Hollywood. For Phoenix, the meeting all but validated Ryan McDonough's early Suns tenure as a success.

Carmelo Anthony also planned to meet with the Bulls, Mavericks, and Lakers, in addition to the Rockets, followed by a final sitdown with the Knicks. New York always boasted the financial advantage for Anthony. Only the Knicks could have offered a five-year, roughly $130 million max contract as Anthony's incumbent team—more than $30 million richer than the

CBA permitted any rival. In Chicago, Derrick Rose and Joakim Noah's hefty salaries limited the Bulls to $20.7 million in available cap space, far below the number Anthony was looking for. But joining a ready-made contender greatly intrigued Anthony.

He first met with Mark Cuban at the Mavericks owner's Dallas mansion, hearing from the front office leaders and superstar forward Dirk Nowitzki, still feeling fresh off their 2011 banner. When Houston hosted Anthony, the Rockets plastered an image of the scorer across the side of the Toyota Center, labeling the All-Star as their key to their championship aspirations. The photoshop had Anthony rocking a red No. 7, his number he'd worn in New York, although it accidentally ignited a social media firestorm.

Jeremy Lin still remained under contract with the Rockets and had worn that No. 7 throughout the 2013–14 season. While Houston's stunt charmed Anthony, it spurned the team's point guard. "If someone slaps you on one cheek, turn to them the other also," Lin tweeted, citing a Bible verse. "If someone takes your coat, do not withhold your shirt from them." Lin and Anthony, after all, hadn't exactly jelled back during their shared days in New York.

Rockets general manager Daryl Morey did himself, and the analytics community, no favors in defending their tactics against naysayers who claimed new-age executives like Sam Hinkie viewed players more like "assets" than people. Morey even had a trade lined up to move Lin's salary and create room to sign Anthony should the free agent choose Houston.

The Lakers, meanwhile, safely manufactured a gold No. 7 jersey for Los Angeles' presentation. Xavier Henry wore the digit all winter, but the bouncy swingman also lingered on the open market, and likely would for a while longer. General manager Mitch Kupchak informed Los Angeles' own free agents his front office wouldn't consider signing anyone before learning the fate of Anthony and, more importantly, LeBron James. The Lakers' moment had finally arrived. "Obviously, they were going after big fish," says Lakers forward Ryan Kelly.

Los Angeles, for example, asked Kelly, a restricted free agent with his rookie deal now expired, not to pursue an offer sheet from a rival franchise. If Kelly agreed to contract terms with another team, the Lakers would have 48 hours to match. However, Los Angeles hoped to keep their stretchy shooter and quietly suggested his patience would ultimately be rewarded with a two-year commitment. "We kinda had this little deal where, if they got a max player, my contract would be X," Kelly says. "And if they didn't, they'd pay me more money because they'd have more salary cap space." Los Angeles even delayed hiring a replacement for Mike D'Antoni as well, representing the lone NBA team without a head coach.

When Anthony arrived at the Lakers' El Segundo facilities, James Worthy escorted the All-Star, his agent, and his business manager inside from the parking lot. "They kind of whisked him through the back door and up to the office," says Clay Moser, the Los Angeles staffer. Kupchak waited alongside Jeanie Buss and Jim Buss. Executives from Anschutz Entertainment Group and Time Warner, locked into a historic 20-year, $4 billion local television deal with the franchise, also attended. Movie producer Joel Silver even created a short film, launching the discussion of how Anthony and his wife, La La Vázquez, a noted television personality, could optimize Hollywood and the Lakers' extended entertainment resources. By meeting's end, Los Angeles offered a four-year maximum contract worth $95 million. The presentation resonated with Anthony as Kupchak escorted the free agent back to his ride. "They even had security outside to keep the media and some fans outside the practice facility gates," Moser says.

This time, Kobe Bryant didn't use the meeting to poke at the star across the table. Unlike his relationship with Dwight Howard, Bryant and Anthony had developed a close friendship, and the Lakers legend revealed he wouldn't attend the sitdown due to a family vacation in Europe. Instead, Bryant joined him for dinner after Anthony met with the Knicks that evening.

The Lakers had convinced Anthony he was not a consolation prize. Los Angeles viewed him as the perfect frontcourt complement to Bryant and big man Pau Gasol. Yet Kupchak still pitched Anthony on the idea of accepting a lower salary if James also flocked west at a discount. Now the Lakers just needed The King's commitment. While Bryant and Anthony chatted over dinner, Kupchak departed for Cleveland to meet with LeBron James' representatives the next morning.

Rich Paul, James' agent, and Mark Termini, the contract guru, hosted meetings on behalf of James in their Klutch Sports agency's Cleveland offices. Suns owner Robert Sarver represented Phoenix along with Ryan McDonough and several top front office personnel. Mark Cuban, the Mavericks owner, flew north too. Chicago executives Gar Forman and John Paxson flanked Michael Reinsdorf, son of Bulls owner Jerry Reinsdorf, having pitched James four years earlier. Each team presented plans for future roster construction and championship contention.

During Los Angeles' meeting, Kupchak divulged the Lakers' positive traction with Anthony. Both he and James could launch the next era of Lakers excellence together, Kupchak preached, accepting the fabled franchise's torch from Bryant.

But Rich Paul quickly squashed any possibility of that dream coming to fruition. James would only accept his full maximum salary, Paul informed each suitor, and the Lakers, of course, had squandered any chance of maintaining two max-salary slots when they signed Bryant's massive extension back in November. "There was no shot at LeBron," Clay Moser says. Some wondered why James' camp even offered the Lakers a meeting.

Despite his success in Miami, forming a repeat champion while receiving a pay cut, James would no longer accept less than his highest possible number. It was the one way, James surmised, he could help fellow stars also maximize their earning potential, rather than be publicly chastised for not considering their team's overall cap situation.

Another stipulation: Paul disclosed his client was considering signing for just one year, with an option for a second season. If James presented a flight risk again in 2015 free agency, he could leverage management away from the cost-saving moves he felt Miami ownership conducted that 2014 spring before falling short against San Antonio. If James was ultimately unsatisfied with his team's front office, he could bolt the next summer. And if he wanted to stay, he could re-sign at an even greater number thanks to the league's ever-rising salary cap, a pool that deepened in part because of that lucrative new television deal with ESPN and TNT. This was far from *The Decision* of 2010; James' reps even implied each team would benefit from keeping quiet on his latest free agent proceedings.

Meanwhile, word circulated of Anthony's growing interest in Los Angeles and Chicago, so the Rockets pivoted to offer Chris Bosh a four-year, $88 million contract. Miami's All-Star forward made no rush to accept, however. On vacation in Dubai and later visiting Ghana for an NBA Africa camp, Bosh also lacked information on James' choice, and he wouldn't make his own commitment before hearing from his Hall of Fame teammate. It seemed the entire basketball world waited for The King's verdict.

"He's LeBron James," says David Griffin, Cleveland's general manager. "He's bigger than we are. He's an entity unto himself and he's completely changed the way the NBA deals with everything: free agency, player power, all of it. It's all tied to him." Why else were teams tanking so egregiously to secure the next superstar of his ilk?

Bosh, Dwyane Wade, and the rest of Miami's organization still clung to a belief James would return to South Beach. The Heat already signed forwards Josh McRoberts and Danny Granger—the veteran who forced his way out of Philadelphia—to fortify their supporting cast for another title run. Little action, though, unfolded elsewhere around the league as James' next decision lingered.

Spencer Hawes did sign a four-year, $23 million Clippers offer on July 4. The former Sixers center met with Phoenix on the first day of free agency, and then visited Portland, but the Suns, albeit objective outsiders on the LeBron James sweepstakes, still had their hands tied. General manager Ryan McDonough couldn't sacrifice any financial flexibility until Phoenix knew for sure they weren't landing James. The margin for error is razor-thin in NBA big-game hunting.

Not only did McDonough lose out on Hawes, but the Suns' original floor-spacing big man, Channing Frye, fled his home state for Orlando's four-year, $32 million offer. He'd hoped to remain in Arizona, but like Hawes, Frye couldn't wait for Phoenix's timeline either. Rob Hennigan's young Orlando core of Elfrid Payton, Victor Oladipo, Aaron Gordon, Tobias Harris, and Nikola Vučević billed as another rising group primed for a punchy season. "The talent, I thought, was better," Frye says. "I was like, 'Dude, we're gonna get *going* out here in Orlando.'"

Cleveland had briefly caught Frye's eye after Cavs point guard Kyrie Irving pitched the franchise on behalf of David Griffin. The Cavs still proceeded with caution approaching James' free agency, skeptical he'd actually ditch Miami. When Paul said James was leaning toward signing a one-year deal, Griffin thought it only confirmed James was returning to South Beach, where he'd chase one more ring—then perhaps sign with Cleveland in 2015. So Griffin handed Irving a list of other players to pursue.

Already a two-time All-Star at just 21 years old, Irving proceeded to phone restricted free agents including Jazz forward Gordon Hayward and Rockets swingman Chandler Parsons. Irving's salesmanship, just like his dazzling handle, impressed Frye and veteran wing defender Trevor Ariza. "He didn't really have to say too much," Frye says. "Kyrie was obviously one of the up-and-coming players in the league at that time."

Cleveland's Plan B was in full effect. Griffin even hired David Blatt, who just led Maccabi Tel Aviv to the EuroLeague title, as the Cavaliers' new head coach. Lacking NBA experience, Blatt's profile matched a growing playoff upstart starring Irving, not a James-led title contender—although Blatt did boast a championship pedigree Cleveland brass thought could oversee a long postseason run if James did decide to return home.

When Griffin finally met with Rich Paul and Mark Termini at Klutch Sports' offices, he conveyed Irving's team-first approach that July. The Cavs extended Irving to a five-year, $90 million agreement back on July 1, and in exchange, Cleveland's young star approached those names of possible Cavaliers additions with Griffin, while acknowledging the LeBron-sized elephant in the room.

Irving was also willing to take a backseat to James. And Griffin's biggest selling point: he knew that Timberwolves boss Flip Saunders preferred Cleveland's potential trade package, featuring Andrew Wiggins, over any rival offer for Kevin Love. Plus, rumor indicated Love would also commit long term to the Cavs, if the trade ultimately teamed him with a newly signed James.

A possible trio of Irving, James, and Love posed as a younger, better-shooting version of Miami's Big Three. Cleveland, however, lacked the cap space to offer James his full max salary. Griffin told Paul the Cavs would finagle ample room should James pledge his signing, but that's not how this saga would unfold. If Cleveland meant business, Paul rebutted, it would need to create the flexibility first.

The Cavs promptly went to work. Owner Dan Gilbert changed plans in order to meet with James in Florida. They aired grievances about their scornful summer of 2010. Gilbert, too, lauded the foundation Cleveland had built with Irving and the Cavs' likelihood of acquiring Love. Then on July 9, Griffin struck a three-team agreement with the Celtics and Nets, mainly shedding the three years and $19 million remaining on Jarrett Jack's contract. Why would rivals help the Cavs clear enough cap space to sign James? "I thought he could play with Deron [Williams]," Brooklyn general manager Billy King says of Jack. At the behest of Nets owner Mikhail Prokhorov, Brooklyn also acquired Russian forward Sergey Karasev in the deal. Danny Ainge, meanwhile, inherited young center Tyler Zeller and a 2016 first-round pick from Cleveland—marking yet another selection for Boston's growing trove of future draft capital.

James did meet a final time with Miami officials while he hosted his basketball camp in Las Vegas. Pat Riley presented the Heat's case, but James' mind was ultimately made. He summoned *Sports Illustrated* scribe Lee Jenkins to his suite on the Wynn's 58th floor. The magazine had recently published first-person essays from longtime Nets forward Jason Collins, in which he came out as the first openly gay active NBA player, and Jabari Parker, when Duke's freshman declined his Mormon mission to enter June's draft. James wanted to usher his announcement in similar form, penning a thoughtful explanation rather than creating another polarizing television event. He unraveled his thoughts to Jenkins over breakfast.

And just after noon Eastern time on July 11, James' free agency choice stopped the basketball world once again.

"I'm Coming Home," the headline read on SI.com.

David Griffin celebrated the news, yet bubbling emotion quickly knocked the executive onto his office floor. The Cavaliers had actualized a pipe dream. Now Cleveland's front office faced no option but delivering Northeast Ohio its elusive first championship since 1964.

FOURTEEN

LeBron James' decision, as always, rippled throughout the NBA.

Carmelo Anthony soon announced he would return to New York, opting for the Knicks' exclusive offer north of $120 million over five seasons. Los Angeles presented a future far too uncertain. Anthony also felt no assurances Bulls head coach Tom Thibodeau would survive ongoing tumult with Chicago's front office.

Chris Bosh and Dwyane Wade both still re-signed with Miami despite James' departure. Houston, first engrossed in landing Anthony and then chasing Bosh, now watched Chandler Parsons sign a three-year, $46 million offer sheet with the Dallas Mavericks.

Having once rostered Parsons on the now-notorious contract dubbed "The Hinkie Special," Rockets general manager Daryl Morey allowed Parsons to test the open market as a restricted free agent, and ultimately walk out the door. "Obviously it was a risk, because what could have happened…happened," Parsons says. Dallas incorporated a clause into Parsons' offer sheet known as a trade kicker, which would reward Parsons with a 15 percent bonus should the Mavericks one day move Parsons. Making the third year of his deal a player option would also let Parsons reach free agency again in just two years. Morey would later say the structure created a virtually untradable contract, sacrificing all of the agreeing team's leverage. "That made that contract hard to match," Parsons says.

The forward put pen to paper with Mark Cuban during the Orlando Pro Summer League. The Mavs owner cut the music and grabbed the mic at a downtown club called Attic. Parsons signed as waitresses delivered bottles of tequila to their table. Houston's four-year, non-guaranteed bargain contract—which Sam Hinkie had now fully indoctrinated in Philadelphia—disappeared as quickly as Parsons and Cuban emptied their shot glasses.

Chicago's alternative plans focused on Pau Gasol. Even with his two championships, the Lakers had kept their All-Star forward idling on free agency's sidelines just like their batch of inexpensive youngsters. "They had kept talking about wanting to bring the big names in," center Robert Sacre says. "We were just basically waiting to see what free agents were gonna do and then go from there."

Now without James or Anthony, reality crashed the Lakers' Hollywood dreams. A healthy Derrick Rose, Joakim Noah, and the rising Jimmy Butler brought far greater title chances than Los Angeles' bleak situation. Who knew how many earnest championship runs Gasol's legs, now 34, still had in reserve?

When Gasol ultimately fled to Chicago for three years and $22.3 million, Lakers general manager Mitch Kupchak was left with his still-barren roster only comprising Sacre's minimum salary plus Kobe Bryant and Steve Nash, both inching ever closer toward retirement. Circumstances again looked ripe for a rebuild in Los Angeles.

The Lakers, however, just as they did a summer earlier, began plugging holes with one-year deals, preserving flexibility once more for another run at top free agents in 2015. "It became kind of a destination place for guys who needed a team that had room," says forward Ryan Kelly. Repeatedly scheming the exact plan, expecting a different outcome despite the same result, is as much the definition of Lakers exceptionalism as it is insanity.

The second season on Jordan Hill's new two-year deal would in fact be a team option. Los Angeles did reward Kelly for his patience, extending a two-year deal worth $3.3 million in guaranteed money. "They ended up basically buying out my player option," Kelly says.

But others, like Kent Bazemore, hadn't been as accommodating after the Lakers didn't pick up his qualifying offer, making him an unrestricted free agent. "That was the end of that," Bazemore says. "Atlanta reached out and gave me guaranteed money and the rest was history." He inked a two-year deal worth $4 million with the Hawks.

Lakers shooter Jodie Meeks also departed Los Angeles for Detroit's three-year, $19.5 million offer. "They wanted to make a big splash and be back to their old-school championship time and all that," Meeks says. "I pretty much knew I wasn't gonna be back unless something happened fast. I wasn't going to sit around all summer and wait."

In their stead, Los Angeles acquired Jeremy Lin from Houston as the Rockets searched for salary relief. Only one year remained on Lin's contract and the Lakers received 2015 first- and second-round picks for their troubles. "He was another serviceable ball handler," says Clay Moser.

More short-term deals followed. Kupchak claimed veteran forward Carlos Boozer off waivers from Chicago. He convinced North Carolina product Ed Davis to sign for two years and just $2 million, with the second year being a player option. Entering his fifth NBA season, Davis needed a safe haven. "All I had that summer was minimum deals," Davis says. "[Kupchak] told me that I'd get an opportunity to play. I could earn it."

Just like Isaiah Thomas felt his success in Sacramento now justified his pay day.

Thomas had thrived since becoming a Kings starter. "He's got a chip on his shoulder," Sacramento's head coach Mike Malone says. "Last pick in the draft, he's got that 'Keep on doubting me' attitude, and he has a passion for the game. He loves being in the gym. A guy that you just like to be around."

Sacramento coaches once hoped for a long inside-out partnership between Thomas and DeMarcus Cousins, valuing his competitive edge and endgame stoicism. "We definitely thought it would be good for our team to bring him back," says assistant Chris Jent. Management, however, characteristically sided with Cousins, who wished for Thomas to play elsewhere.

Vivek Ranadivé saw past Cousins' on-court temperament. The Kings owner believed he understood a misunderstood giant, so uncomfortable in a losing environment. Ranadivé continued to admire Cousins' community involvement. He even made exhaustive efforts, along with advisor Chris Mullin, to help Cousins make USA Basketball's upcoming August outfit for the 2014 FIBA World Cup. To uphold Cousins' positive momentum, at Ranadivé's behest, Sacramento's front office prepared to let Isaiah Thomas walk, without regard to their coaches and without matching any offer sheet he signed in restricted free agency.

General manager Pete D'Alessandro had already attempted to deal Thomas before February's trade deadline. In one view, Thomas was merely a sixth man masquerading as a starter. The Kings projected Darren Collison, the Clippers' sturdy guard, as a more compatible table-setter for Cousins and forward Rudy Gay, and Sacramento landed his services on a three-year, $16 million deal instead.

Thomas did have other suitors. Danny Ainge phoned the minute free agency opened, offering a chance to ignite Boston's up-tempo rebuild. And while Phoenix lost the LeBron James sweepstakes, the Suns were still able to orchestrate a starry presentation for Thomas. There were images of the point guard wearing a Phoenix jersey on a gigantic billboard outside the US Airways Center and inside the arena, flashing on the jumbotron, just as the Rockets had rolled out for Carmelo Anthony. "Wow! Great visit so far!" Thomas' partner, Kayla Wallace, posted on Twitter that afternoon. "Feels weird to be so wanted!"

Similar to Sacramento, Phoenix didn't have a starting position available. But head coach Jeff Hornacek sold Thomas on playing him, Goran Dragić, and Eric Bledsoe often simultaneously, tripling down on the Suns' surprising success with multiple ball handlers from the season prior. All three wouldn't start but would surely close contests amid their 2015 playoff push. General manager Ryan McDonough had publicly declared Phoenix planned to match any offer sheet Bledsoe found in his own restricted free agency. The Suns would be faster and zippier with Thomas also scurrying past retreating foes.

Hornacek began scheming the turbo-charged attack that Ranadivé desired in Sacramento, only the Kings owner's outlandish 112 offensive rating requirement would prove nearly impossible to accomplish without perhaps the league's fastest point guard in Thomas. The Kings nonetheless worked a sign-and-trade to ultimately send Thomas to Phoenix on a four-year, $27 million deal—netting only Alex Oriakhi, the Suns' 2013 second-round pick, who never played in the NBA.

Mike Malone's staff finally believed the scuttle, long indicating Sacramento's front office dissented from the coaches Ranadivé had hired before naming Pete D'Alessandro general manager. "There were rumors about them not appreciating what we were trying to become," says Chris Jent, the Kings assistant. "We were trying to teach defense first in order to build a foundation of winning."

Staffers began hearing several candidates gossiped to soon replace Malone. During one meeting in preparation for July's annual exhibition games in Las Vegas, the head coach even revealed a startling confession.

"We gotta win this Summer League," Malone said.

"What?" a confused Jent responded. Few teams valued the two-week event as more than an instructive period for young players and networking around the league.

"Yeah," Malone continued. "We kinda need to win Summer League, just to get them off my back."

Fear of job security panged Jent's gut: "I was like, 'Oh my gosh. This is not good.'"

Sure enough, as Kings coaches exited La Pescheria one afternoon during Summer League, a seafood spot amongst hundreds of nearby restaurants on The Strip, in walked Vivek Ranadivé and Chris Mullin for their own lunch, accompanied by longtime NBA play caller George Karl. "It was really bizarre," Jent says. All parties insist Karl was simply meeting Ranadivé through mutual connections. He'd coached Mullin during a short late-1980s stint in Golden State, as Pete D'Alessandro studied at Mullin's alma mater, St. John's. And when Ranadivé poached D'Alessandro from Denver back in 2013, Karl was finishing his last season as the Nuggets' head coach. The new-and-improved Warriors eventually upset Karl's group in the playoffs before the coach was terminated.

Now one year later, Karl and Ranadivé reminisced inside La Pescheria about that Golden State series. "The one thing that we coincided with at the time was that the game had to be played fast," Karl recalls. Ranadivé also showed his penchant for hoping to push basketball's ideological envelope.

"Vivek had some wild thoughts. He's an out-of-the-box thinker, as am I," Karl says. "But you know, I just think he had this, in a strange way, an inexperienced enthusiasm that on one side of the fence I admired, but on the other side of the fence it's a little crazy."

Karl wondered if he'd passed the owner's test. It seemed as though Ranadivé was weighing the coach's amenability to his unorthodox philosophies, in contrast to Mike Malone. "I think they were probably taking a pulse on me and I was taking a pulse on them," Karl says. "There was no handshake or no thought of the future other than, 'Good luck.'"

Damage had still been done. The temperature seemed to scorch hotter on Malone's bench. Kings coaches began embracing the possibility of 2014–15 marking their last in Sacramento.

The growing tension in Las Vegas reached a fever pitch inside Cox Pavilion on UNLV's campus. With onlookers overflowing the bandbox gym, security barred any more spectators from Summer League's main event: Andrew Wiggins' Cavaliers against Jabari Parker's Milwaukee Bucks. They clashed for the first time since that November Duke-Kansas matchup and since going No. 1 and No. 2 in June, while Anthony Bennett also saw his first on-court action since injury curtailed his woeful rookie season. Rampant speculation, however, theorized both Wiggins and Bennett could be included in any potential Cleveland trade for Kevin Love. The storyline quickly came to dominate discussion amongst league personnel on the ground in Las Vegas.

LeBron James' official Cavaliers return rightfully stoked the embers of trade chatter between Cleveland and Minnesota. What long seemed possible now appeared probable. Even before James' signing, shortly after the draft, Thaddeus Young's agent, Jim Tanner, phoned Philadelphia's own disgruntled forward. "We got a deal on the table. You're gonna be a part of the Kevin Love trade," Tanner disclosed.

Flip Saunders had continually discussed his potential Love return with the Sixers. Minnesota's dual president-coach understood moving an All-Star would lower his roster's ceiling, and he saw Young's success during 2013–14 as the perfect veteran lighthouse for his eventual group of unproven athletes. "You're gonna be a part of it," Tanner told Young. "You're going to Minnesota."

He would, however, have to wait until August. Cleveland needed to sign Wiggins in order to actually facilitate the blockbuster deal for Kevin Love. Adding Wiggins' $5.5 million check helped the Cavs' outgoing package come within the necessary range of Love's $15.7 million, in accordance with the CBA, as both Cleveland and Minnesota were operating over the salary cap. But per league rules, no trade could be consummated until 30 days after Wiggins inked his rookie deal with Cleveland. The Summer of Love raged onward.

Originally slated to participate in the FIBA World Cup, Love withdrew from Team USA. "The Wolves and the Cavs were like, 'Nah, we need to wait for this trade to go through,'" Love recalls. "It was tough for me." Winning gold at the 2012 London Olympics, after all, originally sparked Love's relationship with LeBron James. They'd overlapped on Nike's campus in Oregon and throughout the AAU circuit as teenagers, but there's something magnetic about the experience collaborating on Team USA for NBA stars. "It's just the pride of playing for your country, kind of a lot of extra shit goes out the window and you're all competing for a common goal," Love says.

Rumor, of course, indicates James, Dwyane Wade, and Chris Bosh first imagined their Miami troika back during the 2008 Beijing Olympics, two years before James and Bosh reached the open market. "There's just nothing better than being around guys that want the same things out of life," Love says. "I think you kind of see where people come from, different walks of life, and to know guys on a higher level than you typically would elsewhere."

Minnesota finally granted Cleveland permission to contact Love in early August. The context of James' short-term contract, having signed a two-year max with a player option for the second season, blanketed not only Cleveland but the NBA at large. Cavs officials couldn't risk renting Love's services for a single winter before he left in free agency, and perhaps James following him out the door. Only after Love divulged his prolonged interest in Cleveland did the Cavaliers agree in principle to soon swap Andrew Wiggins, Anthony Bennett, and a trade exception for Minnesota's All-Star.

"We were kind of in a position where we probably needed to do something," says former Timberwolves executive Rob Babcock. "And to get that level of talent, we felt pretty good about that."

Exactly 30 days after Wiggins signed his rookie contract, Cleveland officially rerouted its No. 1 pick to Minnesota. The Sixers indeed unloaded Thaddeus Young as part of the blockbuster, effectively morphing matters into a three-team swap while landing the Heat's 2016 first-round pick, originally acquired from James' sign-and-trade in 2010.

Sam Hinkie finally netted the future first he'd long required to move Young. The Sixers' president also came away with Alexey Shved, a 26-year-old shooting guard, and, more importantly, Luc Mbah a Moute. With No. 3 pick Joel Embiid staring at a similar lost rookie season to that of Nerlens Noel the year before, Philadelphia now added Embiid's mentor, the fellow Cameroonian who first discovered him playing basketball. Mbah a Moute would also bring much-needed experience and defensive prowess to head coach Brett Brown's rebuilding roster.

Hinkie supporters of course cheered another savvy Sixers acquisition. Patience and pragmatism still ruled the day in Philadelphia, while the NBA world braced for another contender to emerge in Cleveland. Hinkie's Sixers hoped to be ready to compete for a title once James, fast approaching his 30th birthday, slipped out of his prime.

For now, San Antonio had sacked Miami's dynasty, yet The King somehow seemed destined for an even greater effort toward capturing the throne with Kevin Love and Kyrie Irving by his side. "When I got traded there," Love says, "it was a life-changing thing for me."

Sam Hinkie's deputy, Sachin Gupta, had spent the summer determining what assets Philadelphia could extract from the Wolves-Cavs blockbuster for themselves. "Any trade that was rumored," says Lance Pearson, the Sixers' analytics staffer, "he'd figure out, 'How can we benefit somehow by facilitating the trade?'" Even as a marquee move inched LeBron James closer to his third title, the Sixers just had to sneak in and remind everyone of their putrid plan. Sacrificing Young also pushed Philadelphia even closer to the bottom of the NBA standings.

"It became a debate about if it was a justified strategy and people arguing that it was," says one longtime team executive. "There was some fear from the league office, knowing it's a smart thing to do given the rules, but they don't want people doing it. They were afraid of a parade of teams going through that type of rebuilding process."

Rival owners grumbled to commissioner Adam Silver. When Philadelphia visited their market that winter, the home team's attendance and ticket revenue would plummet. "What the NBA is trying to do, I think it's different in football," Bucks co-owner Marc Lasry says. "Because you've got so many more games, you don't want people to lose interest in those games. If there's a race to the bottom, that's not good."

Milwaukee, for example, had compiled the league's worst record in 2013–14 as a last resort. Injuries derailed what was supposed to be a playoff-bound roster. Now with Jabari Parker in the fold, new Bucks ownership wouldn't approve tanking their 2014–15 season. "At the end of the day, my thing is, we're never doing that," Lasry says. "We're going to do whatever we can to win. I get that people say the way to rebuild is through the draft. My view is the way you rebuild is you pick great players."

Some league voices suggested Commissioner Silver even fine Philadelphia for Hinkie's brazen losing. More practically, the league's competition committee and Board of Governors began discussing alternatives to the league's current draft lottery system as the summer sped toward the fall. There did need to be some way to appropriately help bad teams get better talent, but surely there was a better system than the one Hinkie was manipulating. "Like anything else, there are winners and losers," says Nuggets president Tim Connelly. "I like that Adam was proactive and wasn't shying away from it."

Several potential concepts arose, with the most popular being to flatten the odds atop the lottery. Instead of the worst team earning a 25 percent chance at the No. 1 pick, the four lousiest clubs would each have a mere 12 percent chance at the top choice. The worst franchise could even drop as far as fifth, the second all the way to No. 6, etc.

Another suggestion theorized a tournament amongst the league's lottery teams; winner takes the No. 1 pick. Based on their record following the All-Star break, the 14 regular season losers would be seeded appropriately, although some feared teams battling for the eighth seed in their conference's playoff picture might tank into that competition. The 2013–14 Suns, for example, could have won the lottery tournament—and the chance to draft Andrew Wiggins—instead of losing to San Antonio in the first-round like Dallas had. The tournament, though, would encourage winning amongst the league's losers. Teams would no longer rest players down the stretch of the regular season. Youngsters crawling on rebuilding teams would automatically enter a postseason environment despite their year full of defeats.

A portion of league insiders were also interested in Celtics executive Mike Zarren's innovative "Wheel" concept. "Zarren's been godfathering that thing forever," says Wizards general manager Tommy Sheppard. "Every time you ask him about it, it's gonna be at least 45 minutes."

Boston had lived many years at each end of the NBA's competitive spectrum. And whether the Celtics were praying for ping-pong balls like in 2014 or favorable Finals whistles like in 2008, Zarren never much liked the NBA's draft lottery system—albeit Boston choosing to play it toward their advantage. "I think having this safety net provides all sorts of excuses for mediocrity that we shouldn't want both on the court and off it," he says. Zarren believed there was an alternative, cyclical method to determine the league's draft order by some form of chance that didn't inspire organizational losing. "I'll be in favor of any lottery change that reduces the impact of record," he says.

Zarren eventually crafted a PowerPoint presentation with an accompanying law review–style description, even extrapolating how The Wheel would adapt with possible league expansion or retraction. Zarren also included a calculated transition from the current system to his cyclical creation.

His first version required a 30-year rotation. The executive then quickly developed his second iteration on a five-year or six-year scale, grouping the league's 30 teams into buckets of six or five clubs. One year, a team's bucket would, for example, spin for picks between Nos. 1-5, the next season they'd draw for the range of Nos. 5-10, and so on. There would still be lottery drawings and a highly rated television event. It could make for an even livelier broadcast with more spins of the Smartplay machine.

"The downside is, if your superstar pick has a career-ending injury after year one, or your GM does a bad job picking, and you pick someone who's bad the year you have the No. 2 pick, you gotta wait a few years before getting another good one," Zarren says.

Skeptics also feared top prospects would avoid entering their name in the draft if they knew their favorite franchise or a starry market would be drawing for a top pick the following spring. And would LeBron James have left Miami if the Heat, within their bucket's drawing, lucked into the second pick to nab Jabari Parker? "I don't like The Wheel," says Mavericks owner Mark Cuban, "because you could have a team that's dominating get a generational player and it just makes it worse."

The league's competition committee ultimately approved flattening the odds amongst the bottom four teams to just 11 percent, leaving a formal change up to a vote by the NBA's Board of Governors in October. Out of the 30 figures representing each franchise, most commonly the majority owner, 23 would need to vote yes.

At first, lottery reform appeared to be in the league's near future, but those in favor couldn't yet rally a majority by that fall. "There were a couple of teams that continued to discuss the unintended consequences and needed to have more information and have more time to kind of really study it," says Pacers vice president Peter Dinwiddie.

Sixers ownership lobbied hard for votes against the reform. Changing the system mere months before the 2015 lottery would obviously derail Hinkie's strategy entirely. Other cellar dwellers like Boston and Orlando would also have the rug swept out from underneath them, Philly argued. Far too many future draft picks had been traded across the league under vastly different circumstances. "To change it at the beginning of the season when you had no off-season to plan in a certain way, they were right," says former Brooklyn general manager Billy King.

It wasn't that other teams didn't understand Philadelphia's strategy, either. "If you're going to go play the lottery, you're going to play it 10 times. Not one or two," says former Nets assistant GM Bobby Marks.

Oklahoma City president Sam Presti brought needed reinforcements to Philly's cause. Franchises in small markets, like his Thunder, depended on the draft to survive. OKC, of course, had set the gold standard of building through the lottery, selecting Kevin Durant, Russell Westbrook, and James Harden to build a contender, only to then feel compelled to move Harden along to greener pastures. The Thunder couldn't afford to extend Harden his maximum extension while also rewarding center Kendrick Perkins. "In general, a guy's not gonna sign in Oklahoma City for a max if he has an opportunity to go to Dallas," says one former general manager. "You're not fighting the same fight in free agency or in revenue. You don't want to give up another thing that levels the playing field."

Flashy coastal metropolises ineffably draw star athletes. It doesn't hurt the NBA at large either. "Even the league feels that way," the former GM says. Remember that "frozen envelope" curiously delivering Patrick Ewing to New York? And yes, the future OKC franchise landed Kevin Durant No. 2 after Portland selected Greg Oden No. 1 in 2007, but it was a known secret David Stern rued that the phenoms both landed in smaller markets.

Sam Presti's campaign effort began to turn the lottery reform tide. Every team, eventually, relies on the lottery. "There aren't 20-year dynasties other than the Spurs," says one general manager. The Board of Governors ultimately voted not to pass the proposed changes on October 22. Philadelphia and Oklahoma City recruited 11 other franchises to oppose the change: Atlanta, Detroit, Miami, Milwaukee, New Orleans, Phoenix, San Antonio, Utah, and Washington.

"I don't think there's anybody out there who thinks it's a desirable thing to be tanking," says Stan Van Gundy, by then the Pistons' head coach and president. "I haven't heard anybody say this is good for the game. I just think a lot of people don't feel like they have a choice."

Sam Hinkie, though, had certainly determined Philadelphia's fate. And while no lottery reform passed on this attempt, Sixers head coach Brett Brown had continued growing his group as only he knew how. He'd seen the Spurs contend for over a decade with chemistry formed over countless group dinners, flowing with expensive bottles of wine. So when Dario Šarić suited up for his native Croatian national team during the FIBA World Cup, Brown flew Joel Embiid, Michael Carter-Williams, and Nerlens Noel to Spain to cheer their one-day teammate from the stands. "It was really, really, really nice of them. In that position, to show, you know, they really like you and like following you," Šarić says.

The group convened for dinner. "That was the first time I saw Embiid order Shirley Temples," Carter-Williams says. "He proceeded to order like 16 of them." Embiid giggled as the teammates later twirled outside the restaurant to the music of nearby buskers.

"We went dancing in the street a little bit," Noel recalls.

Brown's trip wasn't complete, however, without sitting down with Šarić and his family. Ever since he first chatted with Sixers officials in New York, Šarić maintained his vow: after two more seasons in Turkey, he would debut in Philadelphia. "We knew from the beginning he planned to come [in 2016]," says Miško Ražnatović, Šarić's agent.

It was a tantalizing tease. Brown indeed fell for Šarić's film. "Everybody talked about his talent and his desire to win," says one international NBA scout. "Dude is a winner."

Šarić claimed Croatian League Finals MVP in 2013 and garnered consecutive FIBA European Young Player of the Year awards that season and again in 2014. "You're like, we gotta have this guy come over," says Lance Pearson, the Sixers staffer.

But if Šarić remained in Turkey for a third campaign, he would be past the first three guaranteed years of a rookie contract he could have signed with Philadelphia during that summer in 2014. And if Šarić waited until the 2017–18 season, the CBA would allow him to join the Sixers as a veteran free agent, eligible for a much higher salary—and seemingly the preferred outcome for Šarić's father. Brown understood the math. Šarić signing with the Sixers in 2016 rather than 2017 would make any financial advisor nauseous. "Brett didn't trust that inherently. You're just worried about it," Pearson says.

Returning from Spain, Brown announced a declaration to his staff. Joel Embiid, when healthy, projected as a menacing superstar. Nerlens Noel would fortify the Sixers' defense. And it was Dario Šarić's malleability that could fit alongside either big man. "We need to make sure he feels a part of our program to make sure that he's actually gonna come over," Brown instructed.

The coach would follow Šarić's season over film. Hinkie would text Šarić after big games. Brown often phoned the forward over WhatsApp. Each conversation, Šarić repeated his promise. "I'll be over in two years," he assured. "My word is my word." For Šarić, it was simple. He had already collected most of the hardware a youngster can achieve in Europe. By 2016, he would surely be thirsty for new competition. "I feel like I will need to go to the NBA and play," Šarić recalls. "I wanted the challenge."

In the summers, Brown would deploy assistant Chris Babcock to visit and work out Šarić for upwards of several weeks. Later, shooting specialist Eugene Burroughs also traveled to Croatia. Šarić's sense of humor endeared the coaches, building the relationships Brown hoped to encourage his eventual assimilation into the Sixers' culture. Unlike many rivals, Philadelphia could afford to wait for a player of Šarić's caliber, and for now, there was nothing Adam Silver or opposing owners could do to prevent their leisurely rise.

FIFTEEN

Kobe Bryant readied for his 2014–15 season expecting to lead the Lakers back to the playoffs. This roster wasn't a championship contender, but the postseason had been a given any year Bryant was healthy. He had no plans to gallop quietly into the sunset.

Los Angeles eventually hired Byron Scott as head coach, with Bryant's endorsement. They had been teammates during Bryant's rookie season in 1996 before Scott led several benches around the league. He piloted New Jersey to consecutive Finals appearances in 2002 and 2003. He was later named Coach of the Year in 2007–08, guiding New Orleans to 56 wins. Few Lakers personnel outside of Bryant, though, expected Scott to oversee a truly competitive unit in Los Angeles. He was most recently fired in 2013 after three losing seasons in Cleveland. "You felt Byron was in an absolute no-win situation," says Clay Moser, the Lakers' director of basketball strategy. Scott also only signed an agreement clearly matching the remaining length of Bryant's own contract. "Byron was basically there to kind of be a steward of the ship to get the Lakers through those two years," Moser says.

Bryant maintained they would reach the postseason nonetheless. He refused to let failing tendons and bones derail his storied career. Having rehabbed that troublesome knee from the previous December's injury, he ramped his workload as the 2014 off-season neared its conclusion. Bryant gathered Julius Randle, the Lakers' No. 7 pick, and new acquisition Ed Davis, another client of agent Rob Pelinka, for a grueling stretch of summer training. "He worked his ass off," Davis says. The journeyman forward heard the lore of Bryant's exhaustive practice sessions. Yet word of mouth couldn't possibly prepare Davis for reality.

The 36-year-old paced Davis and Los Angeles' 19-year-old rookie in the devilish 17s drill, in which players must run sideline to sideline 17 times before one minute expires. Full-court sprints followed, this time while handling the ball. Bryant later instructed his teammates to dribble hard from one baseline to the far elbow. And upon reaching their destination, they had to fire jumpers with their off hands. Bryant required each player drain five shots in a row before finishing the workout. While his teammates struggled, Bryant completed the task with ease. "At that point in his career, he wasn't playing for nothing," Davis says. "He knew he wasn't going to win a championship. For him to have that much dedication, it's just crazy."

Conditioning underscored Byron Scott's preseason program as well. The Lakers' new head coach exhausted his roster of short-term-contracted players through endless drills. "I'll probably be in shape from that training camp until I fucking die," Davis says.

While Brett Brown and Philadelphia began prioritizing rest and recovery during the Sixers' 2014 training camp, Scott barked for his players to run day and night. He'd played under Pat Riley throughout the 1980s. Those Showtime Lakers practiced hard enough to easily sprint through live games. "Everybody wants to do it," says Lakers assistant coach Jim Eyen, who joined Scott's staff. "But in order to be able to do it, we gotta pay the price."

Scott's Lakers ran suicides like end-of-practice punishments in high school. Players were allowed only three passes in full-court three-man weaves, no matter the obstacle. Scott placed assistants around the court as human cones. And with each repetition, the coaches stepped farther and farther from center court, stretching the players' weave routes as wide as humanly possible. "Guys would throw these lob passes in the air so you could give yourself a chance to run underneath it," center Robert Sacre says. The few dropped balls garishly echoed off the hardwood, as if reverberating back to Pat Riley's practices and angering the legendary coach. "All you're trying to focus on was not hurling," Sacre says.

Rookie guard Jordan Clarkson dazzled Lakers staffers. The Missouri product had been unguardable during his three-on-three pre-draft visits. Venerable Lakers scout Bill Bertka, who long ago assisted Riley, had fought for general manager Mitch Kupchak to acquire Clarkson in the second round. The rookie didn't disappoint in camp, either. "He was one of those guys, if you gave him a challenge, he'd get after it," says Jim Eyen, the assistant coach.

Los Angeles looked at Clarkson both handling the ball and scoring from the wing. Some coaches felt he had the requisite tenacity to even guard opposing small forwards. And at the end of scrimmages, he wanted the rock. "He had big balls," Eyen says. "He wouldn't make them all, but he would take a big shot. And he made enough of him. I think that's commendable as a rookie. He wasn't fazed."

Clarkson's charisma quickly won over Kobe Bryant, but those crunch time situations would ultimately be decided by Los Angeles' five-time champion. He felt rejuvenated after losing two years to consecutive lower-body injuries. Bryant's legs had grown stronger with each maniacal off-season training session.

Steve Nash, on the other hand, spent his summer contemplating retirement. A full calendar of arduous rehabilitation had drained his mind as much as his body. "It wasn't like he was sitting there fat-cat, happy with the deal he had," says forward Ryan Kelly. Nash heard Lakers fans clamoring for clarity. Los Angeles had sent two first-round picks to Phoenix expecting the former MVP to help Bryant deliver one last title.

"If he were healthy, they probably would have competed for a championship," says Bill Duffy, Nash's agent. "That's what he signed up for."

His first two seasons in Hollywood were nothing short of abject disappointment. And now entering the last year of his contract, Nash still watched from the sideline for much of Scott's taxing conditioning drills, nursing his back and other nagging issues. Noise grew louder about the point guard's $9.7 million salary going to waste. "He got a rash of shit," says Clay Moser.

Guilt swept Nash's conscience. Appeasing the disappointed Lakers supporters fueled most of his internal argument against calling it quits. Duffy also refused to let his diligent client sacrifice money that could benefit his family for generations. "You deserve that," the agent reiterated.

His body ultimately spoke loudest of all. Midway through October, Nash tweaked things again by just carrying his bags. And by October 23, the Lakers confirmed he wasn't yet retiring, but Nash's lingering back dilemma would sideline him throughout the 2014–15 season. He would remain around the team, his shirt drenched in sweat from two hours of core activation and shooting before practices and games. "Dude, talk about a guy who wanted nothing but to play," Ed Davis says. The past two seasons, Nash's sideline stretching inspired hope of future reinforcements. His presence now brought daily reminders of what could have been.

In Philadelphia, Brett Brown could only look forward. He spent countless hours of the off-season engineering his second 76ers training camp. "He obsessed with ways he could improve the program," says Lance Pearson, Philly's analytics staffer. The Sixers set up shop at Stockton College in Galloway Township, New Jersey, a short drive from the beach island that houses Atlantic City. In the mornings, Brown drilled hard conditioning practices, but instead of running for the sake of running, like in Los Angeles, Philadelphia's conditioning activity focused on jump shooting.

Brown constantly called Gregg Popovich and Spurs general manager R.C. Buford, bouncing ideas off his former coworkers. Just as San Antonio captured its latest championship that June while expertly managing its players' minutes, injury prevention emerged as a key area of focus for the Sixers' staff. So in the evenings, instead of drubbing his players with a second session of a grueling two-a-day practice, Brown welcomed a slew of guest speakers. "A Navy Seal one night, a nutritionist another," says assistant coach Vance Walberg. "It was more important to keep those guys together mentally than anything else."

Brown began each film session with detailed discussions on current events. "He wanted us to be aware and not just in a shell," forward Brandon Davies says. "He had a really good perspective on life. It's more than just basketball."

The coaching staff finalized a grading system from Pearson and Walberg, which Brown dubbed Philadelphia's "effort chart." Philly evaluated myriad hustle-type plays for each player. Assistants could then sit down with their assigned players and detail each action, captured on film. The effort chart encouraged individualized goals for players, not just team concepts. How well did they run the floor offensively? How hard did they jet back on defense? Did they contest shots? Did they box out? Deflections, steals, and blocks were all rewarded. "The players were really competing to see who was best in all these different things," Pearson says.

The system inherently highlighted Nerlens Noel's defensive abilities that once projected the string bean as a No. 1 pick. And after a year on the sideline, here he was back healthy. "He was just a freak for a big man with how quick his hands were," Pearson says. The staff implemented the effort chart first during training camp scrimmages and preseason exhibitions. They planned for video coordinators to assist in measuring each player's effort throughout the entirety of every game that season. Coaches would then review their performances over 10-game segments.

"Brett Brown did a great job with laying down the foundation, letting everyone know what the organization was growing to be, and that was a tough, defensive-minded team," rookie forward JaKarr Sampson says.

Philadelphia's expected offensive deficiencies, though, nullified any defensive progress, as the Sixers began the season 0–5. They bungled that fifth game at home to Orlando when Tobias Harris drilled a jumper at the buzzer to give the rebuilding Magic their first win of the year. The Sixers dropped their next in Philadelphia, to Chicago, but Brown's youngsters gained valuable late-game experience in their second consecutive outing.

With 14 seconds remaining, Brown scribbled a back-screen action at the wing before Hollis Thompson's college roommate, 76ers center Henry Sims, fed his fellow Georgetown product for a clutch three. Sims started 25 Sixers games to close the previous regular season after arriving from the deal that shipped Spencer Hawes to Cleveland. Brown empowered the 24-year-old center, and others such as Thompson, unlike most play callers with undrafted journeymen. "He just gave me opportunities to live out a dream," Sims says. "Being in the NBA, being in crunch time, drawing up plays for me for clutch shots and making clutch shots. Those endgame memories will never go away."

On Philadelphia's next possession, Chris Johnson, a 6-foot-6 undrafted wing out of Dayton, splashed a three from the left wing, following a dribble handoff from point guard Tony Wroten, to cut Chicago's lead to 116–115. Bulls guard Kirk Hinrich did ultimately sink two free throws to spoil the fun, dropping the Sixers to 0–6 on the season—the worst start in Philadelphia since the woeful 1972–73 team began 0–15.

Brown praised his group's stingy comeback effort. If the Sixers were going to lose, and it would surely drop the majority of their 2014–15 battles, the head coach continued preaching his gospel. "We ask our guys often, 'What would you want other teams to say about you?'" Brown told reporters postgame. "We want respect. We want to work hard. We want to have a tenacity and a spirit that reflects the city and reflects a bunch of young guys."

Tony Wroten clearly heard the message. His last-second dish to Johnson marked his seventh on the contest, and Wroten himself finished with a career-high 31 points. Starting the first seven games at point guard as Michael Carter-Williams remained sidelined, recovering from May surgery to repair the labrum in his right shoulder, Wroten dropped 21.9 points and 6.7 assists per game, parlaying his incredible speed and energy with a 6-foot-8 wingspan to snatch 2.7 steals each outing. "The talent was obvious," says Lance Pearson. "Those were the types of guys that made sense to the coaches why they were on the team."

Philadelphia's staff viewed Wroten as their third-best active youngster behind Carter-Williams and Noel. At 6-foot-6, Wroten could gallop into the open court like a streaking NFL wideout and fool defenders with a vicious handle, perfected on playgrounds across Seattle. His lone collegiate season at Washington convinced Memphis to select Wroten No. 25 in 2012. "He didn't shoot it great, but he was young," says Dave Joerger, then a Grizzlies assistant coach. "Those guys, they just take time. He could really get to the basket, he could really score." Yet Memphis found just 272 total minutes for its 19-year-old point guard as a rookie. The Grizzlies, bound for the 2013 Western Conference Finals, couldn't spare much time developing a raw athlete amongst a veteran-laden contender. When Sam Hinkie scored Wroten back in August 2013, in exchange for a 2014 second-round selection that never actually conveyed, the executive thought he'd acquired a future postseason contributor for free.

Hinkie clearly valued Wroten more than most players on which he gambled. He coveted Wroten's untapped potential dating back to days scouting him in college. "He thought this was a place [Tony] could be really successful," says Greg Lawrence, then Wroten's agent. Still just 20 years old, Wroten had his parents first fly with him to Philadelphia, and Hinkie greeted the family with a kind smile, his voice hinting at a charming southern twang. "Sam couldn't have been nicer spending time with them," Lawrence recalls. This was not just a transaction to help Memphis cut Wroten's guaranteed salary.

He was still clearly a work in progress, sometimes flinging an ill-advised pass after skipping past his defender's reach. His fancy dribble sometimes stalled the momentum of the Sixers' already-rocky offense. "There was always a constant frustration with Tony's decision-making," Lance Pearson says. Only with Carter-Williams sidelined to start the season, Brett Brown had few players who could handle 35 minutes each night at the point. "There weren't many guys that could actually dribble," Pearson says.

Philadelphia personnel maintained optimism in between Wroten's errant bounces and the Sixers' mounting defeats. "We all signed up for this," says assistant Vance Walberg.

"Even though we were losing," adds veteran guard Jason Richardson, "I could feel something was getting built."

The Sixers' injured No. 3 pick added a key ingredient. Joel Embiid's affable presence warmed teammates and coaches like he'd endeared Kansas personnel and the Cavaliers' brass—this time without the chocolate cake. "People just love being around Joel Embiid," Pearson says. "He's hilarious. He's just a big teddy bear."

Nursing that famously broken right foot, Embiid didn't travel during his first six months as a professional, limited to form shooting while sitting in a chair and stretching his walking boot out along the court. He watched some games in the Sixers' locker room with Pearson and assistant coach Chris Babcock as they logged sequences for their effort chart. Embiid seamlessly joined their conversations like a seasoned basketball lifer, pointing out intriguing matchups. He lamented any Philly shot attempts between the three-point line and the rim. "He's always looking at it almost like an analytics person," Pearson says. "What's the most efficient shot I can get from each situation I find myself on the court?"

At the same time, Embiid masked an excruciating pain. The rapid basketball ascent that already banked millions also separated Embiid from much of his family. It had been four years since he'd seen his younger brother, Arthur, when a phone call on the morning of October 16 shattered Embiid's world. A truck's faulty brakes skid the metal mass into a schoolyard and killed several children—including 13-year-old Arthur. Guilt swept Embiid's apartment in Philadelphia's downtown Ritz-Carlton. Why hadn't he brought his brother to the United States as Luc Mbah a Moute had done for him? "I wouldn't know what to do," says Vance Walberg, the Sixers assistant.

Mbah a Moute, Sam Hinkie, and Brett Brown all rushed to the Ritz to console Embiid. He then flew back to Cameroon for the funeral, returning to Philadelphia three weeks later. Rejoining his teammates helped Embiid heal, but he struggled to stomach sitting on the bench, mere inches from the hardwood. "I think he kinda had a lot of problems with, 'I lost basketball.' And it's hard," Richardson says. "I can't imagine going through that."

At home in the Ritz, Embiid distracted his emotions by spending hours playing FIFA video games. Staffers soon began to notice his added weight. "Joel was more responsible than Nerlens, but you saw the same thing," Pearson says. "When you're not actually out there playing, it's hard to keep yourself motivated and doing all that grinding work when there's no reward for being out on the court."

Hinkie invited Embiid to watch home contests from his arena suite. Despite everything, Embiid still dazzled the executive and Sachin Gupta, Philadelphia's vice president, with astute observations. "They raved about how knowledgeable he was, his basketball IQ, the way he talked about the game," says one Sixers official.

Hinkie showed Embiid his front office's new Slack communication system, a business messenger platform commonly used in media and technology companies. "It just integrated everything," says an active 76ers Slacker. Instead of contacting international scouts on WhatsApp, sharing highlights over Twitter direct messages, or pinging staff groups via email, Philadelphia's basketball ops could filter their conversation in real time, in different channels, to discuss specific topics. Tweets easily uploaded into the platform. Hinkie even hired a programmer to create various bots. One updated every morning with the previous evening's statistics from prospects they were tracking around the globe.

"That was him to a nutshell," one Sixers scout says. "Technology to him is at the forefront of what he knew and how he thought that could help."

Hinkie consistently implemented new methods to streamline productivity. An in-game Slack discussion group allowed every Sixers staffer not seated on the bench to create a communal stream of commentary. "Why are we holding for one shot?" someone would type furiously. "Why aren't we going at this guy who has three fouls in the second quarter?" another would ask. Some of those gut reactions could serve as valuable teaching points in film review. And so during Brett Brown's postgame postmortem, he would receive a log of those best ideas.

Yet even once Carter-Williams returned, Philadelphia dropped to 0–8 at Dallas—and in embarrassing fashion. The Mavericks' 123–70 victory marked the largest win in the history of that franchise. When they entered their November 19 home date with Boston 0–10, Sixers coaches began admitting they feared the worst: their roster might lack the firepower necessary to win even a single game that season. Philadelphia was attempting the sixth-most threes of any team in the NBA yet ranked 29th in converting only 32 percent of those heaves. "Every set that we put together, even when we produced a great shot, the ball just wouldn't go in the basket," Lance Pearson says. "And it was by organizational design. It was just the coaches' perspective that we can't win if we can't shoot."

"We had guys that tried," Vance Walberg adds, chuckling.

They'd make just 33.3 percent of their 21 three-point attempts against Boston. While the Sixers only trailed by five at the end of three quarters, Philadelphia would ultimately fall 101–90 to Brad Stevens' group. Like the end of the Sixers' miserable spring, Brett Brown's youngsters just seemed to find new ways to flounder in the fourth quarter. Defenses sagged off Carter-Williams, unafraid of his crooked jumper. Opponents blew up dribble handoffs on the wings with Nerlens Noel and Henry Sims. Philadelphia's attendance dwindled in tune. But true to the city, the thinning crowd still jeered Evan Turner, having joined Boston in free agency, each time he entered the game and received the ball during the Celtics' victory. "It's not for the weak-hearted," Turner says.

Turner had left Philly in February hearing cheers for his departure. Indiana's postseason run then rendered Turner unusable in the playoffs. When the Pacers didn't extend Turner's qualifying offer, allowing him to become an unrestricted free agent, fans labeled the former No. 2 pick as a bust. A new-found depression gulped him like a sinkhole. "After four years, I was damn near straight over hooping," Turner admits. "I was like, 'Man, this shit ain't even worth it.'"

As he went unsigned on the open market, he saw reports indicating teams viewed the former Buckeye as a character concern. "People just make up shit," Turner says. "I was like, 'This league shit ain't worth it if they're trying to destroy you.'"

Toward the end of the summer, just Boston, Miami, and Minnesota offered either the minimum salary or not much more. "Only three options I had," Turner says. When Los Angeles became a short-contract breeding ground, Phil Jackson lobbied the Lakers to add Turner, represented by Michael Jordan's longtime agent, David Falk, but Mitch Kupchak had no interest.

Pat Riley promised Falk the Heat planned to rest Dwyane Wade, now 32, in a quarter of their 2014–15 games. Once Turner saw increased minutes while the Hall of Famer watched in street clothes, he'd have ample exposure to perform for his next contract. But otherwise, he'd ride the pine.

Timberwolves brass liked Turner dating back to the 2010 NBA Draft. Flip Saunders wanted Turner in his rotation, although Saunders told Falk he'd have to play understudy to Andrew Wiggins. Minnesota couldn't deal an MVP candidate like Kevin Love for the No. 1 pick and prioritize Turner's minutes over Wiggins' development.

Lo and behold, Boston emerged as Turner's only true destination. He joined the Celtics, and their storied media market, apprehensive. Even with his prior relationship with Brad Stevens, Turner still felt unsure about his standing in the NBA. "I was kind of, like, timidly walking back into basketball and being like, 'Man, I hope this shit works out,'" Turner says. "I never went through anything like that, so I walked in eyes wide open praying and hoping it worked out."

Stevens put the ball back in Turner's hands to organize the Celtics' second unit. Stevens and Jay Larranaga often discussed how Sam Hinkie told Boston's assistant, back when Larranaga interviewed for Philly's head coaching job in 2013, that he felt Turner was best deployed at point guard. The move reinvigorated Turner. He challenged rookies and other youngsters one-on-one after practice, unleashing his tricky array of mid-post moves and midrange chicanery. "He and Brad just had an understanding," says Celtics assistant coach Walter McCarty. "Brad knew how to get him into spots where he could be successful." Even during Turner's quieter outings, like his two points against the Sixers, he still contributed on the glass (four rebounds) and helped distribute the rock (three assists). His efforts didn't help net too many early season victories, however.

Boston's win in Philadelphia brought the Celtics' record to 4–6 before a five-game drought plagued Turner's new team. Yet just like Brett Brown piloting his Sixers, Brad Stevens never wavered. "His positive approach was something that helped along the way because it helped us understand him," says forward Jeff Green. "It also gave us confidence as a player to go out there and just play for him."

Stevens' resolve helped conceal the elephant inside Boston's locker room. While the Celtics' previous season had netted Marcus Smart and James Young, with more ensuing draft capital, Danny Ainge still remained active as ever on the NBA's trade market, looking to unload veterans such as Green and Boston's All-Star point guard.

"We knew that [Rajon] Rondo was probably going to be moved," says Walter McCarty, the Celtics assistant. "We just didn't know when and what we'd get in return."

From that first dinner inviting Rondo to his home, Stevens prioritized cultivating a chemistry with the floor general. "When Rondo was hurt, Brad used Rondo almost as an assistant coach," forward Jared Sullinger says. Rondo snuck over to Stevens during practices, suggesting a shooting drill in between more monotonous strategy sessions. And when Rondo returned to the court, Stevens turned to him in late-game huddles, curious for the point guard's call.

"They were just very cerebral and very compatible in terms of knowledge," says Bill Duffy, Rondo's agent. "Two high level basketball minds." Rondo simply didn't want to be part of Boston's rebuild. "He didn't want to be in a situation where they're just young and developing," Duffy says. "He wanted to compete."

Ainge promptly worked the phones, knowing what Rondo could yield on the trade market. A 28-year-old, multi-time All-Star would become rather pricey once his deal expired on July 1. "Rajon at that time was looking for a max," Duffy says. Ainge knew another franchise would pounce at the chance to land Boston's point guard ahead of his free agency. "I don't think [the Celtics] were at that level, so it just kind of made sense for them," Duffy says.

The Lakers, eager to dangle that Rockets pick acquired from the Jeremy Lin trade, made active pursuit. General manager Mitch Kupchak saw an immediate potential makeover for Los Angeles' failed star chases of 2013 and 2014. Acquiring Rondo now would help boost Bryant's penultimate season right away, and allow the Lakers to sign another All-Star into cap space that summer, then re-sign Rondo.

But Ainge declined Kupchak's advances.

Even while hearing his name discussed on the trade block, Rondo still followed Kevin Garnett's playbook. "We always say Rondo graduated from Ticket University," Celtics forward Jared Sullinger says.

As Garnett once guided him, Rondo now instructed Boston's current rookies. "He was really trying to get us ready, me and the young guards," says Marcus Smart, "really trying to teach us what Brad wanted in his system and what it takes to be in this league."

When the Celtics landed in Houston two nights before their first road game, a text pinged first-year forward Dwight Powell's cell. "Hey, rook," Rondo messaged. "Lobby. 6:30." In what became routine, Powell rose before dawn and hurried down to the hotel's first floor to find Rondo waiting. He already snagged their sneakers and a bag of balls from the equipment manager.

"It's never too early for him," Powell says.

They played one-on-one and fired jumpers. Exhausted by day's end, Powell slunk into bed to order room service, when another text from Rondo dinged his phone, requesting Powell be in the lobby again the next morning, this time at 6:00 AM. On game days, the veteran either did an extra lift or activated his muscles with yoga. "Just because you make it as a pro," Powell learned, "doesn't mean you stop working as you get there."

Playing for Boston also reunited Powell with Kelly Olynyk, having first met hooping for Canada's national teams as teens—only their time as teammates would soon prove short-lived. After practice one December afternoon, a group of Powell and his visiting friends were driving to Olynyk's apartment in Waltham when someone yelled, "Yo, Dwight! I think you just got traded."

Powell shrugged off the alert. "What's it say?"

He and Rondo were rumored to Dallas.

"Nah, nah, nah," Powell countered. "If Rondo's in it, it's just a rumor."

Celtics players had heard countless scenarios in which Rondo would depart Boston before the February trade deadline. He'd already been dealt to seven other teams, according to social media.

Then Powell's phone rang. It was general manager Donnie Nelson, welcoming him to the Mavericks.

Stunned, the crew whipped Powell's car around and back toward his home. Olynyk soon arrived for Powell's last night in Boston, helping pack for his morning flight to Dallas. "My closest friends kept getting traded," Olynyk says.

Danny Ainge had moved Powell in the trade that sent Rondo to the Mavericks for pesky forward Jae Crowder, big man Brandan Wright, veteran point guard Jameer Nelson, and what became a 2016 first-round pick. Dallas hoped Rondo would form a seamless pick-and-pop partner with Dirk Nowitzki, having missed out on both Carmelo Anthony and LeBron James in free agency. On the flip side, another key draft asset entered Boston's war chest.

"I was told from the onset that it's a business and to be ready for whatever, and the reason we get paid is not just to perform but to be able to pick up and move at a drop of a hat," Powell says.

No teammates scrambled to Rondo's home before he ventured south. He texted several Celtics, but otherwise left the only franchise he'd known without even a whisper. "Once the trade happened," Sullinger says, "Rondo was gone."

When Jameer Nelson learned of the deal, he was out Christmas shopping for several in-need families he'd "adopted" through a holiday gift program. "I got traded in the mall," he chuckles. "It is what it is."

Jae Crowder watched his living room television intently as the news was airing on ESPN. His agent quickly dialed in. "I knew I was going to a unique situation with a new team, a rebuilding team," Crowder says. "I just wanted to make the most of it."

Crowder could hear the excitement in Ainge's voice when Boston's lead executive called. The 34th pick in 2012 after two impressive seasons at Marquette, Crowder looked the part of an NFL defensive end at 6-foot-6 and 235 pounds, and Ainge envisioned Crowder potentially starting long term on the wing. He could bully opponents on one end and space the floor with his shooting on the other. Crowder had only one qualm about joining Boston. En route to his new city, he read countless articles detailing Ainge's diligent rebuild, saying Crowder marked just the latest Celtics acquisition in a series of roster shakeups. More trades were coming, and Ainge's front office was apparently unconcerned about another trip to the lottery.

Boston indeed fumbled four straight games in late December, falling to 10–18. Crowder grew worried. He pulled Brad Stevens to the side after one practice.

"Are we tanking?" Crowder asked. "And if so, let me know."

Stevens sighed. His tone dropped lower, more empathetic. "I don't coach this game to lose," he responded. "I'd never coach this game to lose." They were just fighting an uphill battle.

Crowder nodded, shook Stevens' hand, and proceeded back to the locker room. Boston's second-year play caller gained another loyal soldier. "We always, what I like to say is, keep it real with each other," Crowder says. "We'd talk whatever was on our minds. He was my first coach at this level to open up that way."

And despite his tinkering, Ainge, too, kept one eye trained toward contention. The executive's patience only lasted so long. The Celtics' putrid 2006–07 campaign immediately birthed Boston's 2008 title, one may recall. As the new year crept closer, Ainge kept searching for trades that both brought back future draft picks plus young players boasting upside— such as Crowder, perhaps capable of soon contributing in the postseason while still playing on a relatively inexpensive rookie contract. Then maybe Boston's growing hoard of future draft ammo could deliver the next unsatisfied superstar, like Kevin Love or Kevin Garnett before him. "Clearly there were some of us who were spending a while hunting unprotected first-round picks," Celtics assistant general manager Mike Zarren says.

Sam Hinkie boldly chased first-rounders as well, except Philadelphia's president also spent exhaustive hours mining the NBA's bargain bin, hoping to land another Chandler Parsons on a similarly team-friendly contract.

While those deals brought players on incredibly low salaries, relatively speaking, Hinkie was also filling Brett Brown's rotation with the youngest roster in the league. Philadelphia thus dropped its next six games following that loss to Boston, stumbling all the way to 0–17. The Sixers' drought set the new worst-ever opening stretch in Philadelphia. One more loss would also match the 2009–10 Nets for the poorest start in NBA history.

Hinkie had heard his coaching staff's dismay. So just like he'd done to begin the second round of the 2013 draft, the Sixers president phoned Robert Covington's representative, Chris Patrick. "Sam had been kicking himself," Lance Pearson says. "He was always looking for an opportunity to get Rob Covington signed."

Houston had waived Covington after training camp that fall. Several teams called, but Patrick still held out for a richer offer before signing his client to a new NBA club. Covington thus became the unanimous No. 1 pick in the D-League draft, only for Hinkie to dial Patrick the same day as Covington's scheduled regular season debut for the Grand Rapids Drive. Once Hinkie loaded his patented four-year, minimum deal with more guaranteed money up front, Patrick finally encouraged Covington to take the deal. Patrick had spoken to Brown; there would be minutes galore for the young marksman to fire from deep.

And by the Sixers' December 3 trip to Minneapolis, staring down the Nets' historic 0–18 start, Covington had fully integrated into Brett Brown's rotation. He poured in 17 points during 31 minutes off the bench against the Wolves. His bomb with 1:15 remaining gave Philadelphia an 81–77 lead to quell Minnesota's final run. Blue sleeves hugging each of his arms, Covington splashed a trio of his triples during the fourth quarter to help clinch the Sixers' first win. "Having Cov come in and be able to knock as many threes down as he did, it helped to open up the court for us," says rookie forward Jerami Grant.

Two games later, Covington led Philadelphia with 25 points in a 108–101 overtime win at Detroit. There were still obvious reasons someone as talented as Robert Covington toiled on the NBA's margin. He could rain from distance but struggled putting the ball on the floor. He could fire over most defenders with a towering release point, but Rio Grande Valley's frenetic system engrained tendencies Philly's coach staff deemed suboptimal. "That was a carnival, just jacking threes," Brett Brown says of Houston's D-League experimentation. "The whole thing was based on shooting 60 threes and it's a science project. And so he came in here and started, like, you'd sort of squint and say, 'Really?'"

Brown needed time to iron out Covington's shot selection and improve his basketball IQ. In turn, more experienced opponents kept taking games. The Sixers lost five straight after winning two of three. Both Philadelphia and Minnesota would carry more than 20 losses into the new year, toggling back and forth atop Tankathon's inverted standings. After one season tanking toward the bottom, Andrew Wiggins, Anthony Bennett, and the Wolves' 2015 first-round pick would surely lead Minnesota toward the postseason. And removing nightly pressure to win games allowed Brown's coaches to perhaps grow their young phenoms into inexpensive stars. With Covington on board, Hinkie believed he finally secured his greatest opportunity at a basketball reclamation project yet.

SIXTEEN

Byron Scott's 2014–15 Lakers also stumbled out of the gate. Despite the annual postseason aspirations in Hollywood, Los Angeles dropped nine of its first 10, the worst start since the 1957–58 Minneapolis Lakers fumbled their first seven. Even still, no word of tanking trickled through the front office. "Never ever did that conversation come up," says Clay Moser, the longtime Lakers staffer.

The losses nonetheless persisted, with Kobe Bryant still attacking like Los Angeles could vie for a playoff spot. He scored 27.3 points per game in November, only the Lakers trailed opponents by 14 points per 100 possessions when Bryant was on the floor. Another four-game losing streak slunk the Lakers to 3–13 after their November 28 loss to the equally futile Timberwolves. Bryant dinked a three-pointer as time expired in the Target Center. Each not-enough fourth-quarter comeback carried increasing weight in the Lakers' locker room. "Frustration and anger is going through my head right now," Scott told reporters postgame.

Bryant boiled over on December 11.

Nursing his aging body, the All-Star spent much of those Lakers practices receiving treatment. Meanwhile, Scott ran the rest of his roster through an arduous series of drills this particular morning, hopefully capable of springing momentum for a string of wins. While Bryant's teammates clutched their knees, he leapt off the training table ready for a 10-minute closing scrimmage. "Guys were already out there tired," says Xavier Henry.

Bryant began barking at fatigued teammates the moment play began. "He came out and just laid into the guys," assistant coach Jim Eyen says. "A lot of our guys were young. If not rookies, a few years in the league. Their eyes got as big as saucers."

Nick Young didn't cower. The man referred to himself as Swaggy P, after all. "Nick talks. Period," says center Ed Davis. "Before, after, during, missing, making. It don't matter, he's talking shit." He began chirping back at Bryant after one basket. The Mamba took umbrage. "That's really what woke him up," Davis says.

Bryant and Young went back and forth, trading a few jumpers. The Hall of Famer flashed a series of fadeaways that would make Michael Jordan blush. He knifed through the defense like it was 2001. "And then he started calling dudes soft," says Xavier Henry. Bryant began comparing his interior teammates to a specific brand of toilet paper.

"You motherfuckers are soft like Charmin in this motherfucker!" he shouted.

Bryant then switched onto Jeremy Lin, who'd upstaged him back in 2012 at Madison Square Garden. Bryant swiped the point guard's pocket and taunted Lin throughout his ensuing breakout lay-in. "Jeremy Lin's not a talker," Ed Davis says.

The Lakers all huddled briefly before opening their practice doors to the awaiting media. As Scott wound the discussion down, ready to return to scrimmage action, Bryant resumed his toilet paper tirade. "You're a bunch of pussies!" he eventually spat. Most Lakers players fell silent.

"He let them know, 'I'm still that guy,'" Xavier Henry says.

Reserve guard Ronnie Price broke the hush. Directly at Bryant, he shouted back: "I ain't no fucking pussy!" Both sides garbled at each other as they broke the huddle to resume play.

"I loved it," Eyen says.

Mitch Kupchak sat there attuned as local reporters filled the rest of the sideline. "Cameras came in, that really took him over the top," Davis says. "Kobe's a real calculated guy, real smart, sharp. He know what he doing."

Nick Young stayed on Bryant. But despite Young's best efforts, the veteran cashed one crucial bucket after another. Bryant spouted off again.

"Fuck, is this the type of bullshit that's going on in these practices!?" he chirped louder. "Now I see why we've lost 20 fucking games. We're soft like Charmin! We're soft like Charmin in this motherfucker!"

All onlookers were treated to a vintage Bryant performance. "It was that takeover that you hadn't seen in a while," Henry says. Lakers staffers sensed a deeper message to Bryant's madness. He certainly handled these later years with intention. Los Angeles now sat under a pile of losses too deep to climb out from and into the postseason. The front office's summer clearly hadn't boosted Bryant toward contention.

"His tirade was basically at Mitch," Clay Moser says. "It could have been directed at everybody."

Indeed, as Bryant stormed off the court following his demonstrative victory, he aimed his anger toward Kupchak. "I'm supposed to practice and get better, Mitch! I'm supposed to practice and get better!" Bryant hollered. He paused to catch his breath. "These motherfuckers ain't doing shit for me!" His teammates weren't just unskilled enough to win games—they were apparently too soft to even push him in practice.

"Kobe knows, and everyone in this league knows, ain't nothing soft about me," says Ed Davis. No matter his toughness, the North Carolina product represented another Kupchak addition not yet qualified for playoff minutes. "My whole focus was just to get the fuck off a minimum deal," Davis admits.

Bryant's squabble with Kupchak mirrored the ongoing friction between the front office and basketball operations. In a joint ESPN.com interview that ran the very next day, Jeanie Buss and Jim Buss confirmed they were speaking only when necessary. The siblings did present a unified front against questions about the Lakers tanking. Jim retorted he was insulted by the comment. Jeanie delivered a monologue any public relations official would approve. "The teams that use tanking as a strategy are doing damage," she said. "If you're in tanking mode, that means you've got young players who you're teaching bad habits to. I think that's unforgivable."

Los Angeles' dire situation was, however, evident. The franchise owed its upcoming first-rounder to Phoenix unless they selected within the top five. Already lingering amid the league's cellar, fans started counting ping-pong balls. Would the lowly Lakers even keep their pick?

Los Angeles had never made consecutive trips to the lottery under Buss family ownership. With the Lakers amid their second of three years Jim once said it would take to turn the franchise around, Jeanie was asked for her thoughts on that timeline. She concluded her response telling ESPN: "I think that, just like any business, if you're not meeting your expectations in an organization, you should expect a change."

Any new direction held mum in Los Angeles, however. Jim Buss and Mitch Kupchak would head into free agency in July as planned, and now potentially with another top lottery pick—so long as it didn't convey to Phoenix.

As the calendar turned toward 2015, the only upheaval in the NBA came on Sacramento's bench.

The Kings' thrilling double-overtime victory at Phoenix had brought the team to 5–1 back on November 7. They stood at 9–6 on November 26 before DeMarcus Cousins developed a debilitating case of viral meningitis.

The balletic giant scored 24.2 points and mauled 13 rebounds per game during November. He had joined a few Kings practices in Las Vegas during Summer League and buzzed excitedly throughout training camp. Coaches wondered if Cousins' Team USA experience had exposed their All-Star talent to better, winning habits. "He was a leader of the practice and the hardest worker," assistant Chris Jent says. "It was just very different."

But Sacramento couldn't muster much with the 24-year-old sidelined. The Kings went just 2–7 without Cousins before axing Mike Malone late on Sunday evening, December 14, bringing those long-whispered rumors to rest. Pete D'Alessandro maintains the decision came from ownership. Vivek Ranadivé claims he merely approved the choice that his general manager and advisor, Chris Mullin, pitched.

Malone's staff believed Ranadivé. They'd already seen D'Alessandro let go of Shareef Abdur-Rahim in September. Sacramento's former director of player personnel was the only front office holdover from the Kings' old regime, and Abdur-Rahim staunchly supported drafting Elfrid Payton over

Nik Stauskas all of June. Many staffers believed D'Alessandro ultimately fired Abdur-Rahim for continued disagreement on personnel decisions.

Ben McLemore was shooting inside Sacramento's facility when Kings point guard Ray McCallum texted the news of Malone's ouster. The coach rang McLemore's phone soon after. "I kind of got teary-eyed," McLemore says. "I was devastated."

The Kings' full roster echoed that sentiment. "I think that whole situation was messed up," says forward Rudy Gay. "He was getting his feet wet. You gotta give your coach a chance." Players and assistants recognized the obvious timing of the decision. Cousins' sickness presented the perfect excuse to make a change at head coach. And even with Sacramento looking like a playoff team before Boogie got sick, reports immediately linked George Karl, quite expectedly, as the leading candidate to replace Malone.

Ranadivé first lobbied for Mullin to assume the post. When he declined, Mullin sensed he began falling out of favor with the owner. In the interim, Pete D'Alessandro met with Malone's staff individually that next morning and explained assistant Tyrone Corbin would handle head coaching duties. "It wasn't really a why, it was, 'This is how it is,'" Chris Jent says. By the end of their discussion, Jent resigned out of loyalty to Malone. "I was so jacked up," Jent says. "I just couldn't wrap my mind around why it was happening. I was just like, 'I can't do this.'"

Firing Malone angered Cousins as well. He'd finally found a coach who he trusted could shepherd the franchise toward contention, in a style that he enjoyed. Malone never called Cousins out in the press. They handled their business face to face. On the first day of training camp, Malone hollered at Cousins in front of everyone. He threatened to kick the burgeoning All-Star out of practice. "As a rookie, I was like, 'Oh, okay. This coach obviously means business,'" Kings guard Nik Stauskas recalls. Malone's screams were underscored with a care that shaped his criticisms as constructive. "All the coaches we had, Mike Malone was actually the guy that kept DeMarcus in check," Stauskas says.

Losing Malone, without any prior warning, gutted the star big man. "He was really, really frustrated and felt betrayed," Jent says. How could the

Kings ever forge forward if their leadership was constantly trying to survive a game of Ranadivé's musical chairs?

Corbin stood no match for Cousins' outbursts. Kings players knew the coach was nothing more than a lame duck stopgap. "Tyrone had no control," Stauskas says.

Cousins particularly jawed at the Kings' first-round pick. It was no secret Stauskas' representation had attempted to steer the Michigan product away from Sacramento. Walking off the court one early practice, Stauskas even told Jent his agent said he'd be traded by Christmas. "When he revealed that to me, I was like, 'Oh boy. This is gonna be tough,'" the assistant says.

When Cousins taunted teammates, he would specifically target Stauskas, searching for greener grass within a different franchise. "That's just how DeMarcus expressed his feelings and wanted to help the next guy in line," explains McLemore.

Cousins loudly questioned Stauskas' toughness during five-on-five action. Not unlike Kobe Bryant's "Charmin" chastising, Cousins routinely called for Stauskas to toughen up after plowing him with a screen. He shouted with each of the noted shooter's misses. "It's just hard on a young player," Jent says. "You gotta have thick skin and it was tough for him to take. When it's tough to take, you become a bigger target."

Stauskas' practice struggles manifested in games. He made just 26.1 percent of his threes before the All-Star break. Cousins continued to chirp. "As a rookie to begin with, you're gonna have it tough," Stauskas explains, "but Boogie's...he's an interesting guy. That's all I can say." By the new year, Stauskas finally understood his agent's warnings. "I started thinking, 'Is this how it is everywhere?'" Stauskas says. "It's just chaos and drama all the time."

During one pregame locker room, Rudy Gay turned to counsel the floundering rookie. "You'll probably move on to other teams," Gay began, "you'll learn from your mistakes. This isn't a normal situation. From here on out, it's only gonna go up for you." But the Kings skidded to just 17–29 by the end of January. Another lottery trip seemed predetermined for Sacramento, where Los Angeles was sure to join.

Misery kept plaguing the Lakers. Head coach Byron Scott took a measly 12–30 record into New Orleans on January 21, where Kobe Bryant rejoined the team having skipped the first two of L.A.'s four-game road trip to rest. His previous appearance, albeit in another Lakers loss, Bryant dished a career-high 17 assists. And midway through the third quarter in New Orleans, he looked amid another solid performance, having posted 12 points on 5-for-12 shooting with five rebounds, two assists, and a block.

He danced past Pelicans forward Dante Cunningham in the right corner for his latest bucket, gliding baseline for a routine two-hand jam. Only while retreating back on defense, Bryant gingerly touched his shooting shoulder in obvious discomfort. "He went up and down the court three or four times with his right arm dangling down to his knees, basically," Clay Moser says. When Bryant next caught a handoff at the elbow, he took three shaky dribbles with his off hand before relinquishing the ball and signaling to the Lakers' bench in need of a breather.

His right arm still drooped as Bryant jogged off the floor. Yet he professed to coaches the pain didn't matter. Bryant's left hand still worked, he reassured any skeptics. "It was, 'Oh, I can still play. I can keep this off my mind,'" says Xavier Henry.

"He was hurt, but the way his swag is, man, it's unbelievable," adds Robert Sacre. "His swag made it seem like it was nothing. That guy had crazy pain tolerance. It's sick. It's disgusting."

Bryant iced his ailing shoulder for most of the fourth, lobbying all the while to return to the game. Sure enough, his first touch back in battle, Bryant gathered the ball at the mid-post against Pelicans wing Quincy Pondexter, ready to pounce. "We threw it in to him in the post, and he made this incredibly beautiful, shimmy-shake, Hakeem Olajuwon, Michael Jordan–esque post move with his left hand and buried it," Moser says.

The action appeared far from natural, but Bryant made the motion look fluid. "He was like, 'I've just been practicing all these shots,'" Sacre says. "I couldn't doubt him, you know?"

Ed Davis and Julius Randle confirmed Bryant's preparation. Their demanding summer workout, not finished until burying five consecutive off-handed jumpers, suddenly proved eerily prescient. "He was locked the fuck in," Davis says.

Then just five days later, the Lakers ultimately ruled Bryant out for the remainder of 2014–15. He'd played those last few minutes, hoisting a lefty runner to boot, with a torn rotator cuff. Like in his previous two season-ending injuries, Bryant still refused to sit out of the action in New Orleans, despite the grim end to his career seeping into reality.

"That's one of those quietly great, forgotten moments of Kobe lore," says forward Ryan Kelly.

With Bryant joining Nash on the sideline, the Lakers' Groundhog Day continued on. No matter Mitch Kupchak's efforts, Los Angeles was doomed for another lottery appearance. And they could possibly surrender that pick to Phoenix as part of the sign-and-trade that delivered Nash in the first place.

While Boston sat pretty, inheriting future draft capital left and right, having preemptively moved on from Kevin Garnett, Paul Pierce, and now Rajon Rondo as well, the Lakers were terrible and owed as many first-rounders as they were due from rival teams. Plus in Boston, Brad Stevens was implementing a system that the refurbished Celtics would one day utilize in the postseason.

Byron Scott, meanwhile, moved Ryan Kelly to the wing to fill Bryant's immediate vacancy. "We just didn't have any people left," says Clay Moser. Accustomed to hedging over picks, Kelly was now getting caught on those same screens while defending the ball handler. Quicker opponents skipped past his stance.

"I was starting games on Dwyane Wade," Kelly says. The sophomore found a statistical breakdown that tracked average heights at each position. "There were only two players 6-foot-11 and higher playing significant minutes at small forward," Kelly recalls, "and it was me—and Kevin Durant."

It's hard to fault Byron Scott's attempt. A single injury can force coaches to scrap entire swathes of their playbook. Losing Bryant, of all players, and his nightly 20.4 field goal attempts, eliminated the Lakers' alpha and omega.

Jacque Vaughn was experiencing similar tribulations adapting his own rotation in Orlando. Injuries had sidelined one Magic youngster after another. And after dropping a December 30 home contest against Detroit 109–86, Orlando slogged through its next five losses to reach 13–27 on the season. The Magic even handed Scott's lowly Lakers a rare victory on January 9.

While veteran additions like Channing Frye and Ben Gordon were supposed to step Orlando closer to the postseason, it was the Magic's nucleus of lottery picks that management expected to decide games. "We really wanted to get a group of guys who liked each other and wanted to grow together," says a Magic executive.

General manager Rob Hennigan, however, couldn't exact his Thunder rebuilding model without Orlando's phenoms sharing the floor. An errant elbow first fractured Victor Oladipo's face during practice, keeping him out of the team's first nine games. Oladipo only returned for two outings before Aaron Gordon, the No. 4 pick in June, broke his left foot and missed the next 32 contests. And then Orlando's starting big, Nikola Vučević, missed six straight to open December. Tobias Harris, the burgeoning wing, next sat five straight games in the beginning of January.

The constant lineup juggling prevented any sort of pecking order to emerge within Jacque Vaughn's offense. He'd scrapped experimenting Oladipo at point guard by the end of December, instead sliding rookie Elfrid Payton into his starting lineup. The change sparked noticeable tension within the Magic locker room. "If you don't know what position you want a guy, you have all this talent, it's too much indecision," Channing Frye says. "It's too much. You can't do that." Oladipo, after all, was considered Orlando's face just a year ago. "Do you like this guy or not?" Frye says. "If you pick him and that's your guy, you make the hierarchy, put the ball in his hands, let's go. Pick the guy, everyone else will fall in. They could've picked five guys."

Nikola Vučević had emerged as a pole of Orlando's offense. He cajoled opponents with nifty footwork on the block. He posted 19.3 points and 10.9 rebounds per night by 2014–15, yet Vučević still longed for a constructive voice to help push him and his inexperienced teammates. Channing Frye brought mentorship but lacked the scoring chops to force others in line. "There isn't that one guy to tell you, 'Hey, young fella. This is what you have to do. You have to do it that way,'" Vučević says. "I think that was the main issue with us." Rob Hennigan's Magic couldn't determine their Paul George, like Indiana had, and Orlando lacked its David West to then hold him accountable.

Moving Victor Oladipo off the ball also interrupted minutes for Evan Fournier, a sweet-shooting 22-year-old guard acquired from Denver that summer for Arron Afflalo. And another body on the wing meant less opportunity to try Aaron Gordon on the perimeter, while Tobias Harris also toggled between forward positions. "Unanswered questions creep in daily," says reserve center Kyle O'Quinn. "I think it started to take its toll over 82 games."

Magic coaches considered finding guys more playing time with their D-League affiliate, the Erie BayHawks. Only they'd learned assigning a player from Disney World to Erie, Pennsylvania, read more as a punishment than an opportunity. "It's kind of like when you have kids and you give one candy, or if you give some more than the other, there was almost a little bit of that," says a Magic assistant coach.

The fact Harris faced a potentially lucrative contract extension that summer further muddied the waters. Orlando was headed back to the lottery, but Harris would be due for a payday without having ever been part of a winning season. "When everybody thinks it's their year to bust out and be this person, it takes away. It's like rats trying to climb up a ladder," Channing Frye says. "They're all fighting each other instead of just taking turns going up there."

Victor Oladipo sought the counsel of Dwyane Wade, having shared a college coach in Tom Crean, pondering what the superstar learned about blending different personalities during Miami's four-year title window. The Magic needed any advice they could find. A 110–103 loss at San Antonio on February 4 capped a 10-game drought that sank Orlando to 15–37 on the year. "I just felt like the team wasn't listening anymore," Channing Frye says. "When you've lost trust for a coach as a team, it puts a coach at a disadvantage."

Yet despite another defeat that night against the Spurs, assistants found Vaughn relaxed in their postgame dressing room. "Jacque was in a different mood," one coach recalls. "He seemed looser, almost, like, relieved." The group laughed more than they'd had throughout the entire miserable stretch. Besides, only a few games remained before the refreshing All-Star break.

Then, back in Orlando, somewhere amid the Magic players' warmups at practice the following afternoon, assistant coach Wes Unseld Jr. closed his office door, carrying out a full bag, tucking several other belongings within his grasp. Assistant Brett Gunning and scouting video guru Zach Guthrie also stepped across the court with their personal items. "The day was starting, and they were leaving," one Magic staffer says. The trio were unusual casualties to Rob Hennigan firing Jacque Vaughn that morning, February 5.

"When you're young, you think the coach you have and the team you're on, it's going to be that way forever," Kyle O'Quinn says. "And then when the news came it was kind of like, 'Why? What did he do? We love him!' My mom, she was like, 'What happened!?'"

Frye translated the situation to his naive teammates—and apparently their parents as well. "There was so much indecision of who was the man and what direction we were going into, everybody kind of was just like, 'You know what? Alright, enough of this.' It's sad," he says. "I think [Vaughn] can coach. I just think, in my honest opinion, we needed to choose who was the big dog and that's the person we were gonna ride with." Midway through his third season, Vaughn simply hadn't yet developed a Kevin Durant or Russell Westbrook for Hennigan's rebuild.

Frye phoned interim head coach James Borrego that evening. With just 30 games left, he understood the 37-year-old coach would benefit from finding so-far-untapped success with Orlando's young core. He wouldn't complain if Borrego needed to send him to the bench. "Do I want to play? Of course. But don't play me because you feel like you have to. Play me because I'm the right fit," Frye advised.

Despite Vaughn's ouster, perhaps Borrego, another Spurs disciple, could keep that branch of Gregg Popovich's coaching tree alive.

Another former San Antonio assistant, Mike Budenholzer, coached the All-Star Game on February 15 having led Atlanta to the East's best record at the season's midway point. Brett Brown, meanwhile, fought admirably to keep Philadelphia's sinking ship afloat.

Joel Embiid had begun traveling with the Sixers. Brown hoped it would help the rehabbing rookie feel connected to the team, and his charisma might prove infectious within the rest of Philly's roster. His appetite also became something of lore. And by January, rumor suggested Embiid ballooned close to 300 pounds. Unable to play, his work ethic stalled like rush hour traffic. Philadelphia personnel contemplated different methods to teach Embiid accountability. "He had to do certain things, pass tests," says Michael Carter Williams.

Sixers medical staffers routinely logged the giant's weight. Supposed to join Philly on their road trips just like everyone else, Embiid suddenly felt he'd become a training room sideshow. He erupted at strength coach Jesse Wright one session. "JoJo was kind of to the point of saying, 'Fuck it, I'm not doing it,'" says Vance Walberg. His outburst prompted Brown to send Embiid back to Philadelphia.

Jason Richardson watched Embiid berate Wright while riding a nearby stationary bike. Richardson felt Embiid, like Noel before him, had blown off too many conditioning drills while the veteran was giving everything he could to work back and play. Richardson would ride the bike for hours each day to regain strength in the knee that cost his entire previous season. "You gotta stick with it. I know it's tough, I know it seems like you're not getting ready for anything, but you gotta continue at this," Richardson advised Embiid. Once the rookie cooled off, Embiid accepted Richardson's advice and acknowledged his shortcomings. "And he got better at doing stuff, started taking it a little more seriously." Richardson says. "He wanted to play. That was the whole thing. He didn't want to sit out that whole year."

On the court, Brett Brown's defense had actually emerged as a bona fide force. The Sixers won more games in January (six) than the previous two months combined. Philadelphia's five-man unit of Michael Carter-Williams, K.J. McDaniels, Robert Covington, Luc Mbah a Moute, and Nerlens Noel entered the All-Star break first in the entire NBA in defensive efficiency. They allowed just 86 points per 100 possessions, a mark that far bested Golden State's league-best 97.3 team rating. By the break, Philadelphia ranked 12th in overall team defensive efficiency. Even better, Brown's crew was eighth in defense since January 1.

Brown had removed Henry Sims from the starting lineup in favor of a smaller combination where Mbah a Moute and Covington battled opposing forwards. Each member of Brown's new group could seamlessly switch assignments while defending screens, quick enough and long enough to guard each rival player, no matter their position. The Warriors, under new head coach Steve Kerr, popularized the technique while storming to the top of the West. And switching allowed Noel to fully flex his athleticism and instincts, gobbling 1.6 steals and 2.4 blocks per contest throughout January and February. "I was able to play 25-30 minutes a game and we were a top defensive team. I always knew that to be the case," Noel says. "If I'm out there, I'm gonna change the game any way possible. I'm gonna stuff the stat sheet and change the game."

K.J. McDaniels' success not only benefited the defense but also, perhaps, showcased the rookie to front offices around the league. Sam Hinkie's No. 32 pick in 2014, McDaniels felt he should have been a first-round selection. When his original agent was unsuccessful negotiating a contract greater than Hinkie's typical four-year, non-guaranteed special, McDaniels hired the noted Mark Bartelstein instead. "Sam had a philosophy of how he wanted those contracts to be signed and what he wanted to get out of them," Bartelstein says. Hinkie earnestly planned to reward those players once they'd completed that first deal, unlike how Houston let Chandler Parsons walk in free agency. But this way he could keep banking those prospects for the long term at little risk to Philadelphia, while still handing 20-year-olds significant paydays by laymen's standards.

Hinkie was indeed successful in signing Jerami Grant, drafted at No. 39, to a four-year agreement that guaranteed just over $1 million, but nothing past Grant's first two seasons. And Grant would eventually fire his agent as well when he learned how the contract's length had no advantages for players. "At all," Grant says. "Once you sign it, at that point you're stuck in that."

Mark Bartelstein thus pitched his new client on a different option. McDaniels ultimately accepted Philadelphia's qualifying offer, the standing, one-year deal any team can extend to a player on their books. That qualifying offer would only net McDaniels' minimum salary, but he'd quickly reach restricted free agency in July, where any front office could throw millions of guaranteed dollars at him—three years before Grant would even reach the open market. "I had big confidence in myself," McDaniels says.

His athleticism did pop in the pros just like it had at Clemson. And as McDaniels shot over 35 percent from deep to begin the season, Hinkie began gauging his value on the trade market. Perhaps a rival would want to incorporate McDaniels before he became a free agent, similar to how Dallas jumped early to add Rajon Rondo.

Injuries, though, soon crept up on Philadelphia just like they had in Los Angeles, and the Sixers' defense lost its pair of rangy point guards. A nagging toe injury sidelined Carter-Williams for their last three games before the All-Star break. Even worse, Tony Wroten tore his right ACL in mid-January, curtailing a season of growth. Coaches had seen him, too, make strides as a disciplined defender. And without Wroten, Philadelphia suddenly had no traditional option to handle the already-subpar offense.

By the Sixers' February 6 contest in Boston, Brett Brown planned to start the undrafted forward JaKarr Sampson at point guard. Desperate for another ball handler, Philadelphia also reached out to Tim Frazier, the Penn State product who bested Dante Exum pre-draft. Frazier had been starring for the nearby Maine Red Claws, Boston's affiliate club. He'd been named a D-League All-Star and shown enough for Hinkie to extend a 10-day contract before that Celtics game. Boston had cut Frazier from their training camp back in October. Now Philadelphia summoned a luxury sedan to chauffeur him from Maine to Massachusetts that morning to make his NBA debut. "It really just was a dream setting falling in place," Frazier says.

Frazier raced over to the Red Claws' quarters at the Portland Exposition Building, only to find the facility's locked doors wouldn't budge. Frazier's sneaker collection remained inside, and every Red Claws employee with key access had already migrated south to attend his NBA debut. Frazier soon remembered Celtics guard Avery Bradley wore the same size shoe. So when

Frazier entered midway through the first quarter for Philadelphia, he wore black-and-red Adidas The KOBEs from Bradley's collection.

Originally released in 2000, back when Frazier was in middle school, Bryant's old signature shoe was designed to look like the Audi TT Roadster. They're clunky, the antithesis of Flywire, lightweight technology that had swept basketball's sneaker industry. "But they were Kobes, so it's all good," Frazier says. Heavy sneakers be damned, Frazier scurried around the TD Garden parquet, dishing 11 assists to just two turnovers in 35 minutes off the bench.

Yet sure enough, at the end of Frazier's second 10-day, Sam Hinkie once again offered a four-year, non-guaranteed minimum deal. Frazier declined. As much as the executive remained firm in his negotiations, so too did Frazier's agent, Andre Buck. While Portland would ultimately sign Frazier to a multi-year contract, solidifying his NBA career, the Sixers' front office upheld there would be countless other Tim Fraziers for Philadelphia to gamble on.

Instead, Hinkie zeroed in on the rapidly approaching trade deadline.

His front office lieutenants frequently asked coaches for feedback on players, asking to project their development and on what timeline. All of Brown's staff liked Carter-Williams personally, but when Sixers executives kept quizzing assistants on the long-term trajectory of his shooting, Philly's assistants didn't hold back. "The coaches realized the limitations of his game," says one staffer.

Carter-Williams presented the most difficult Sixers player to rebound for after practice. If Wroten missed short, for example, his next miss would likely be long. Carter-Williams' wonky mechanics rendered far more inconsistent, unpredictable results. "You had no idea in the world where that ball was gonna miss at," a Sixers coach says. They weren't bullish on K.J. McDaniels' jumper either. Coaches valued his athleticism and defensive effort but saw him as more of a rotation player than a future starter.

As always, Brown's staff prepared for any possibility. Both Carter-Williams and McDaniels could net something of value on the trade market. For all franchises, especially those actively rebuilding, players can be moved at any moment.

Rumors naturally continued to swirl. And as the 3:00 PM deadline on February 19 inched closer, one NBA mainstay surprisingly appeared destined for a new home: Phoenix Suns star Goran Dragić.

SEVENTEEN

Mere 48 hours before the 2015 NBA trade deadline, just like Kevin Love's representatives had in Minnesota, Goran Dragić's camp abruptly informed Phoenix officials he planned to walk in July's free agency if the Suns didn't move him sooner.

General manager Ryan McDonough left the meeting with a list of Dragić's seven preferred trade destinations, leading with New York, Miami, and the Lakers. Word predictably spread across the NBA like wildfire. Another All-Star-caliber player was now available on the open market. Which team's stockpile of young players and future draft capital would reel in this big fish?

Reporters engulfed Phoenix's point guard after practice that Wednesday afternoon, wondering what straw finally broke The Dragon's back. "I don't trust them anymore," Dragić said, alluding to McDonough's front office. "It happens too many times, two or three times, they give promises they don't keep."

Dragić had only returned to Phoenix in 2012 as team owner Robert Sarver's heir apparent to Steve Nash. Then just a year later, Sarver hired McDonough, and even though the executive promised Dragić would remain the Suns' centerpiece, Phoenix soon acquired Eric Bledsoe. The pair, of course, shared obvious success in their first year together, nearly reaching the postseason, but while Dragić was named Third Team All-NBA after his brilliant 2013–14, he ultimately felt he'd been snubbed from the All-Star

Game because he shared his backcourt with Bledsoe, rather than running the show solo like, say, Damian Lillard in Portland. Then McDonough spent Phoenix's 2014 off-season adding yet another point guard in Isaiah Thomas and caved during extension talks with Bledsoe. Re-upping Bledsoe on a five-year, $70 million deal in September helped assure Phoenix's future, but also significantly limited flexibility for Dragić's next contract.

The Suns did sign Dragić's brother, Zoran. Handing the younger Dragić a two-year deal worth more than $4 million would hopefully help sway their All-NBA guard to re-sign in Phoenix. "[Goran] was Sarver's guy," says center Miles Plumlee. "If there was a No. 1 guy on the team, it was him. Like, 'Oh, I can get my brother to come play here.' And then he always showed up. He was competitive as hell, worked his ass off."

But Jeff Hornacek's 2014–15 three-guard lineup fell far short of what the coach had pitched back during Thomas' free agent visit. Bledsoe, Dragić, and Thomas appeared in 187 minutes over 37 games together, whirring seven sequences per 100 possessions faster than the Warriors' league-best pace and netting a 112.1 offensive rating, which would have tied Golden State for second in the league. Yet the Suns' trio allowed 110 points per 100 possessions on the opposite end, extrapolating as the 27th-worst defensive mark in the NBA. "And I think he saw the writing on the wall," Plumlee says of Dragić. "It wasn't going to be the place that he could see himself winning a lot going forward."

Dragić also wanted to star like Stephen Curry at the epicenter of the Warriors' attack, an All-Star in his own right, now drawing comparisons to Nash himself as Curry emerged as the league's leading MVP candidate. "It was just too many guys at that one position," Dragić recalls. "It was just an awkward feeling, all three at the same time, and there was only one ball."

Late-game substitutions presented an especially thorny challenge for Hornacek. The previous winter, Dragić and Bledsoe took turns until the veteran typically handled crunch time possessions. But when Isaiah Thomas went on a run leading Phoenix's second unit to open fourth quarters, Hornacek would leave Thomas on the ball, just like Mike Malone had done in Sacramento, bringing Dragić and Bledsoe back in to flank him. "There were times where [Thomas] was rolling with us and we just let him go ahead and do it," Hornacek says.

Most floor generals command the court with a strong personality. It's unsurprising those types of temperaments can struggle to coexist in any workspace, let alone under the NBA microscope, with increased pressure to make the postseason. Phoenix did reach the All-Star break at 29–25, but the Suns had dropped five of their last six games before the midseason pause. Bledsoe found Plumlee following one late-game blunder.

"I'm pretty fucking frustrated," Bledsoe vented.

"I get it," Plumlee said. "We had the perfect amount of a good thing last year, and now we have too much of a good thing this year."

No point guard particularly enjoyed watching another isolate with Phoenix's fate on the line. "Somebody had to take a backseat every game," forward P.J. Tucker says. "If Isaiah got it going, Bled had to sit back. If Bled got it going, maybe Goran had to sit back."

Dragić's agents finally played their hand just before Thursday's February 19 deadline, although the public nature of his request prickled Phoenix management. Hornacek and Sarver had visited Dragić's family in the hospital when his son was born. Suns officials felt it was out of Dragić's character, and his agents were the ones greasing the wheels by gossiping to the media.

Their ploy worked nonetheless. McDonough's phone line buzzed with a flurry of calls. No news had come by the time Suns players filed onto the team bus inside Phoenix's arena that Thursday afternoon, due for the airport ahead of Friday night's contest at Minnesota. But after some haggling, Miami ultimately surrendered its 2017 and 2021 first-round picks to Phoenix in a three-team, seven-player swap that landed Dragić in South Beach, along with Zoran, primed to re-sign the point guard for nearly $100 million. The brothers shuffled off Phoenix's bus soon after the trade broke. Only 15 minutes remained before the 3:00 PM deadline.

Ryan McDonough's front office then dialed Milwaukee. Dragić's demand had forced Suns brass to ponder his replacement for Hornacek's frenetic system, and Brandon Knight quickly emerged as Phoenix's top target. Knight garnered All-Star consideration of his own that February, averaging 17.8 points, 4.3 rebounds, and 5.4 assists for a playoff contender.

He also wasn't a pure point guard, which would theoretically blend far better alongside Bledsoe. While Knight was finishing Bucks practice at the Al McGuire Center, general manager John Hammond neared an agreement with Phoenix, setting his sights on another point guard to include in the evolving trade as well.

A month before the deadline, Hammond and Sam Hinkie went through both of their teams' rosters over the phone. When Hammond revealed his interest in Michael Carter-Williams, Hinkie began preparing for a later negotiation, readying to land his largest haul possible. "We had this vision of this big, long team and liked Michael's length," Hammond says. "You knew there was that upside with him also. You value a player, you acquire him."

Hinkie, however, didn't value any of the players Hammond had made available. All of Giannis Antetokounmpo, Jabari Parker, and Khris Middleton were deemed untouchable. Only when Phoenix expressed interest in Brandon Knight did the Suns add the necessary juice to make Carter-Williams a Buck. "Sam was the one that basically spearheaded that," Hammond says.

Hinkie valued the Lakers' 2015 first-rounder Phoenix owned from the Steve Nash trade far more than most players on the Suns or Bucks. Top-five-protected for that May's lottery, the pick would become just top-three-protected in 2016 and 2017 and eventually unprotected in 2018.

With the Lakers set to miss the playoffs for a second straight season, Los Angeles seemed likely to keep its 2015 pick with a fortunate bounce of ping-pong balls. But what if the Lakers failed once again to sign a marquee free agent in July? Kobe Bryant would be entering his final year after rehabbing a third straight season-ending injury. Perhaps Los Angeles' 2016 pick would convey to Philadelphia somewhere outside of the top three but still in the lottery, just like how New Orleans had handed the Sixers No. 10 in 2014's draft. These were the elusive assets at the forefront of teams' chase to acquire future draft ammo. "I was pretty surprised that Philly was able to get that pick from Phoenix," Celtics assistant general manager Mike Zarren recalls.

Little time remained before the buzzer when all three of Philadelphia, Phoenix, and Milwaukee quietly came to agreement. "It was truly a last-minute deal," says Dave Babcock, the Bucks' vice president of player personnel.

Yet on the surface, Thursday's deadline came and went without any noise of their transaction. The official trade call still waited in queue on the league office's phones. And so Suns players rallied on Phoenix's bus, unknowingly assuming this would be their core unit to refocus for a playoff push. "This is the group we're gonna have," Isaiah Thomas said. "Let's finish this year off strong."

Then Miles Plumlee's phone rang. The center, along with point guard Tyler Ennis, were actually headed to Milwaukee in part of the three-teamer with Philadelphia, and they needed to deboard Phoenix's ride.

A few minutes later, a news alert pinged another players' cell. "IT!" he shouted. "You just got traded!"

Thomas cackled. "No, I didn't!" With Dragić already bound for South Beach, Thomas was under the impression he and Bledsoe were going to thrive like Phoenix's duo a year prior.

Markieff Morris rushed to log on to Twitter and confirm the scuttle. Only when a phone was handed to Thomas did he realize this was no fib. The Celtics indeed swept in before the deadline to acquire Thomas, mostly in exchange for the 2016 first-round pick Boston had landed from Cleveland that off-season during the Cavs' efforts to clear space to re-sign LeBron James.

"I was like, 'What the fuck?'" Markieff Morris says. In less than 20 minutes, five Phoenix players were rapidly sent elsewhere. A Suns staffer soon waded to the back of the bus and asked Thomas to follow. He dapped teammates good-bye before being led directly to a sitdown with the Suns' front office.

Boston, remember, had tried to sign Thomas in free agency before Phoenix ultimately offered more money. Danny Ainge then phoned Ryan McDonough in December after a six-game stretch dropped Phoenix to 12–14 on the season. By that time, whispers of the Suns' backcourt drama had reached rival front offices. "There was already discontent," Celtics exec

Mike Zarren says. And even though McDonough rebuffed Boston's initial attempts, the Celtics kept calling nonetheless.

Ainge rang again roughly 90 minutes before the deadline. "Ryan had made us believe there wasn't a trade to be had," Zarren recalls. Ainge even buzzed Brad Stevens, notifying his head coach, "It doesn't look like we're gonna do anything."

Only in Phoenix, Suns officials began worrying that incorporating Knight might still spark animosity amongst he, Bledsoe, and Thomas, especially being that Hornacek still planned to bring Thomas off the bench. So McDonough dialed Ainge back. "Alright, fine," he relented. "Let's do something."

Ainge reached back out to Stevens while Zarren ironed out the particulars. Thomas was headed to Boston in another three-team trade, which would leave the Celtics with just nine available players the next evening for their game in Sacramento.

Stevens' plans for his meeting with the Celtics' active players, due to begin in a few minutes, were now completely obsolete. "We were looking at our roster for that night," Stevens says. What on earth would his rotation look like?

He began the meeting, diagramming plans that tweaked their scheme for the second half of the season without yet acknowledging Thomas would be brought into the fold. "My mind's spinning," Stevens recalls. Boston's players nodded in agreement until center Tyler Zeller, perched in the back, blurted out, "Is Marcus Thornton here?"

The scoring guard poked his head up. "Yeah. What's up?" Thornton asked.

"You just got traded, bro," Zeller announced.

Thornton promptly exited the room to phone his agent. A few beats later, he broke the Thomas trade news to Boston's roster. Thornton was in fact headed to Phoenix in the deal.

Thomas was already en route to the Celtics' Waltham headquarters to undergo his physical. After one last meeting with Suns officials, he scooped a few sneakers from Phoenix's locker room and his fiancée dropped him at the airport. Later that evening, Stevens first connected with Thomas over

FaceTime to break down Boston's playbook, replete with accompanying video.

Amid Danny Ainge's flurry of trades, the second-year coach always placed a premium on his player relationships. "One thing Brad said was, 'I never want these guys to leave not knowing they were cared about as people,'" says Celtics assistant Ron Nored. It was hard in certain situations, like when Jeff Green was traded to Memphis minutes before a game tipped.

Michael Carter-Williams, meanwhile, was driving with several friends after the deadline had passed when his agent called to disrupt their ride. "It was definitely shocking," Carter-Williams says. "I was disappointed." He had lost track of the times Sam Hinkie said he was part of Philadelphia's foundation. Carter-Williams' Rookie of the Year campaign had seemed to validate he was the first building block of a one-day Sixers dynasty.

"We thought he was pretty much going to be the face of the organization," says Philadelphia forward JaKarr Sampson. Now he was flying first thing the next morning to Milwaukee.

"You have to pick up and go," Carter-Williams says.

The point guard wasn't the only player to suggest Hinkie reneged his assurances on the trade market that season. When Philadelphia acquired Andrei Kirilenko back on December 10 from Brooklyn, Nets officials finalized the deal expecting the veteran would quickly leave the Sixers to join a contender, just as Danny Granger had done the year before. "I thought [Hinkie] was gonna trade for [Kirilenko] and cut him and then he could go sign," Nets general manager Billy King says.

But once Hinkie told Brett Brown of Philadelphia's new acquisition, as the Sixers continued sputtering, the coach gleefully accepted the idea of adding a defensive stalwart like Kirilenko into his development program. Luc Mbah a Moute had already been an enormous presence. Philadelphia staffers soon began talking of Kirilenko's imminent arrival. And so Hinkie called Kirilenko's agent hoping the veteran would report to Philadelphia. "He said that Brett wanted Andrei there," recalls Marc Fleisher, Kirilenko's representative.

Fleisher never collaborated with Hinkie during his Houston tenure, and fellow agents had warned Fleisher about the Sixers executive's unique dealings. "I was reading stories left and right about him being not the most trustworthy of guys in the world," Fleisher says. Other international players—like fellow Russian Alexey Shved, traded by Hinkie in December—advised Kirilenko to seek a buyout instead of playing within Philly's rebuild. "They were just all about losing and it would have been frustrating," Fleisher says.

The agent also gave Hinkie legitimate reason for his client not to join the Sixers. Kirilenko's wife, Masha, had struggled throughout the winter with a difficult pregnancy. Her doctors prescribed bed rest until the child was born. Now 33, Kirilenko was only open to uprooting his family from Brooklyn, which would require finding new medical support, if it meant joining a championship contender. He wouldn't go through that trouble for the bottoming Sixers. "We told them if they waited until after she gave birth in February, we would at least talk at that point," Fleisher says.

The agent believed Hinkie was blaming Brown's interest in Kirilenko while he also hoped to showcase the swingman and move him again before the February 19 deadline. "He was just kind of one of those guys that grated on you," Fleisher says of Hinkie. "He was the kind of guy that thought he was smarter than everyone else and he acted like it. Maybe he is."

Agents across the league added this Kirilenko discrepancy to a running list of grievances against Hinkie. "You want them to be able to trust what your intentions are," says Billy King, the Nets' general manager. "That was a concern from some."

Philadelphia nonetheless maintained its position that Kirilenko wasn't reporting. "They started fining him something crazy, like $25,000 a day," Fleisher says. "It kept getting bigger and bigger." On January 9, Brett Brown confirmed the Sixers suspended Kirilenko without pay. "I said, 'If you don't believe me [about Masha's condition], here's the doctor. Call him,'" Fleisher recalls. "The Nets knew all about her medical situation."

As January stretched into February, the Sixers continued withholding each of Kirilenko's checks without much further explanation. "It was impossible to get Sam on the phone," Fleisher says. "And every time you would talk to him it was a different story." The agent eventually lobbied for assistance from the union. And once the player's association and league office ultimately settled matters privately, Hinkie mercifully waived Kirilenko on February 21.

Hinkie next released JaVale McGee on March 1. In addition to having already moved Carter-Williams, the Sixers acquired McGee from Denver before the deadline in exchange for a top-18-protected 2015 first-round pick, originally belonging to Oklahoma City. Hinkie also landed another 2015 second-rounder from Houston as Philadelphia sent K.J. McDaniels and his ensuing restricted free agency to the Rockets. "Philly, you knew, if you put in a second-round pick, Sam would take it," says Billy King.

"They were the team that you could call when you needed to move money," adds Nets assistant GM Bobby Marks.

With each transaction, Brett Brown's roster thinned even more. Hinkie recouped draft asset after draft asset, but then waived the player whose salary he'd inherited to receive that pick. And even though the coaches agreed Carter-Williams wasn't a true foundational piece, he was their lead ball handler. Now Brown could only hand the keys of his offense to 23-year-old Isaiah Canaan, a sophomore second-round pick out of Murray State who arrived in the McDaniels trade with the Rockets. "We were maybe on our 12th point guard at that point?" says Sixers assistant Lloyd Pierce.

Shockingly moving Carter-Williams also infuriated Philadelphia's business operations. Two days before the deadline, while Goran Dragić's agents met with Phoenix officials, the Sixers unveiled a new marketing slogan, "This Starts Now," teasing new uniforms that summer and featuring Nerlens Noel, Joel Embiid, and Carter-Williams as key aspects of the Sixers' blueprint for a championship. With all three healthy, Philadelphia's sales team could finally smell a playoff push. But now with Carter-Williams headed to Milwaukee, CEO Scott O'Neil fumed, embarrassed by Hinkie's trade upending the team's marketing strategy. "We knew that he raised a large stink about it," Sixers analytics staffer Lance Pearson says of O'Neil. "That's his purview. That's what he should be concerned about. But that should be the last thing on Sam's mind."

Philadelphia lost a valued assistant as well. In a rare occurrence, Vance Walberg left Brown's staff midseason to join Sacramento, and that franchise's new soon-to-be play caller.

The Kings ended all speculation by officially hiring George Karl that February to close Tyrone Corbin's stint as interim head coach. Karl, after all, boasted plenty of experience turning lottery losers into postseason participants. "I thought that with a little tinkering and hopefully a little magic along the way, you could turn it into a playoff team," Karl says.

The 63-year-old coach paid no mind to the musical chairs at the end of Sacramento's bench. A man who identifies first and foremost as a basketball mind, Karl was unsure when his next head coaching opportunity would come, if ever again. "I think it's a gift to be offered a job in the NBA," Karl says.

Another new voice doesn't always benefit a roster, however. Karl did mark the Kings' third head coach of the season, and fifth in three years. "As a young player, it's tough," Ben McLemore says. "That experience was pretty wild."

With Karl signing a four-year, $15 million contract, he garnered enough power within Vivek Ranadivé's ever-shaky franchise to nudge Tyrone Corbin off his staff and into a front office advisory role. Vance Walberg, having previously assisted Karl in Denver, then arrived in Sacramento shortly after the trade deadline. But it takes organizational stability to foster the necessary trust and communication to compete for the playoffs, let alone a title. Those two loose threads obviously dangled from Sacramento's cultural fabric.

"Every time we had a [coaching] change, the rotations changed, the sets we were running changed, the culture changed. It was a lot to deal with," Nik Stauskas says. "There was no point of the season where I could feel myself getting into a solid rhythm."

Karl felt the remnants from DeMarcus Cousins repeatedly upstaging Corbin's authority. "Is there a coach he has treated with respect?" Karl says now.

Vance Walberg saw similarities to how Brett Brown oversaw Nerlens Noel's turbulent rookie campaign. "DeMarcus ran that whole situation there," Walberg says. "Whatever he said would go. They kowtow to him and he was in control." Karl and Walberg also appreciated Cousins' community involvement and charisma when meeting with the Kings' business operations, but found no excuse for his on-court disruption. It floored Walberg that management had never fined the moody center. "DeMarcus did what DeMarcus wanted," Walberg says.

After general manager Pete D'Alessandro told Cousins it was Ranadivé who pushed for hiring Karl, it further watered Cousins' growing suspicion of Sacramento's owner, dating back to Mike Malone's ouster in December. "He would just react back," guard Ben McLemore says. Cousins didn't respond to Karl's new vision, especially when the old-school play caller hounded him in practice. While Malone's barbs were presented practically, Kings players viewed Karl's approach as more of an attack. "He knew what kind of buttons to push with DeMarcus," McLemore says.

By March, in another curious maneuver by Ranadivé, Sacramento hired former Kings All-Star center Vlade Divac as vice president of basketball and franchise operations. Ranadivé hoped the big man, who'd helped power Sacramento's golden era of the early 2000s, could infuse stability within his rocky organization.

Divac's early directive was clear: cultivate a partnership with Sacramento's current All-Star giant. And so Divac joined the Kings' four-game road trip to close the month. Only he slumped down next to Walberg at one point into their week-long junket. "Fuck, I'm trying to work with Cousins," Divac sighed. "You know what he said? 'What the fuck are you going to do to help me?'"

Divac had served as president of the Serbian Olympic Committee, yet despite no NBA personnel experience, the Kings announced he would both advise the front office and coaching staff while helping "facilitate talent evaluation."

"They wanted to make a change," Walberg translates. "They wanted Vlade to take over Pete's job."

Kings officials began gossiping about D'Alesandro's job security, just like they'd once done about Malone. Sacramento personnel were already contemplating Chris Mullin's infrequent appearances around the facility, like television viewers wondering why a character had been killed off their favorite show. Room only exists for so many at the top of a power struggle. "There were probably too many opinions being heard from Vlade, to Vivek, to Peter, to me," George Karl recalls. "Everybody had a microphone."

Most staffers recognized the Kings' tectonic plates shifting. Divac seemed to gain more influence each day. In two years of ownership, Ranadivé delegated power whenever and in any direction he saw fit. "I personally felt there were so many mistakes made," says Walberg.

The Kings would soon regret one of those blunders. Their former point guard, Isaiah Thomas, caught a wave of stardom in his new home in Boston.

He missed the shorthanded Celtics' loss in Sacramento during that first game following the trade deadline, but their next outing, in Los Angeles, Thomas torched the depleted Lakers for 21 points in 25 minutes.

One night later, Boston arrived at the US Airways Center to face Phoenix. "It was kind of a crazy whirlwind there," Brad Stevens says. In the second quarter, Brandon Knight fouled Thomas on a nifty layup for an impressive and-one. Thomas then crossed Eric Bledsoe a few plays later, burying a triple in his grill. He notched eight of his 21 points in the final 1:37, beginning with a four-point play thanks to Knight bodying Thomas once again. The vengeful guard stared at Phoenix's bench with each late bucket, smirking like the Grinch.

"He didn't know too many plays and we still killing 'em," says Boston wing Jae Crowder.

Back at home, the Celtics obliterated New York by 21 and then took one from Charlotte. "We all trusted one another, we knew exactly what everybody liked and…bam," says Marcus Smart. "The rest is history for us." They nearly defeated Golden State but squandered a 26-point lead over the juggernaut Warriors.

LeBron James, Kyrie Irving, Kevin Love, and the Cavs then served a slice of humble pie with a 110–79 rout in Cleveland on March 3. Jae Crowder worried once again of Boston's alleged tanking.

"That's when I pulled Brad to the side and was like, 'We have some guys who really just want to play, want to win, and want to prove themselves,'" Crowder says. "And Brad was like, 'I'm all in as well.'"

The Celtics won seven of their next eight, beginning with a theatrical win against Utah on March 4. Stevens called timeout trailing the Jazz 84–83 with just two seconds left. The Celtics all braced for a dash of Stevens' play calling wizardry. "He'll draw something up in the moment, he'll send the guys out there, and before the ball's handed to the player from the official, he'll say, 'We got 'em,'" says Celtics assistant Walter McCarty. "He just knew it from the way the other team lined up."

Kelly Olynyk recalls one huddle: "He was like, 'You go here, you go here, you go here, here, here, come off this screen, and I want you to throw it now. And then when this guy comes off, he'll be wide open. But throw it early.'" Someone asked what the second option would be if the pass wasn't available. Stevens simply dropped the clipboard. "It will be open," he deadpanned.

"And of course," says Olynyk, "it works."

Stevens knew Utah, on this occasion, would switch any screen while fronting his players toward the weak side, hoping to force a treacherous pass over 7-foot-1 center Rudy Gobert, guarding Boston's inbounder. Thomas darted toward the left corner. Avery Bradley and Tyler Zeller shifted to double-screen for Crowder at the foul line. And for a split second, the Jazz jumped at Crowder's burst up to the three-point line, allowing Zeller to seal inside position on the smaller Rodney Hood while his man, forward Derrick Favors, chased Crowder instead. "That was one of the best ATOs I've ever seen in my life," Crowder says.

Marcus Smart lobbed Zeller a softball at the rim, and he banked in the game-winner before the buzzer. "Brad can just think outside the box in a limited amount of time," Smart says. "Not a lot of people can do that."

Stevens encouraged all players to utilize their strengths. Everyone was free to shoot threes if they had room to launch. Stevens gave Thomas carte blanche to batter his way to the rim. Boston faithful quickly fell in love with their new point guard. "His type of energy had the city on fire," says Evan Turner.

The coach's insatiable appetite for film study gave way to Boston's fluid offense. "He's studied his roster to a T," Crowder says. With Danny Ainge gathering a trove of malleable wings, Stevens designed schemes where each player could slide into every spot.

"We were a machine," Avery Bradley says. "I could do one-through-five. I knew every set. Every guy was interchangeable."

Unlike rivals' typical shooting-heavy sessions, Boston would run sets for 45 minutes straight in practice. "We knew the wrinkles of it," Turner says. "We squeezed everything out that Sam's Club tomato ketchup."

Their April 1 victory over Indiana suddenly brought the Celtics within a half game of the East's final playoff spot. Few had expected this Boston unit to compete to such a degree. Isaiah Thomas, Jae Crowder, and Evan Turner had all been discarded by the teams that drafted them. Jared Sullinger tumbled on draft night back in 2012. Some scouts deemed Kelly Olynyk too slow. Even Stevens, so many doubting his transition from college, operated with an underdog mentality. "I feel like we were forgottens in a sense," Turner says. "Nobody expected much from us and we kind of banded together."

After one dreadful first-half shooting effort, Stevens stormed into Boston's locker room. He handed each player and staffer a crisp, freshly printed stat sheet. "Everybody, crumple it up," Stevens ordered. The coach then dragged a garbage can into the center and tossed his paper ball into the bin. Some Celtics laughed at the demonstration. "We're going to make shots this half. Last half is over," Stevens said.

"He was hype!" Bradley recalls. His assistants began shooting their sheets into the trash. Those laughing players soon joined in. "It was a small thing, but it gave us that confidence," Bradley says. Boston indeed claimed victory in the second half.

The Celtics' playoff push arrived in Toronto on April 4. After a seesaw battle that required overtime, Lou Williams canned a triple with five seconds left in the extra period, swiping his Raptors a 116–115 edge.

Boston surrounded Stevens once more with a win on the line. The Celtics still had one timeout to use as Stevens scribbled his play. When Boston took the court, the coach surveyed Toronto's defense and Stevens called for a second huddle.

"Yup!" Lou Williams crowed, walking back to the Raptors' bench. "We lost."

Celtics players hustled back to their sideline. "Alright, this is the real play," Stevens announced, flipping his clipboard to reveal an entirely different, already-diagrammed set. "I just wanted to see what they were in," he said.

Isaiah Thomas thus rocketed full speed off a Kelly Olynyk screen near half-court. He drew so much attention, it left Marcus Smart wide open to flick a last-second putback for the win.

"Brad's a genius, man," Evan Turner says.

EIGHTEEN

Boston closed the regular season 40–42 to sneak into the playoffs, drawing a date with LeBron James and the revamped Cleveland Cavaliers. "Seventh seed," guard Avery Bradley says, "but we made it."

Less than 24 months removed from trading Kevin Garnett and Paul Pierce, not to mention also sending Rajon Rondo to Dallas back in December, Danny Ainge's Celtics already returned to the postseason, with a motley crew of 25-and-unders, piloted by a brilliant young head coach. Plus the Celtics still owned Brooklyn's 2016 and 2018 unprotected first-round picks—and the right to swap 2017 firsts. All while the Nets' days of reaching the postseason now appeared to be numbered.

Brooklyn had already moved on from Kevin Garnett at the trade deadline. The Nets did sneak into the playoffs one slot behind the Celtics, but Atlanta took care of Brooklyn in six games—sending Paul Pierce into free agency nothing short of dissatisfied with his Nets tenure. If Pierce, now expectedly, walked in July, and Brooklyn slipped even further down the East next season, that 2016 pick owed to Danny Ainge's Celtics could become even more valuable than the Lakers pick Sam Hinkie acquired in return for Michael Carter-Williams.

Boston's own 2015 postseason appearance didn't last longer than Brooklyn's. Cleveland quickly swept the young Celtics even after Kevin Love injured his shoulder early in Game 4, tangling with Kelly Olynyk for a rebound. Love beelined for Cleveland's locker room once he wrangled free of

Olynyk. Many players soon claimed Olynyk tugged Love's arm on purpose. The reputation has, unfairly, followed him around the NBA. "If it was intentional, you would do it in Game 1," Olynyk says. "Why would you fucking do it in Game 4?"

The incident still provided fuel for the Cavs' fire. Late in the second quarter, Boston's former center Kendrick Perkins, now wearing the Cavaliers' navy alternates, leveled Jae Crowder with a powerful screen. Cavs guard J.R. Smith then caught Crowder with an elbow in the third quarter, drawing an ejection. And with the Cavs dealing Brad Stevens' young Celtics their first taste of postseason warfare, LeBron James and Kyrie Irving's brilliance still powered a Loveless Cleveland offense with ease. Facing the same opponent each night posed new challenges for the inexperienced Boston unit. "We learned the margin of error is very short, very small, very limited," says rookie guard Marcus Smart. Especially as James still ruled the East.

Cleveland ultimately rolled through the rest of the conference. But despite James reaching his fifth straight Finals, Golden State proved too much. Losing Irving to injury in Game 1 certainly didn't help James overcome the Warriors' small-ball combination. With a five-man lineup of MVP Steph Curry, Klay Thompson, defensive specialist and Finals MVP Andre Iguodala, swingman Harrison Barnes, and 6-foot-6 swiss army knife Draymond Green, Golden State raced past Cleveland in transition, while Green was still able to protect the rim.

Few days remained where giants routinely posted up. And debate regarding the modern state of big men only continued raging atop the 2015 NBA Draft class.

Traditional thought pointed to Jahlil Okafor as the obvious top prospect that June. A massive 6-foot-10 brute on the block, Okafor led Duke to the national title after a decorated Chicago prep career. Big men with equal strength and skill had carried NBA offenses and organizations for decades. However, the speed of the smaller Warriors forced the Cavaliers to sit their starting center, Timofey Mozgov, for whom general manager David Griffin sent two first-round picks to Denver, and Cleveland still lost the championship.

Modern theory suggested only nimble bigs, like Kentucky's athletic big man Karl-Anthony Towns, could overpower smaller foes like Golden State while matching the Warriors' quick pace on defense.

Scouts across the NBA did reach a near consensus opinion: both Okafor and Towns were still obvious top-three prospects, and perhaps the only viable candidates for the No. 1 pick, which NBA deputy commissioner Mark Tatum revealed during the league's annual draft lottery.

Oklahoma City had landed No. 14 after the Thunder dipped just outside the postseason without Kevin Durant, who underwent foot surgery back in March.

Phoenix then collected the No. 13 pick. Jeff Hornacek's feisty upstart once again fell shy of the playoffs, this time stumbling in 10 of their last 11 games after once standing 38–33. Instead of replacing Goran Dragić, Brandon Knight injured his ankle on March 9, only to play in one of the Suns' final 17 games. After Hornacek's three guards spent all winter yearning for the ball, only Eric Bledsoe remained available to lead the Suns, and he wasn't yet enough to shoulder a franchise into the postseason.

Picks No. 12 and 11 in the draft went to Utah and Indiana, respectively. It would be the Pacers' first lottery selection since nabbing its superstar Paul George 10th back in 2010. The draft order held firm as Mark Tatum continued announcing picks.

Vlade Divac braced himself as the deputy commissioner opened the envelope to declare the sixth pick. If Tatum didn't reveal the Kings' logo, that would mean Sacramento had leapt into the top three.

Divac not only sat as the Kings' dais representative; he now brandished the nominal position of Sacramento's top decision-maker. After weeks of hearsay, Pete D'Alessandro's days as Kings general manager were clearly numbered. Ranadivé kept swapping his basketball operations leaders as frequently as other rebuilding franchises, like the Sixers, auditioned possible players for their future playoff team. In as short a time as Boston tore down and rebuilt a postseason contender, Ranadivé was now on his third head coach and second lead executive.

The jury was still out on Divac's prowess as a front office figure, but he didn't bring any luck to the Kings in the lottery. Mark Tatum indeed revealed Sacramento landed the No. 6 pick.

Lakers executives cheered back in Los Angeles. Philadelphia owned their pick if it landed outside of the top five thanks to that Michael Carter-Williams trade, but now the Lakers, with the fourth-worst record and an 11.9 percent chance at No. 1, were guaranteed a high choice they sorely needed.

As Los Angeles hovered in the standings, floating around that Mendoza Line of No. 5 throughout March and April, staffers constantly calculated the chances of keeping their selection. "Like, 'Where are we now? What's the odds of us keeping this pick?'" says Clay Moser, the Lakers' director of basketball strategy. "And it wasn't from a tanking standpoint, it was more of a planning and organizing standpoint." Lakers officials maintain they never rooted for losses. "We were more concerned with what Philadelphia was up to," Moser says.

Orlando earned pick No. 5, keeping the lottery results as expected thus far. General manager Rob Hennigan hoped the Magic had landed high enough to draft Lithuanian phenom Kristaps Porziņģis. After Orlando failed to convince Porziņģis to remain in the 2013 draft, he'd risen up draft boards since his promising year overseas. Orlando upheld its promise nonetheless: Hennigan wouldn't blink at selecting Porziņģis fifth if he got past the first four.

New York, in dire need of a franchise face, would make that fourth and final choice before Orlando. The recently hired president Phil Jackson now spearheaded the Knicks' decision tree. New York had lured the champion coach to Madison Square Garden in March thanks to a five-year deal worth $12 million annually. The Knicks believed Jackson could reverse their miserable 2014–15 fortune, finishing just 17–65, the second-worst record in the league behind only Minnesota and even one loss more than the tanking Philadelphia 76ers. Not one, but two teams won fewer games than Sam Hinkie's intentionally poor roster.

But as New Yorkers complained across the city, ping-pong balls didn't bounce in Jackson's favor on lottery night. Falling to the fourth pick also meant Jackson's old Lakers actually leapt New York for a top-three choice. ESPN's broadcast of the lottery, true to fashion, cut to commercial, leaving Los Angeles, Philadelphia, and Minnesota with a franchise-altering cliffhanger.

Overjoyed with a top-three pick, a horde of Sixers fans overflowed a Buffalo Wild Wings in Northeast Philly. *ESPN The Magazine* writer Pablo Torre had formally introduced the phrase "Trust the Process" inside his January article featuring Sam Hinkie's polarizing rebuild. "We talk a lot about process, not outcome," Hinkie did say back during his May 2013 introduction. Joel Embiid had tweeted "TRUST THE PROCESS!!!!" back on November 18, 2014. When Spike Eskin and Michael Levin read Tony Wroten say, "They tell us every game, every day, 'Trust the Process.' Just continue to build," within Torre's article, *The Rights to Ricky Sanchez* podcast hosts adapted it as their war cry.

Eskin printed black T-shirts from a local vendor. White ink depicted Hinkie spinning a lottery machine. Hundreds of fans then purchased the design to pick up and wear at the podcast's lottery watch party at that aforementioned Buffalo Wild Wings. They invited Torre to make an appearance, but the journalist needed to film ESPN's *Around the Horn* that afternoon in Manhattan. He asked for a shirt instead, and showcased the original Hinkie apparel on national television. "That was when 'Trust the Process' became a thing," Eskin says.

Eskin arrived at Buffalo Wild Wings hours before the lottery began. Many of *The Ricky* podcast's listeners were already tailgating in the parking lot. Dozens of Sixers fans were turned away after they'd stuffed the establishment to capacity. The bar ran out of clean glasses. A waitress eventually wailed, overwhelmed by the demand from so many customers. They were thirsty for cheap beer and the No. 1 pick.

So, too, was Byron Scott. The Lakers' head coach represented Los Angeles onstage at the lottery. Nerlens Noel, looking dapper in a navy suit, towered over Scott. He already flashed a preview of Philadelphia's new jerseys, stitched inside his jacket lining.

Timberwolves owner Glen Taylor flanked Noel's right. Minnesota, of course, had plunged to the league's worst record after trading Kevin Love to Cleveland. This was why the lottery existed, auctioning the chance for a downtrodden franchise to recoup another superstar atop the draft. With a successful pick and the right roster maneuvers, the Wolves could possibly bounce back into the playoff picture after one poor season, just like Brad Stevens' group in Boston—unlike Hinkie's yearly drought in Philadelphia, many league voices continued clamoring.

Perhaps Lady Luck punished the Sixers at the 2015 lottery in response. Mark Tatum announced Philly would choose third for the second straight draft. The Lakers came up next at No. 2. And as Mark Tatum officially declared Minnesota landed the No. 1 pick, rumor quickly swirled across NBA front offices: having to decide between the draft's two talented towers, Timberwolves president Flip Saunders apparently favored Jahlil Okafor over Karl-Anthony Towns.

Philadelphia officials prayed for that reality. Up and down the front office, Sixers brass fawned over Towns' versatility at his enormous size. No matter the fit with Noel and Joel Embiid, Towns was such an incredible prospect, it was even worth contemplating trying to trade up to No. 1. But if Minnesota selected Okafor, that meant Philly would land either Towns or Ohio State point guard D'Angelo Russell, whoever remained after Los Angeles picked second.

From his first Buckeyes practice, Russell mesmerized Ohio State head coach Thad Matta with his vision and passing. "If you're not ready," Matta told his roster, "you're gonna have a Nike swoosh tattooed on your forehead about 10 times this season." Russell could throw chest passes the full length of the court, on a rope and on the numbers. He dropped 33 points in a preseason scrimmage against West Virginia's relentless press defense. On the bus driving home, Matta turned to his staff. "Fellas, we gotta get another guard," Matta sighed. "That kid's out of here. He's the best guard in the country."

By season's end, Russell projected as a clear top prospect in the 2015 draft. At 6-foot-5, he had great length and shooting touch. Scouts only doubted his foot speed to defend opposing ball handlers. But there were also questions about his maturity.

Minnesota promptly brought Russell in for a workout. "You want to make sure you cover yourself and make a good decision," Wolves executive Rob Babcock says. "In order to do that you need to bring everyone in."

That included Emmanuel Mudiay, widely considered the second-best point guard behind Russell. A 6-foot-3 Congolese phenom, Mudiay joined China's Guangdong Southern Tigers for 2014–15 after playing prep ball in Texas. The Timberwolves couldn't get Kristaps Porziņģis in for a workout, but Babcock had spent five days in Spain scouting his Sevilla club's practices and games.

Besides, Minnesota quickly focused on favoring either Okafor or Towns for its No. 1 pick. Both giants soon flocked north, conducting a workout and having meals with various Wolves executives. "They both were good guys," Babcock says. "Towns' skill level was probably what stood out more than anything. His versatility, his ability to score in different ways, to handle the ball, to shoot the ball. He was very impressive in his workout. Okafor was so much more limited in what he could do." They both met privately with Saunders. Minnesota's president still kept drumming up trade interest for the top choice as well. Perhaps a team like Philly would surrender something valuable to slide up to No. 1.

When a team holds the top pick, rival front offices always call. And with word still suggesting Saunders might take Okafor, the phones kept ringing. The chance at landing Towns was too tantalizing. "Flip's philosophy was he'd say different things to different reporters and keep everyone guessing," Babcock says.

By January, Towns had surpassed Okafor in the eyes of many scouts. John Calipari's Wildcats famously chased an undefeated season, a quest he'd marketed since the summer. Drake, the world's biggest rapper, even joined Kentucky's starting lineup announcement during its Midnight Madness event. Waiting backstage with Kentucky's roster, the visitor seemed anxious. "He was just kind of bouncing around, shaking his hands," says Tod Lanter, the Kentucky walk-on. Drake downplayed his nerves, joking the moment felt like readying to perform a concert. Sure enough, when his first turn came in the team's layup line, Drake took Lanter's pass and completely whiffed his midrange jumper. "The jitters caused an airball," Lanter says.

The Wildcats, though, were as good as advertised, winning 38 straight before falling to Wisconsin in the Final Four. Calipari defined clear roles for each of his phenoms in their successful offense. He parked Towns down low. "I told him, 'If you listen and we go do this together, you'll be the No. 1 pick,'" Calipari says. While NBA scouts valued Towns' perimeter prowess, firing from distance throughout high school, he needed to learn how to score efficiently within a team construct that in turn created for teammates.

"It's tough to catch the ball in the short corner and think, 'Oh, I can go one-on-one against this guy, but Cal's telling me I need to do this and get this switch to happen,'" Lanter says.

Calipari soon watched his offense hum behind Towns. The Wildcats seemingly couldn't lose. "When it was winning time, we brought it together," says Devin Booker, another Kentucky freshman phenom.

Now two weeks before the draft, Calipari was hearing Flip Saunders might pass on Towns?

Kentucky's coach frantically phoned Minnesota's lead executive. "If you're not taking him, trade the pick and you'll get whatever you want," Calipari advised.

"Cal, are you out of your mind?" Saunders replied. Even college basketball's greatest pitchman had fallen for Saunders' charade.

Sure enough, when Adam Silver announced Minnesota's selection to the Barclays Center green room, it was Karl-Anthony Towns who rose and grabbed a Timberwolves cap. "We knew his potential was through the roof," says Andrew Wiggins, the Timberwolves wing and fellow No. 1 pick.

As Towns strolled onto the stage, Bill Duffy readied to finally learn the fate of his newest star client. Seated at Jahlil Okafor's green room table, Duffy turned to find D'Angelo Russell's group. He locked eyes with the point guard's representative, Aaron Mintz of CAA Sports.

The agent business can be cutthroat, replete with backstabbing and shadow dealings. Many representatives, too, have formed competitive friendships with their rivals, sharing in the unique moments their profession brings. And as the clock ticked down on Los Angeles' No. 2 selection, Duffy jutted his palms toward the arena's rafters, shrugging to Mintz he had no clue what the Lakers were about to decide. Mintz shook his head in return, scrunching his shoulders in equal uncertainty.

Mitch Kupchak revealed nothing over the phone. "He'd say, 'We haven't made up our mind. We haven't made up our mind,'" Duffy recalls. "He said that repeatedly."

Few Lakers officials truly knew their general manager's preference until the morning of the draft. "The way Mitch Kupchak ran things, it was very covert," says Clay Moser, the longtime Los Angeles staffer.

"We couldn't figure out what was gonna happen," Jahlil Okafor recalls. "I didn't know. I was super nervous." The Duke center visited Los Angeles twice pre-draft. Lakers staff bordered the sideline to watch his full-court workout. With media attending his second session, Okafor flashed his mid-range jumper. Okafor hadn't played live basketball since the championship game in April, and his physique looked as such. Even still, Okafor impressed Lakers officials with athleticism and skill level.

The giant wanted to be the next of Los Angeles' great centers, only Lakers brass were just as enamored by D'Angelo Russell's dexterity.

Russell's workouts hadn't gone as smoothly. He bombed his first Los Angeles visit so badly, the Lakers called his agent to organize another visit, where Russell once again struggled in a three-on-three game with other, lower-ranked prospects. "I sucked, man," Russell says. "I didn't think I was going to be a Laker. I'll tell you that."

Lakers evaluators worried the pressure had gotten to Russell's head. As much as they loved his skill set, they fretted the activity between his ears. "There were real concerns about D'Angelo's kind of emotional maturity makeup," Moser says.

Los Angeles then dialed Andy Miller of ASM Sports. The powerbroker who represented Nerlens Noel now managed Kristaps Porziņģis, and the Latvian couldn't miss during his agency's Las Vegas pro day in mid-June. ESPN even filmed a *SportsCenter* segment from the gym. "There was so much hype," recalls one ASM figure.

Some teams questioned Porziņģis' toughness, but a closed workout was the perfect environment to showcase Porziņģis' speed and shooting stroke at such size. "He's like 7-foot-4 out there with an 8-foot-5 wingspan and incredible touch," says Dirk Nowitzki, the original Hall of Fame shooting big. "He can move, he can put it on the floor."

Before the ASM showcase, Miller made one directive clear: Sam Hinkie was not permitted to speak to Porziņģis. ASM staffers would allow Knicks president Phil Jackson to meet their client. However, Miller detested Hinkie's free agency inactivity. While Sixers supporters cheered Philadelphia's $20 million in cap space that preserved flexibility for future trades, able to take on bad contracts at the cost of extra draft capital, the strategy clearly burned agents like Miller economically. One fewer team bidding on players shrunk the free agent marketplace and downsized the scope of player reps' leverage. Hinkie also hardly returned Miller's phone calls.

With a media groundswell boosting Porziņģis' draft stock, Miller could get away with stonewalling the Sixers' president. "Andy did that whole thing," says one ASM figure. He refused to disclose Porziņģis' medical, just like Joel Embiid's camp had done with several teams the previous June. Only Minnesota, Los Angeles, and New York received Porziņģis' information, although Orlando retained his 2014 medical on file. "Without that physical, no owner was gonna draft him," says the ASM voice. "He's this big-ass name, and if you don't have his physical and something's wrong with him, then you look like a complete idiot."

If Philadelphia did pass on Porziņģis, Miller would have successfully steered his client to the Knicks, a franchise in dire need of a running mate for Carmelo Anthony who could bridge the future of Madison Square Garden. And now Porziņģis' pro-day performance inspired the Lakers to host him for a more intimate evaluation. Miller couldn't have accepted the invitation quicker. Los Angeles, even more so than New York, bred superstars. "I was like, 'Oh shit,'" Porziņģis recalls. "'I would love to be a Laker.'"

He and his brother Janis drove directly west from Las Vegas, quibbling over music choices on the stereo. They couldn't have known their four-hour trek, fresh off Porziņģis' pro day, would leave him depleted for his Los Angeles visit. "I was just so tired in that moment and it was a tough workout," Porziņģis says. His jumper looked flat as shot after shot clanked off iron. Porziņģis saw his chance at No. 2 slipping away with each miss. "I didn't feel like I showed what I could actually do," Porziņģis says. "I felt like that opportunity wasn't there anymore."

Indeed, just before draft night, Kupchak phoned Ohio State head coach Thad Matta one last time. The general manager kept highlighting how Golden State's five-man "Death Lineup" of Steph Curry and interchangeable wings dismantled the great LeBron James during the Finals.

"What position are those guys playing?" Kupchak asked Matta, rhetorically. "They're just playmakers. That's the way the NBA's going right now, is playmakers."

Matta chuckled on the other end of the line. "And D'Angelo is definitely a playmaker," he said.

Arriving back at the Barclays Center podium, commissioner Adam Silver made things official when he announced Russell as the Lakers' No. 2 selection. "I think Steph shifted that there," says Bill Duffy.

"The NBA was changing," adds a Duke staffer. "Jah got caught up right in the middle of it."

Jahlil Okafor didn't seem to fit Brett Brown's philosophy or Sam Hinkie's typical prospect, either. The first two years of their Sixers tenure brought long athlete after long athlete though Philly, not a post presence who held the ball. And while Brown hadn't won many games, Philadelphia did see firsthand how quicker, smaller units wreaked defensive havoc. The Sixers improved drastically when sending Henry Sims to the bench in favor of the smaller Robert Covington.

Hinkie had continued efforts to meet with Porziņģis, only his agent, Andy Miller, never acquiesced. "I didn't do anything with Philadelphia," Porziņģis says. "It was kind of my team's decision." At one point, Miller agreed to a workout at PCOM, but cancelled the night before. Hinkie then asked to sit down with Porziņģis in Manhattan the week of the draft and Miller originally cooperated, before scrapping the plan, claiming his client had food poisoning.

"You gotta be honest," one ASM staffer says of the pre-draft process, "but you gotta bluff a little bit too."

Phil Jackson, for example, guaranteed New York would select Porziņģis No. 4 after his pro day in Las Vegas, yet Hinkie didn't need to learn that. And from Jackson's promise, Andy Miller remained determined Hinkie wouldn't have any access to his client. So Philadelphia kept hosting more amenable prospects. Just as during Hinkie's two previous drafts processes, the Sixers worked out more than 100 players before the June 25 draft.

The point guard Emmanuel Mudiay impressed Sixers onlookers during his visit. "There was a real debate of who you would rather have leading your team, D'Angelo Russell or Emmanuel Mudiay, for the non-basketball stuff, the intangibles," says Lance Pearson, Philly's analytics staffer. Jahlil Okafor's college teammate, freshman forward Justise Winslow, also impressed with his athleticism and defensive versatility, but few Philadelphia officials thought either Winslow or Mudiay was worthy of the No. 3 pick.

As the clock dwindled on Philadelphia's third selection, that third choice suddenly felt far less valuable than it had during the celebrity commercial break on lottery night. Sixers fans, like the many packed into Buffalo Wild Wings that May, had once dreamed of pairing D'Angelo Russell with a healthy Nerlens Noel and Joel Embiid, forming some East Coast version of the Clippers' Lob City with Chris Paul, Blake Griffin, and DeAndre Jordan. But now Russell was already off to the Lakers, and the status of Embiid's return to play was once again uncertain.

Embiid had spent the spring gearing back toward full clearance. When coaches taught him footwork that typically took other youngsters several practices to grow comfortable completing, Embiid polished it within minutes. "Anytime you'd teach him anything, within two or three repetitions, he would have pretty much mastered the fluidity of the movement," Lance Pearson says. Embiid grasped smaller details unlike most players. He watched videos of James Harden's evolving step-back jumpers and Kevin Durant's rip-through, dissecting how clever scorers can create contact to draw fouls. "Joel Embiid is a basketball genius," Pearson says.

Embiid soon dominated three-on-threes. "It was almost like the same thing with Andrew Bynum," says Jason Richardson.

The center was upgraded to four-on-four before he departed in early June to train for the summer in Los Angeles. There were no referees or fouls, and coaches jumped at the chance to pit him against Nerlens Noel, himself making a rare appearance at voluntary off-season practices. "Embiid tried to impose his will," Pearson says.

One dunk sent Noel stumbling backward. Embiid screamed in his teammate's face, calling him soft and spouting, "You're a pussy!"

Then in Southern California, almost a year to the day Embiid fractured his foot in Cleveland, a routine CT scan revealed an issue in the injury's healing process. Doctors soon determined Embiid re-broke the navicular bone that had already cost Embiid's first season. Another surgery was likely, and would eliminate his 2015–16 campaign.

Promise of the next Hakeem Olajuwon wearing Sixers red immediately seemed to evaporate across Philadelphia. How would Embiid's unpredictable status impact the Sixers' third choice atop June's draft?

As the clock neared zeroes, a contingent of Sixers evaluators still believed Jahlil Okafor to be the best prospect available at No. 3. He was so unguardable in college, converting 66.4 percent of his field goals, Philadelphia had difficulty projecting his NBA production. "It was such an outlier," Lance Pearson says, "models tended to minimize how good he was."

Sixers scouts were rightfully concerned about Okafor's ability to guard pick-and-rolls, but believed his wingspan and footspeed on the block could allow him to drop in coverage and barricade the basket from ball handlers. And with the growing possibility of Embiid never playing for Philadelphia, just like Andrew Bynum before him, Okafor did present a Band-Aid for Hinkie's polarizing No. 3 selection from the year prior. "We could eat what would be perceived by most people as a mistake," says Pearson.

Adam Silver returned to the podium in Brooklyn. Andy Miller sighed relief when the commissioner announced the Sixers indeed selected Okafor with the third pick. Even with all of Miller's chicanery to save Porziņģis for New York at No. 4, the agent still worried Philadelphia would scoop him third. "Andy had basically made his chess move," an ASM staffer says "He didn't know if Hinkie would make the ultimate one." Now with the Knicks officially on the clock, Miller knew he'd won this round.

Across the green room, Bill Duffy kept his cool when he embraced Okafor. "You have to have enthusiasm for your client even though you're disappointed," Duffy says. He hadn't wanted Okafor to land in Philadelphia's crowded frontcourt as much as Miller didn't wish that situation upon Porziņģis. Besides, Duffy knew Hinkie prioritized compiling assets. Perhaps the Sixers merely selected Okafor, who many regarded as the best prospect available, and Philadelphia would soon move him to another franchise.

As Okafor shook Silver's hand, he still scanned down the draft board posted onstage behind the commissioner, contemplating possible landing spots for his imminent trade. "I was still nervous," Okafor says. "I looked down. I didn't know where I was going to end up." It wasn't until he spoke to Hinkie that Okafor and Duffy realized reality: Duke's star was due in Philadelphia the following morning for an introductory press conference.

The clock ticked on with New York's pick.

In Boston, Danny Ainge expected the Knicks would choose Justise Winslow. Okafor's running mate had met with Phil Jackson and Winslow was later spotted at a Yankees game with Carmelo Anthony. Knicks fans were clamoring for the versatile athlete.

Winslow's confidence often wavered early into his Duke tenure. "When I was playing throughout the season, the NBA and all that was fucking me up," Winslow says. But the freshman found his outside stroke in the second half of the year. On the other end, he clamped opponents' best scorers as the Blue Devils won the title—all while playing with cracked ribs.

"He was arguably our best player down the stretch," says a Duke staffer.

The Knicks also hosted Emmanuel Mudiay. He watched film with Phil Jackson as the Hall of Fame coach explained videos of Kobe Bryant and Michael Jordan running his fabled Triangle offense.

Adam Silver, no matter, returned to the podium in Brooklyn to declare New York's pick was in fact Kristaps Porziņģis. On cue, Knicks fans heartily booed the news. Taking a European shooter, commonly labeled as "soft" by his skeptics, seemed like the perfect recipe for another New York draft bust.

Magic executives were equally disappointed as they sunk inside their Orlando war room. General manager Rob Hennigan expected New York would draft Porziņģis, but the finality still stung. Orlando never even had the chance to uphold its 14-month promise. The Magic instead regrouped to select another European phenom, Croatian wing Mario Hezonja.

Orlando felt he boasted the highest ceiling of any prospect remaining. NBA personnel had been tracking his progress since Hezonja was 17. He scored 18 points in 25 minutes during a Spanish ACB Finals game at just 20 years old.

That brought Sacramento on the clock at No. 6. Just five minutes separated Vlade Divac from his first draft pick as a lead executive. Ending all confusion, Pete D'Alessandro had left his post as general manager to rejoin Denver's front office. His footing had just grown too fractured in California.

Back on May 31, Divac called a meeting with D'Alessandro, assistant GM Mike Bratz, George Karl, and several assistants. This time, instead of an offensive rating requirement, Divac announced Kings owner Vivek Ranadivé demanded a 50-win season in 2015–16. "Give us a plan on how to do it," Divac said.

Karl took to the conference room's whiteboard. He listed every Kings player by position and crossed off names until only five remained, representing the few he believed could help a 50-win rotation. In order to get more players capable of reaching Ranadivé's goal, Karl harkened back to how his Nuggets had moved Carmelo Anthony to New York for a collection of players that later earned the third seed in the West in 2013. "If you trade DeMarcus," the coach began, "you can probably get two or three pieces plus a draft pick, plus our [No. 6] draft pick, and we pick up a free agent, that would be the best way for us to get to 50."

Divac and Ranadivé started making calls. Karl also phoned Lakers general manager Mitch Kupchak, hoping to pry the No. 2 pick. "I had heard he had interest in Cousins," Karl says. Just 10 days after that fateful meeting, D'Alessandro left for Denver. He'd been fully boxed out of the Kings' decision-making like others before him.

Karl maintains he didn't canvas for Cousins trade destinations. "I might have talked to one or two other guys in the league and asked them, 'What's the value of Cousins?'" Karl says. "But I'm not a phone guy, and I'm definitely not a talk-to-an-executive guy. Look, I'm a gym guy. I'm a basketball guy."

Yet rumor leaked around the league of Kings-Lakers discussions sur-rounding Cousins, which predictably angered Sacramento's All-Star. He was on the trade block and nobody had the courtesy to tell him? "This is what created all the crap with Boogie and George," assistant coach Vance Walberg says.

Divac hadn't struck a trade for Cousins before Sacramento's No. 6 pick arrived on draft night. The Kings had tracked another Kentucky product, junior center Willie Cauley-Stein, since his freshman season in Lexington. At the time, Vance Walberg thought he was a better prospect than presump-tive No. 1 pick Nerlens Noel. "He could just run and jump and protect the rim," the assistant coach says.

Yet Cauley-Stein waited two more seasons to declare pro, even after he helped the Wildcats to the 2014 championship game. "He surprised me when he wanted to come back," John Calipari recalls. "He just said, 'I want to compete for a national title. I'm not ready mentally for [the NBA].'"

The Kings also liked Emmanuel Mudiay, but he'd refused to work out for any team drafting below No. 4. Sacramento contemplated Wisconsin big Frank Kaminsky as well, but ultimately had concerns about his defense. And if the Kings didn't move Cousins, Cauley-Stein boasted the malleability to guard whichever frontcourt opponent Boogie couldn't match. "He was going to be a defensive-minded, hustle, energy guy that plays 20-25 minutes a game," George Karl says. Cauley-Stein officially came off the board once Adam Silver announced their pick.

Nuggets brass leapt to scoop Mudiay at No. 7. He'd yet set foot in Denver, but he was officially a top-10 NBA draft pick. "Seven is pretty high too," Mudiay smiles.

Detroit came on the clock at No. 8. The Pistons, led by dual president-coach Stan Van Gundy, felt their roster was one talented wing short of a playoff push. They zeroed in on Justise Winslow and Arizona forward Stanley Johnson, hopeful both chiseled athletes could grow into fluid shooters. "Devin Booker wasn't really on everybody's radar at that point in the draft," Van Gundy says. When Danny Ainge called Detroit, offering a hoard of draft capital for the Pistons' eighth pick, he too coveted Winslow, and not Booker, the Kentucky sharpshooter.

Stanley Johnson felt his range began with Detroit, but Miami, holding No. 10, hosted a rare two-on-none workout—as opposed to top prospects typically working out as individuals—when Johnson and Frank Kaminsky visited South Beach simultaneously. They were both clients of Bill Duffy, who pitched the idea to Heat brass. "'You want to do it together?'" Johnson recalls being asked. "Yeah, fuck it."

He and Kaminsky went through routine shooting drills and sparred two-on-two against Miami assistants Chris Quinn and Juwan Howard, the latter a former NBA All-Star. "We did a lot of intense me-and-him in ball screens and pick-and-rolls going full court," Kaminsky says. "It was more of a cardio workout than it was anything else." The tropical humidity burned their lungs with each gasp for air. "It got kind of brutal toward the end," Kaminsky says.

Miami, though, wouldn't have the chance to select Johnson. Even after one front office contingent's final push for Devin Booker, Detroit ultimately declined Danny Ainge's efforts for the eighth pick, and chose Johnson. He boasted a bigger frame, more ready to battle NBA wings and was "who we thought was more what we needed," Van Gundy says.

With Winslow still available, Ainge dialed the Hornets. Nearing his breaking point, Boston's chief executive offered a total of six draft picks, including four first-rounders. If Charlotte traded No. 9, the Hornets would have netted Boston's picks at Nos. 16 and 28, Brooklyn's 2016 unprotected first-rounder, and Memphis' 2019 top-8-protected first the Celtics acquired in January when trading Jeff Green. Boston even worked a contingency trade with Atlanta that could have sent Charlotte the Hawks' No. 15 pick instead of the Celtics' 28th.

This wasn't an unhappy impending free agent like Kevin Love or Goran Dragić; Ainge was going all in on a 19-year-old. "There was a time when I thought, 'Whoa, this is getting a little out of control. We're putting a lot of eggs in one young player's basket,'" Ainge told reporters later that evening. Yet despite the bountiful offer, Charlotte still declined Boston's advances.

As the Hornets focused on drafting the top prospect on their board, Devin Booker readied to hear Silver call his name. "Charlotte didn't have a good shooter," he says. Only Adam Silver announced the Hornets had rejected Ainge's mega-offer in order to draft Frank Kaminsky. Booker still sat in the green room, as surprised as the skeptics around the league, growing ever-dubious as word circulated Charlotte turned down such a massive haul from Boston.

At No. 10, Miami rebuffed Ainge's attempts as well. This time, the Heat happily scooped Winslow for themselves. Boston would have to wait to pick someone else at No. 16.

Indiana grabbed Texas center Myles Turner next with the 11th pick, bringing Utah on the clock at No. 12. The Jazz had hoped to work out Booker pre-draft, but the Kentucky freshman refused to visit Jazz headquarters—the only team he'd declined a pre-draft invitation from. "It was Utah," Booker says. "My life, my situation. I didn't feel like it was the best situation for me."

The Jazz selected Booker's Wildcats teammate, fellow freshman Trey Lyles, instead. Utah's intel suggested the talented forward was actually open to playing in Salt Lake. "You're just trying to get these guys in and find a core," says a Jazz executive.

With each pick that left Booker available, Phoenix executives leaned toward the television. "As it kind of got closer to us, we got more confident," says assistant general manager Pat Connelly. While rivals passed on the 6-foot-5 marksman, Suns brass imagined Booker draining kickouts from Eric Bledsoe and Brandon Knight's penetration. Booker had also flashed the potential to attack gaps and finish at the rim as well. "Obviously, his shooting was his main piece, but the rest of his package was also really appealing," Connelly says.

Booker was Phoenix's pick at No. 13. Suns officials had no way of knowing how selecting him would ultimately impact Ryan McDonough's front office.

Oklahoma City selected Murray State point guard Cameron Payne 14th in the 2015 NBA Draft. Kansas wing Kelly Oubre Jr. went 15th, landing in Washington via a three-team trade. With No. 16, Boston selected Louisville point guard Terry Rozier.

Another long perimeter defender, Rozier's wingspan stretched 6-foot-8, allowing the 6-foot-1 ball handler to potentially guard three positions within head coach Brad Stevens' defense. Like many rising teams around the league, most notably the reigning-champion Warriors, the Celtics were now predicated on switching all screens. Adding more players like Rozier to a Boston group already boasting Jae Crowder, Marcus Smart, and Avery Bradley would continue pestering opposing backcourts, while helping Isaiah Thomas match up with his bigger assignments.

The first round continued onward. Los Angeles, Boston's storied bitter rival, would pick again down at No. 27, thanks to the first-rounder acquired from Houston for having taken on Jeremy Lin's contract.

With commissioner Adam Silver declaring the Lakers on the clock, Los Angeles eagerly readied to select Larry Nance Jr. out of Wyoming. Lakers brass valued Nance's pedigree, son of the three-time All-Star, and the athleticism his dad had clearly passed along. During Nance's pre-draft visit, Jr. easily logged a 44-inch vertical on his first jump. Mitch Kupchak stood staring up at the measuring device. "Can you do that again?" the general manager asked. Nance kept leaping and kept registering either 43 or 44 inches off the floor.

"We thought he was going to be a steal," says Clay Moser, the Lakers' director of basketball strategy.

One pick later, at No. 28—the Clippers selection Danny Ainge first acquired when trading Doc Rivers two years prior—Boston drafted R.J. Hunter, a lanky, 6-foot-5 sharpshooter out of Georgia State. The Celtics grabbed another long, versatile defender in LSU forward Jordan Mickey at No. 33. If there were any remaining questions about Boston's team-building strategy, onlookers clearly weren't paying attention.

NINETEEN

Philadelphia returned on the clock at No. 35 for the first of Sam Hinkie's five second-round selections, the most by a single team during one draft in modern NBA history—tying the mark Hinkie *himself* had just set in 2014. And the Sixers still moved No. 35, which became Spanish big Willy Hernangómez, to New York for two more second-round picks, one coming in 2020 and the other not conveying until 2021.

"There was some frustration in the room that we were trading away this pick when this was a guy that we really felt could come in and actually contribute," says Lance Pearson, the Sixers analytics staffer.

Many Philly scouts were hoping to draft athletic UCLA guard Norman Powell. They sighed relief when, two slots later, Hinkie actually selected big man Richaun Holmes with the intention to keep the Bowling Green product. Holmes had risen up draft boards during the pre-draft circuit. He visited with 13 teams after flashing elite shot blocking and athleticism during the Portsmouth Invitational Tournament in April, which showcases college seniors from around the country. Holmes' performance, coupled with an encouraging shooting stroke in school, also landed an invite to the draft combine. His block and steal rate projected a defensive difference maker for Brett Brown's bench unit. "He was an analytics darling," Lance Pearson says.

Holmes' agent, Keith Kreiter, knew the numbers. Many evaluators had Holmes ranked as a first-round prospect, and Kreiter wanted his client to be paid as such. Yet true to form, Hinkie maintained his offer of a four-year, team-controlled contract. He even suggested both Holmes and J.P. Tokoto, Philadelphia's No. 58 pick, play overseas before joining Brown's roster.

Holmes' situation would require far more negotiation. At the union's annual agent meetings that summer, NBPA officials warned the gathered player reps against taking Hinkie's four-year, non-guaranteed minimum "special." Agents who accepted that contract, the union explained, inherently damaged all of its members. Just like LeBron James taking his maximum salary raised the bar for every player to command his richest earnings possible, a youngster accepting the Hinkie Special lowered the floor for all players and their respective agents.

"It was generally frowned upon," one player representative says.

"You always want to put a player in a position where there's a chance for stability," says Mark Bartelstein, the noted agent, "a chance to build something where you feel like there's an equal investment on both sides."

Even still, Houston maintained the same practice. Boston also signed Jordan Mickey, the No. 33 pick, to a four-year deal that assured roughly $2.5 million over the first two seasons, but the Celtics weren't committed for either of the last two years. "Jordan Mickey never would have made as much money in the first two years, guaranteed, if he hadn't signed a third and fourth year non-guaranteed," says Mike Zarren, the Celtics assistant general manager. "I think the issue that the Sixers were having is they were only guaranteeing one year."

Keith Kreiter followed the union's playbook. When he met with Sam Hinkie in Las Vegas during Summer League, Philadelphia's president again hinted at Richaun Holmes playing overseas. The agent rebuffed. His client was an NBA player, Kreiter believed, and Ryan McDonough's Phoenix Suns were waiting to trade for Holmes' draft rights if Hinkie couldn't reach an agreement.

"No. No, no, no, we love him. That's not our plan," Hinkie countered. "I don't want you to go down that road. We want him here."

"I can't listen to a stash," Kreiter said. "That's not what's of best interest for the kid."

Hinkie nodded. On the spot, he offered Holmes $1.7 million over his first two seasons, but the next two years were, of course, not guaranteed.

Hinkie argued that contract was similar to a late-first-round-pick's deal. "You got a little bit more than Jerami Grant," he said, referring to Philly's 2014 second-rounder, who fired his agent for advising that agreement.

Kreiter suggested the four-year deal worth over $4 million that Joe Young, the No. 43 pick in the 2015 draft, recently inked with Indiana. If Hinkie couldn't offer Holmes that number or higher, then they would request a trade.

Hinkie needed time to consider. And two days later, he indeed phoned back offering to meet Joe Young's numbers. But while Kreiter's hardball effectively guaranteed Holmes $2.1 million over his first two seasons, having steered Hinkie away from his infamous minimum special, Holmes' modest agreement would actually mark the richest deal Philadelphia negotiated during all of July free agency.

Maddened agents continued watching the Sixers' cap space go unused on the open market. Andy Miller had prohibited Hinkie from meeting with Kristaps Porziņģis partially for this exact reason. "He protected the Sixers," says one player rep. "They could always make flexible moves because they weren't cash-strapped." The best agents are hagglers by nature, unsatisfied until securing the yes. They were accustomed to traditional team executives treating them to lunch, leveraging meetings with the agents' All-Star clients. "Sam Hinkie wasn't doing none of that shit," says the player rep.

Philadelphia was planning its first splash into free agency for 2016. Three years of cultivating young phenoms would hopefully produce an attractive destination for established veterans. So while Hinkie didn't add any marquee players in 2015, he did poach Texas strength and conditioning coach Todd Wright, who was known to have a strong connection with Kevin Durant, a former Longhorn set for free agency the following July. "Sam was constantly doing those sorts of things, hiring people that had a connection to people you might really want on your team," Lance Pearson says. Sixers player development ace Chris Babcock had followed Brett Brown to Philadelphia from San Antonio, but he too was a former Texas staffer. Hinkie also targeted Royal Ivey as a possible development coach, who established a friendship with Durant as teammates back in Oklahoma City.

Sixers assistant coach Billy Lange, a former Villanova assistant, shared a bond with soon-to-be free agent, and fellow Wildcat, Kyle Lowry. Defensive specialist Lloyd Pierce had sparked a connection with LeBron James during his time with Cleveland from 2007 to 2010. Perhaps Hinkie would soon lean on those staffers, annually pitching free agents like his predecessor Daryl Morey in Houston.

For now, Hinkie kept juicing Brown's roster with high-upside prospects.

One year after Brown lamented losing Nik Stauskas in the 2014 draft, the Sixers landed him in a trade with Sacramento. As Vlade Divac hoped to clear cap space for his own momentous off-season, the Kings' new lead executive also traded Hinkie Sacramento's 2019 unprotected first-round pick, plus the rights to swap 2016 and 2017 first rounders, to shed Carl Landry and Jason Thompson's contracts. All Philadelphia surrendered in exchange were the rights to Hinkie's other 2015 second-round selections, international prospects Artūras Gudaitis (No. 47) and Luka Mitrović (No. 60), neither of whom would ever log an NBA minute.

If the Sixers trailed Danny Ainge's Celtics in future draft capital, this deal surely narrowed the margin between them. The Kings, meanwhile, used their newfound flexibility to sign point guard Rajon Rondo (having never meshed in Dallas), sharpshooter Marco Belinelli, center Kosta Koufos, and swingman Omri Casspi—a veteran group few rivals expected would help win Sacramento owner Vivek Ranadivé's mandated 50 games. Perhaps this was Divac's inexperience atop an NBA front office coming to fruition.

Process-trusting Sixers supporters, of course, hailed another Hinkie trade haul. If Stauskas found his shooting stroke within a more nurturing Philly program, he'd add another young lottery pick to a potentially enticing roster for premier free agents when the time did come.

Fellow rebuilders Los Angeles and Phoenix were already making different versions of that same sales pitch to LaMarcus Aldridge that very July.

The Lakers first met with the All-Star forward in a conference room at Wasserman Media Group's Los Angeles offices. In marched more AEG officials and Time Warner executives conducting a similar performance for Aldridge they'd pitched Carmelo Anthony a year earlier. The big man understood. Having played in Portland for years, Aldridge needed to learn about the opportunities that come with major markets. But Aldridge cared more about basketball and the futures of D'Angelo Russell and Julius Randle, he whispered to Kobe Bryant, seated next to him within the large meeting. Throughout the Lakers' official presentation, Aldridge and Bryant quietly chatted offensive philosophy. They both famously boasted deadly midrange games.

Bryant made impassioned pleas about his love for Los Angeles and the power of Lakers lore, but when Aldridge arrived at Wasserman's offices the next morning, Tyson Chandler surprised him in the lobby. While the Lakers got first dibs at pitching Aldridge, Suns general manager Ryan McDonough spent the opening night of free agency signing Chandler for four years and $52 million. Phoenix brass knew Aldridge preferred to play power forward and had particularly viewed Chandler as a welcomed frontcourt partner. A recent Defensive Player of the Year, Chandler's rim protection had cemented Dallas' championship defense in 2011—to which Philadelphia hoped Nerlens Noel could aspire.

McDonough planned to shock Aldridge with Phoenix's new All-Star center that morning, and Aldridge reciprocated with awe. Newly hired Suns assistant coach Earl Watson, a John Wooden disciple who teamed with Aldridge in Portland, joined the meeting as well as Eric Bledsoe, Brandon Knight, and others. Aldridge and Chandler could team up front while Bledsoe, Knight, and Devin Booker danced on the perimeter. Alex Len, entering his third season, would be ready to replace Chandler at the end of his contract.

Aldridge left the meeting envisioning life in the desert. One year after missing out on LeBron James, Phoenix now seemed the improbable leader to land the biggest name on the 2015 free agent market.

San Antonio, though, offered a similar warm climate, and proximity to two of Aldridge's children; he'd played college ball for the Longhorns as well. Texas already felt like home, and San Antonio's presentation soon made Aldridge feel like he was talking hoops with family. Multiple players were dressed in sweats. Head coach Gregg Popovich wore jeans and a T-shirt. Everyone sat on the couch and engaged in a free-flowing, casual conversation.

There were no bells and whistles among a busy presentation. And within an hour of making his decision on the morning of July 4, Aldridge signed a four-year, $80 million deal with San Antonio instead of Phoenix.

McDonough tasted another lick of the Suns' now-annual losses in free agency. Making matters worse, not only would acquiring Aldridge have impacted Markieff Morris' playing time, Suns executives had already angered their versatile forward when Phoenix traded his twin brother, Marcus, to Detroit, solely to open space for Aldridge's potential contract—as Cleveland had done before ultimately securing LeBron James. If you carve cap room for a superstar, you better not miss.

It was only last summer, as James returned to Ohio, that the Morris twins sat down with McDonough and former Suns exec Lon Babby and negotiated bargain deals to remain with Phoenix in tandem. "As long as we together, I don't give a fuck," Markieff told McDonough. "We'll take a little bit of money." Now the Suns moved Marcus without any notice, and Markieff was furious. All trust he'd built with the front office evaporated just as it had for Goran Dragić before him. Markieff demanded to be traded as well, eventually posting his wish on Twitter. "Sometimes that's what you gotta do to make shit happen, man. I know I got a fine for it," Markieff says. The fabric of Phoenix's rising 2013–14 contender continued to unravel.

Los Angeles nonetheless rinsed and repeated its summer strategy. Among other cost-effective moves, the Lakers signed Lou Williams and Brandon Bass to inexpensive deals, added Brazilian point guard Marcelo Huertas, and re-signed former Lakers wing Metta World Peace. If this unit wasn't post-season bound, the 2015–16 season would bring tons of fanfare with Kobe Bryant's retirement tour around the association. Perhaps that spotlight could then enamor upcoming free agents like Kevin Durant, after Bryant's contract slid off the Lakers' books and freed space for two max salaries. Maybe Durant and James could bring an unbeatable pairing come next July?

By then, Los Angeles would no longer be offering a share of Bryant's baton. L.A. staffers had begun wondering if playing in Bryant's shadow ultimately steered stars away from the Lakers. Even to his greatest contemporaries,

Bryant's legacy stood as large and intimidating as any among modern NBA lore—as evidenced throughout his rousing final lap around the league that winter.

In an open letter on November 29, Bryant indeed announced 2015–16 would be his last. Los Angeles left a copy enclosed inside black envelopes on every seat across Staples Center before that night's game against Indiana.

Two nights later, on December 1, Philadelphia would house the first hallmark moment of Bryant's final season. A raucous crowd filled the Wells Fargo Center eager to watch Bryant's final game in town, where he starred at nearby Lower Merion high school in the early 1990s. "You're doing your best to focus on playing your game and winning," says Lakers forward Ryan Kelly, "but no question that created a little bit different of an environment."

Sixers faithful also packed the arena desperately hoping for Philly's first win, having begun 0–18—tied again for the worst start in NBA history—for a consecutive year.

Sam Hinkie's group was still so young. Twelve of 15 players on Brett Brown's opening night roster had two years or less experience. With point guards Tony Wroten and newly signed Kendall Marshall both injured, the former second-rounder Isaiah Canaan began the season still running Philadelphia's offense. Brown's attack felt more than cluttered with Nerlens Noel and Jahlil Okafor attempting to fit alongside one another. "It was different," Noel says.

"We had no spacing whatsoever," recalls Nik Stauskas.

By their fourth outing, Brown even tried T.J. McConnell as his starting floor general. Undrafted after four years at Duquesne and Arizona, McConnell reminded Brown of Australian point guard Matthew Dellavedova. Both smaller players compensated tenacity for their lack of elite athleticism. "For us, trying to uncover point guards, it's a really good opportunity for him, and I think for us," Brown said at the time. McConnell pestered opponents for 94 feet. He dove for every loose ball.

"You think he's so annoying because he's this little white guy who just doesn't stop," Stauskas says. They'd had no prior relationship except sparring in Michigan-Arizona games. "I thought T.J. was the biggest prick of all time," Stauskas says.

Yet after the Sixers' first training camp practice, in which McConnell battled three other ball handlers for his spot, he approached Stauskas, sweaty and vulnerable, wondering what Stauskas thought of his chances to make Brown's roster. Stauskas scrunched his face. Honestly, he felt McConnell had no proverbial shot so long as he lacked a pure shooting stroke. But Stauskas knew all too well of the point guard's grizzled gift. "You just have to be a motherfucker," he told his new teammate.

Each practice, McConnell polled a new teammate, asking if they believed he could make the team. "Just tried to send out some feelers to see what people thought my chances were," he says. He'd done the same line of questioning back at Arizona.

"T.J. thought he was going to get cut every day during that season, til the end of the season," says fellow rookie Richaun Holmes.

"Even though I think I belong," McConnell says, "I'm gonna fight like people don't think I do."

He developed a strong pick-and-roll chemistry with Noel. He texted the center highlight videos of Steve Nash and Amar'e Stoudemire. "T.J.'s one of the most communicative point guards I've ever played with," Noel says.

The Sixers still couldn't find the win column with McConnell starting, however, and Brett Brown moved him back to the bench by late November. It coincidentally gave McConnell a front row seat for Kobe Bryant's first-quarter eruption to begin his final game in Philadelphia.

Whenever he visited the Sixers, Bryant always had a way of puncturing the crowd noise, draining fadeaways that each seemed more unfathomable than the last. "It was a madhouse," Lakers assistant Jim Eyen says. More gold speckled the roaring crowd than any color as Bryant poured in 13 points on 5-for-10 shooting through the opening frame.

"The way he started the game," McConnell says, "I thought he was going for 60."

Bryant canned three triples to score Los Angeles' first nine points, then shook Robert Covington at the top of the key for a long jumper.

Only then Bryant missed five of his six attempts in the second quarter. The Lakers still managed a 58–50 advantage at halftime, although Philly turned the tables with a dominant third, outscoring L.A. by 13 in the frame.

Bryant's struggles continued. "There was a period in the game where he missed like 12 straight jumpers," Stauskas says. The Lakers featured few other weapons, yet he still willed Los Angeles' attack.

As the horn sounded, spectators both cheered the Sixers' win and Bryant's ultimate performance. Once again, Philadelphia narrowly avoided setting that new record for NBA futility. "It felt like the fucking championship," recalls Spike Eskin, *The Rights to Ricky Sanchez* co-host and local radio figure.

In the locker room, Sixers players and staffers sprayed each other with water bottles and Gatorade. "We had gone so long without winning," Richaun Holmes says. It would be another while before Philadelphia returned to the win column, especially after losing Jahlil Okafor.

The morning after defeating Bryant's Lakers, the Sixers announced a newsworthy two-game suspension for their most recent No. 3 pick.

TWENTY

Barhopping around Boston's Copley Square, Nik Stauskas and a group of prep school friends bumped into Jahlil Okafor's crew—including rookie center Christian Wood, another undrafted athlete Sam Hinkie long coveted. It was the evening before Thanksgiving, and despite a morning flight to Houston, many Sixers youngsters joined the local party following that night's loss to the Celtics.

Okafor and Wood were headed to the nearby nightclub Storyville. By evening's end, the 19- and 20-year-olds had enjoyed several drinks. "I wasn't really in the right state of mind," Okafor says.

Wood ordered an Uber as they left the club to head back to the Ritz-Carlton, but their first driver cancelled. The players' new ride was five minutes away—just enough time for Celtics fans exiting the bar to notice two rival players from that evening's game.

"You suck! The Sixers are trash!" they hollered.

"You have no money!" someone shouted.

Granular details are fuzzy for Okafor. "I do remember being heckled," he says. "I've been heckled before. I've handled it much better, 99 times out of a 100. But it only takes one time."

Okafor turned toward the hecklers. He'd just hung 19 points and nine boards against the Celtics. He was the No. 3 pick in the draft with multiple endorsements. "We got money!" he shouted.

Wood and friends urged Okafor to walk away, nearer the Uber's exact pickup destination. "But then they started coming up to us," Wood says. "And then they started talking about his family."

Okafor jawed right back. He forcefully shoved one heckler. "The guy swung," Wood says. "After that, it was crazy."

The fracas stumbled up Huntington Avenue and down the next side street, behind a Star Market grocery. Okafor lunged to swing at someone. At one point, a man in the melee ultimately slammed into a storefront's glass door. "It's something I regret," Okafor says now.

In the morning, Stauskas saw Wood waiting to catch the hotel elevator downstairs, only Wood downplayed the fresh shiner darkening his eye. Whispers later buzzed across the Sixers' team plane, and minutes before takeoff, TMZ released a video capturing the beginning of Okafor's fight. "It was the worst timing forever," Stauskas says. Synced to in-flight Wi-Fi, players were able to follow the firestorm kindling that Thanksgiving morning online.

Brown summoned Okafor and Wood to his seat at the back of their plane. The head coach needed their recounting of the incident. Okafor maintained his actions were out of self-defense. "He didn't get on me, he wasn't upset with me. He was just making sure I had the support that was necessary," Okafor says now of his head coach. Brown and the Sixers needed time determining how to handle the evolving situation.

Wood remained glued to Brown's bench over the coming games, but Okafor played the next night in Houston, then in Memphis and against the Lakers for Kobe Bryant's Philadelphia finale. All the while, TMZ released a second, longer video from later in the brawl. "Shit went left from there," Wood says.

Police began investigating Okafor for assault and battery after a person pressed charges in Boston. CSN Philadelphia then uncovered that, months earlier, a stranger pulled a gun on Okafor after he'd drunkenly pawed at the man through his car window. The *Philadelphia Inquirer* also reported Okafor had been issued a speeding ticket back in October for racing 108 miles per hour on the Ben Franklin Bridge.

With each news item, the 76ers somehow remained silent. Neither ownership nor Sam Hinkie addressed the developing situation regarding their top pick in June's draft, just after Philadelphia's porous 0–18 hole stole its share of headlines from Golden State's historic 24–0 start across the aisle.

Critics lambasted the Sixers' losing environment, especially when it was left to Brett Brown during his pregame presser, before the Sixers' December 2 game in New York, to offer an official comment on Okafor's eventual two-game suspension. Hinkie had traveled with the team to Manhattan but declined to speak on the record to reporters that night. "I think that was the final straw from the commissioner's office that, 'Hey, we need a senior person in here to kinda run things,'" says Bobby Marks, the longtime Nets executive.

The controversy indeed angered Adam Silver. He mandated both Okafor and Wood speak with league security officials. The commissioner was stunned Sixers players had been out independent of any safety presence from Philadelphia. "In college we didn't have any security guards," Okafor says. "But now looking at it, it was odd that we didn't have any security from the team."

Several league insiders suggest Blue Devils coach Mike Krzyzewski even phoned Silver, a 1984 Duke graduate, urging the commissioner wield whatever power his office held over Sixers leadership and install another executive atop Philadelphia' front office, if not encourage Hinkie's ouster. ("I've never heard of that theory," counters one Duke staffer.) The implication was that Krzyzewski couldn't sit idly by as Okafor's incident left a black eye on his illustrious Blue Devils program as garish as Christian Wood's dented face.

Sixers officials knew the league office didn't exactly support Hinkie's brazen strategy. "They don't care that people tank," says Lance Pearson, "they just don't want ESPN talking about it."

Local media and critical Philly fans had long clamored for Hinkie to communicate more frequently than he'd chosen. He merely spoke on the record during his press conferences after the trade deadline and NBA draft. Now Adam Silver, too, sat incredulous at the executive's silence amid such a national public relations catastrophe.

"You've pissed off agents, fans, and now the league. Eventually that's going to be your demise," says one player representative.

Philadelphia personnel maintain Silver and Joshua Harris had mutual interest to alleviate the situation, and when the Sixers' managing partner asked the commissioner for advice, Silver eagerly offered to put Harris in touch with former Suns owner and longtime executive Jerry Colangelo.

Then the patriarch of USA Basketball, of which none other than Mike Krzyzewski coached the men's national team, Colangelo maintained the relationships amongst league cadre Hinkie so blatantly disregarded. To Joshua Harris' group of billionaires, Colangelo billed as Hinkie's perfect counterbalance. "The owners don't really know what's going on anyway," Pearson says. "This is mainly an investment for them. It's a cool investment for them."

And so before hosting San Antonio on December 7, the Sixers called a press conference to introduce Harris' new advisor and chairman of basketball operations. Colangelo asserted he'd been part of four rebuilds in Phoenix. He promised to satisfy the media and league insiders while Hinkie remained focused on tactical team advancements. Philadelphia's president wore a welcoming face on the podium, but Hinkie's loyal staffers already smelled his blood in the Delaware River. "It was like, 'Oh shit,'" one Sixers scout says. "'Ohhh fuck!'"

A shocked Spike Eskin watched the Colangelo announcement from a Chickie's & Pete's restaurant in South Philly. "At first I was like, 'Here's a guy who has a good history with the league and they're just adding him,'" says Eskin, *The Rights to Ricky Sanchez* podcast co-host. "But I think it took me less than three hours to be like, 'Wait a minute…this is not good!'"

Sixers players gossiped in their pregame locker room, pondering more about Hinkie's job security than their chances against the Spurs. "Everybody thought he was going to get fired," Christian Wood says. They would lose by 51 points that evening.

Harris assured hiring Colangelo was "not a deviation from our plan." Hinkie ostensibly maintained final say over basketball operations decisions, but Colangelo continuously lobbied firm suggestions to Harris that were ultimately passed down to the analytical president. Colangelo pushed hard for Philadelphia to add another veteran presence on Brown's roster. "In the

NBA you have to have mentoring, a sense of transition to have all this money, all this freedom, all this notoriety," says Bill Duffy, Jahlil Okafor's agent.

Carl Landry, the veteran forward acquired from Sacramento, could only do so much on his own. So Colangelo dialed longtime agent David Falk. And after his client Elton Brand—another Duke product—sought counsel from his old coach Mike Krzyzewski, Brand accepted a breakfast meeting with Sam Hinkie near PCOM's facilities. A former Sixer, Brand had chatted with Hinkie back at Philadelphia Country Club's July 4 event. Brand still wanted to play, but at 36, no team rang Falk looking for the old All-Star's services. He'd declined television offers and coaching opportunities. Brand even turned down Atlanta's assistant general manager job.

Hinkie planned to issue a team credit card with which Brand could treat players to dinner, espousing professional wisdom to every youngster, especially Jahlil Okafor. Perhaps he could fill some form of on-court player development position too. Brand didn't have great interest. He still yearned to hoop, but the unique role did intrigue him. "It felt like giving back to the game that had given me so much," Brand says. Needing time to consider, he left for a 10-day family vacation in Jamaica while Colangelo continued through his Rolodex.

The Sixers' new chairman called the trailblazing coach he once tapped to unleash Phoenix's seven-second revolution. Mike D'Antoni answered from his home in West Virginia.

"Will you come to Philadelphia?" Colangelo asked.

D'Antoni initially resisted. He respected Brett Brown and recognized the optics of joining a one-win team midseason. But assisting Brown would offer him a subtle NBA return, Colangelo argued, allowing D'Antoni to dip his toe back in the game before jumping into another head coaching role. "You can't say no to him. It's inevitable," D'Antoni says. "Whatever it was, you're gonna get the yes. So I might as well do it."

Philadelphia still sorely lacked sufficient ball handlers. Even with Kendall Marshall and Tony Wroten making their season debuts that month, Colangelo pressed for greater reinforcements. On December 24, Philadelphia traded 2016 and 2017 second-round picks to bring Ish Smith back to the Sixers. "I'm like, 'Ho now!'" Smith recalls, having already been traded four times in five seasons. "I'm not just a throw-in!" He'd started for Brett Brown to close out 2014–15 as another late-season Hinkie auditionee.

On the surface, the transaction appeared antithetical to Hinkie's recent record, stockpiling historic troves of second-round selections to invest in teenage prospects, not journeyman point guards. "You knew Sam was not in control anymore," Spike Eskin says. "It felt like it was over."

To clear room for Smith, Hinkie even waived Wroten without warning on Christmas Eve. "That was the only time I had a glimpse of Sam doing something that would infuriate the agents and stuff, and I don't think he meant it," says Greg Lawrence, Wroten's former representative. "I just think maybe sometimes he didn't think it all the way through." Hinkie had picked up the $2.2 million team option on Wroten's contract for that season, guaranteeing a full salary regardless of his roster spot. The situation forced Hinkie's admission, far sooner than he'd preferred, that betting on Wroten had netted little return.

Ish Smith thus joined the Sixers in Phoenix on Christmas night. And despite Colangelo's growing Sixers influence, he still resided in Arizona. He took Philadelphia's entire traveling party for an Italian feast within a reserved back room inside one of his favorite local haunts. The longtime executive sat in the middle of the private dining area like an emperor reigning over his honored guests. He followed each story with another tale of his personal basketball lore. Colangelo spared no name drop of a famous ally.

The next morning, Colangelo entered Philadelphia's locker room before the Sixers' shootaround at Talking Stick Resort Arena. "We're going to turn this program around," he promised. His authoritative voice cut through the silence. They would not continue this torrid streak of losing. "It might not always be pretty right now, but this is the start of a new beginning," Colangelo preached. Sixers players, once fearing Hinkie's ouster, quickly felt rejuvenated.

"We all looked at each other and just said, 'This guy is the real deal,'" T.J. McConnell says.

"We were just looking for a fresh start," adds Isaiah Canaan.

Out on the court, Brown began the Sixers' walkthrough as usual. Mike D'Antoni had already approached the head coach and addressed the elephant in the room. "I'm with ya," D'Antoni says. "I wouldn't like it if I was you." Colangelo, after all, elevated D'Antoni to Phoenix's head coach back in 2003 after Frank Johnson started 8–13. Brown still yielded the floor for D'Antoni to install a few new sets, but the offensive guru made it clear he was only looking to aid Philadelphia's attack en route to a new head job elsewhere.

"He let Brett do his thing," McConnell says.

The coaches were aligned in championing up-tempo basketball, and D'Antoni introduced a series of "pistol" actions—which feature multiple high screens shortly after the ball handler crosses half-court in transition. Ish Smith promptly scored 14 points and dished five assists in the Sixers' 111–104 win over Jeff Hornacek's struggling Suns. "I come in and we win right away!" D'Antoni teased in the postgame locker room.

They nearly beat Utah two nights later and then sacked the Kings in the third game of Philly's annual West Coast trip. Smith dropped 18 and nine in the five-point win at Sacramento, where D'Antoni's influence pushed the game to a frenetic 104.9 pace that would have led the NBA that season by a wide margin. "He didn't want you thinking, he just wanted you to quick-read and react," Smith says.

Philadelphia's momentum then stopped in Southern California on New Year's Day. Even with Los Angeles' own putrid start—and another lottery pick on the way should it fall in the top three during May's lottery—Kobe Bryant's 7–27 Lakers held home court over the Sixers 93–84.

Los Angeles' 15–4 run midway through the fourth quarter proved to be the game's deciding spurt. Yet Byron Scott yanked D'Angelo Russell with 5:13 remaining after helping lead the Lakers' charge. Beside Bryant's magnanimous retirement tour, Scott's curious endgame substitutions regarding his rookie point guard rippled throughout Los Angeles' third consecutive losing season.

Lakers coaches were preoccupied with how Hollywood's spotlight could impact a 19-year-old. Many had minted Russell as Los Angeles' next star to succeed Bryant. Then he converted only 32.7 percent of his 223 threes through January, after shooting 41 percent at Ohio State. Local sports talk hosts began comparing his production to that of Jahlil Okafor and Kristaps Porzingis, who both averaged over 14 points and seven rebounds as first-years.

Palpable pressure expected Russell to still make the NBA's All-Rookie team. There's nowhere in Los Angeles the Lakers' heir apparent can hide.

After practices, assistant coach Jim Eyen sat Russell down for film study. "As he's learning the pro game, you don't really want him to get caught up in stats," Eyen says. He made sure to highlight Russell's hockey assists more than the helpers that registered in box scores. "'This was great. You did this right. No you didn't score here, but you made the play that led to the pass that led to the score,'" Eyen explained. "'You read the situation exactly like you needed to.'"

Scott would pull Russell when he thought the rookie was freelancing instead of setting the table for teammates. He'd offer varying reasons as to why he benched Russell during crunch time situations. "I think Byron coached D'Angelo from the heart. He did what he thought the best thing for D'Angelo was. It would have been easier had he just taken the path of least resistance," Eyen says. "But he didn't. It's a lot more difficult to try to do it, what you feel is the right way, and discipline when you need to discipline. Pat him on the butt and give him accolades when he deserves it and just do what you feel you need to do for not only the team, but for the long term of the player."

Russell, frankly, disagrees. Scott didn't handle sophomore forward Julius Randle with the same kid gloves. "He's an idiot," Russell says of his coach.

Russell felt Scott often yanked him from close contests purely to spark controversy and attention for his postgame media availability. "I just think he was malicious for no reason," Russell says. "He's a solid man. But as a coach, he was bad. He was just bad at his job."

When Scott summoned Russell back to the bench, Russell would take his most circuitous path in order to duck high-fiving the coaching staff. "I was just young. I used to do all types of shit to avoid talking to him," Russell says. The guard bristled in his seat at the end of Los Angeles' pine. Lakers officials diagnosed the dynamic as evidence of Russell's immaturity issues scouts across the league had flagged before the draft.

Those skeptics didn't hear Russell badger Lou Williams for scoring tricks or ask Metta World Peace how to handle public scrutiny. The teenager often hung out with one of Bryant's private security guards on the road too. One night in Houston, Bryant returned back to his room after meeting with Tim Cook in the hotel lobby.

"Guys go out and party in every city," the Hall of Famer told Russell. "I'm meeting with the CEO of Apple. Think about what you want to do when you're done playing and work on it now, so when the basketball's done for you, you've already built a brand."

Russell admits he failed to grasp many of Bryant's teachings then. "Everything he said to me comes back around all the time," Russell says now. "He used to say this, he used to say that, drop the jewels here." They'd break down specific play sets and how to read various defenses. Russell was young, but he had veterans to check his swagger.

Jerry Colangelo maintained Philadelphia needed a similar figure on Brett Brown's roster.

When Elton Brand returned from vacation, Hinkie amended his offer to a veteran minimum contract. "And you won't have to play," the Sixers' president assured.

Brand accepted, with the caveat that he wanted to learn aspects of team management. Receiving Atlanta's offer helped Brand clarify he hoped to one day run a front office of his own, but he recognized his shortcomings regarding the job's nuances. "You don't know you're responsible for people with dreams, aspirations, raises, who want to feel safe," Brand says.

Hinkie flashed a glimpse of such leadership to clear cap space for the 16-year veteran. Unlike how he cut bait with Tony Wroten, Hinkie explained the maneuver to Christian Wood when he released the promising big man. "I absolutely plan on bringing you back," Hinkie said. "Just kill the D-League, kill that role, and you'll be back in no time."

Whether they were scrappy like T.J. McConnell or rather promising like Robert Covington, when Hinkie developed a fondness for draft prospects such as Wood, he'd harbor that endearment throughout those player's careers. Those youngsters and their agents never complained about his communication style or lack of transparency. "He definitely had a soft spot for some guys," Christian Wood says. "I was glad I was one."

With Brand on board, Okafor seemed to follow wherever he went. "I feel like Elton's main assignment was to mentor Jah and teach Jah the ways, teach him tricks, teach him how to live a healthy NBA lifestyle," guard Nik Stauskas says. Duke players considered themselves a brotherhood, and the big men clearly established such a kinship in Philadelphia.

Brand was charmed by the youngster's compassion. Despite his early season extracurriculars, Okafor has since been widely admired around the league. "Jah's honestly one of the greatest dudes I've ever been around," T.J. McConnell says. "A take-his-shirt-off-his-back-for-you kind of guy."

Okafor and the Sixers bested Karl-Anthony Towns' Timberwolves in Brand's first game on January 4. They thumped Portland 114–89 on January 16 and outplayed Orlando 96 87 on January 20. Philadelphia even swept its season series with Phoenix after a 113–103 win on January 26.

Despite losing out on LaMarcus Aldridge, Suns management still expected head coach Jeff Hornacek's formidable lineup to finally reach the postseason, not drop winnable games to the tanking Sixers.

Starring Brandon Knight and Eric Bledsoe, plus Tyson Chandler teaming up front with Markieff Morris, and P.J. Tucker hounding opposing wings, Phoenix looked dangerous on paper and even started 7–5. Then a four-game drought in late November grew worse after Chandler strained his hamstring. Hornacek's group fumbled five of eight games with third-year Alex Len at center.

After Markieff Morris missed the Suns' December 9 game against Orlando due to a sinus infection, he curiously didn't play during the next four outings even though Morris was active. His trade request still loomed over the franchise. "They really started treating me a lot differently," Morris says. "Some games I'd play, some games I wouldn't."

Morris then earned a two-game suspension for chucking a towel toward Hornacek after the coach yanked him from one fourth quarter. And while Morris watched from the sideline serving his ban, he winced as Eric Bledsoe crashed to the deck during one second quarter. Tyson Chandler and a Suns trainer had to carry the hobbled point guard back to Phoenix's locker room.

Team officials originally hoped Bledsoe would return in six weeks, but a torn left meniscus ultimately ended his 2015–16 campaign. In Bledsoe's stead, rookie guard Devin Booker became the youngest starter in franchise history. The Kentucky product's response—13.8 points and 2.6 assists per game—brought some silver lining to Phoenix's sputtering season, but the Suns' overall demise clouded his promising play. "A lot of losing," Booker says of his rookie year. Phoenix's second blunder against Philadelphia on January 26 dropped Hornacek's group to 14–32 on the season, and marked only the beginning of a treacherous 13-game losing streak.

Suns owner Robert Sarver began polling trusted confidants around the NBA about changing his head coach. This was an unacceptable third year of Hornacek's partnership with general manager Ryan McDonough. "It's been well-documented how emotional he is as an owner," says a Sarver acquaintance. "Just because you're smart doesn't mean you have common sense. He just can't help himself."

Sarver made his millions in real estate development. And like many owners, he sought to apply his success to Phoenix's basketball operations as well. Sarver chatted agents during the pre-draft process. He grew close to certain Suns personnel while hanging around the facilities. And just as Sarver, a lifelong Phoenix fan, had developed a connection with Hornacek during the Suns guard's playing days, the owner was now growing fond of Earl Watson during the assistant's first season with the franchise. "That's repetitively, over the years of Sarver owning the team, that's what happened," says his colleague.

Watson cut his coaching teeth a year earlier with the Spurs' D-League affiliate and harbored the presence many executives thought could make a successful head man one day. A 13-year NBA veteran, Watson emulated his fabled UCLA coach John Wooden, carrying himself with concerted poise and preachy, inspirational quips. Sarver appreciated Watson's approach and began envisioning his future as a play caller. When Phoenix fired assistants Mike Longabardi and Jerry Sichting in late December, the Suns promoted Watson to the front of their bench.

But soon after, the injury bug next nipped Brandon Knight, leaving him with an abductor strain that would require sports hernia surgery, and

T.J. Warren was then lost to a season-ending foot injury. The majority of Phoenix's scoring attack was stuck in the training room. And with the losses mounting, Hornacek ultimately learned his fate from McDonough following the Suns' January 31 defeat in Dallas, their 19th loss in 21 games.

McDonough interviewed Watson, along with assistants Corey Gaines and Nate Bjorkgren, to replace Hornacek, but this was Sarver's one-horse race. The front office hoped Watson could refocus Phoenix's rickety roster and instructed he showcase Markieff Morris before the upcoming trade deadline. In his first move as interim head coach, Watson promptly placed Morris back in the starting lineup and watched the forward score 30 points, grab 11 rebounds, and dish six assists in 41 minutes.

With Hornacek ousted and the trade deadline fast approaching, NBA coaching chatter now shifted to George Karl's status in Sacramento.

The Kings, too, had stumbled out of the postseason picture, standing just 21–31 after dropping eight of nine. By their February 9 off day in Philadelphia before a potential streak-ending victory against the ever-tanking Sixers, Vlade Divac met with Karl, planning to inform the coach he'd be fired during the impending All-Star break.

After falling by 20 the night earlier in Cleveland, DeMarcus Cousins unleashed his latest postgame tirade directed at Karl. The coach often said, "Playing hard in the NBA is a talent, not an attitude," and each time Karl uttered the expression, it boiled Cousins' blood. The All-Star interpreted Karl's coded message as a direct shot. "Boogie had been tainted on George before he got there, anyway," says a Kings assistant.

Before Jarinn Akana, one of Cousins' representatives, became an agent, he spent six seasons with the Nuggets. That is until a later-hired George Karl initiated Akana's removal from his Denver staff. And whenever Cousins now spouted at Karl in Sacramento's coach, he'd accuse the coach of caring more about his standing on the NBA's all-time-wins leaderboard, rather than caring about the Kings' players. Why else would Karl have suggested trading Cousins for a better shot at 50 wins? When rumor first speculated the coach tried to move Sacramento's star ahead of June's draft, Cousins slyly tweeted an emoticon of a snake bookended by two blades of grass. Karl's assistants believed Cousins first heard that concept from Akana.

Karl thought he had swept any underlying tension under the rug during July's Summer League. While assistants ran one of the Kings' practices at a nearby Nevada high school gym, Karl, Cousins, and Vlade Divac regrouped in the cafeteria down the hallway. They poured sodas from the still-plugged-in drink dispensers and cleared the air.

Karl and Divac assured Cousins he was no longer on the trade block. "After the meeting, I thought everybody felt pretty good about it," Karl says. Divac even recruited Caron Butler, his former Lakers teammate in 2004–05, to serve as an intermediary between coach and superstar on the Kings' roster.

"Seriously, I was gonna retire," Butler says. Yet after exchanging pleasantries, Divac asked if the 13-year veteran was still in shape. When Butler confirmed he could still hoop, Sacramento's new chief executive didn't begin negotiating. He instantly offered Butler a two-year deal worth roughly $3 million. "Yeah, I'll fucking play," Butler recalls, chuckling.

While the swingman put pen to paper, Divac assigned him one responsibility: Butler needed to relate to Cousins, unlike Divac's failed attempts. And then he needed to foster a connection between Cousins and Karl.

"Make sure they come together," Divac instructed. "Teach him the business of the game. Talk to Boogie about how the business of basketball works. It's okay to have disagreements and still move forward."

Sacramento's 1–7 start, however, killed any opportunity for harmony that season. Following a 106–88 loss versus San Antonio, frustration burbled throughout the Kings' locker room. Karl addressed the team as normal: he'd watch the film and have more to say the next morning. Each time the coach paused his speech, Cousins grumbled something from his stall. His free throws with 48 seconds left in the third quarter trimmed the Spurs' lead to two, yet San Antonio built a 96–80 edge by the 4:30 mark of the fourth.

"All of a sudden, DeMarcus just goes off. 'Fuck you, Coach! Fuck you! You think you're a motherfucking Hall of Famer coach? You ain't shit!'" assistant Vance Walberg recalls. "'All the fuck you care about is wins. Fuck you!'"

Caron Butler rushed to bring Divac into the locker room, hoping the Kings executive could defuse matters. "He didn't do a damn thing," Walberg says. Cousins made clear he thought Karl's Las Vegas spiel was bullshit, and that Divac was still fishing to trade him.

"I actually thought that when it happened, it was going to be a good thing for us," Karl says. "I felt it had to happen."

But the air was far from cleared. Most teammates supported Cousins. Karl pushed all of their buttons during practices, especially Boogie's. "It was kind of funny, but not funny at the same time," says Kings guard Seth Curry. "Every day they got into it about something and every day I'd come home with a different story."

Coaches pleaded for Divac, along with Peja Stojaković, another Kings legend Sacramento had hired as director of player personnel, to hand Cousins a five-game suspension for his outburst in San Antonio. They needed to establish an organizational hierarchy. "He motherfucked George left and right," Walberg says. "What kind of control do you have as a coach the rest of the year? You've lost the locker room. Players can say anything and do anything they want."

Divac ultimately determined they would merely fine Cousins. He and Stojaković somehow marked the members of Sacramento's front office with the most power, yet least experience. "Vlade sabotaged that season right then and there when he made that decision," Walberg says.

"I think DeMarcus felt he still had control," adds Karl.

Even some of Cousins' allies on the roster felt he needed to be reprimanded in some capacity. No players-only meeting would ever help overcome Cousins and Karl's irreparable divide. "We could never get past that," Caron Butler says. Sure enough, Cousins' postgame antics in Cleveland three months later followed a nearly identical script.

And so Divac met Karl in Philadelphia on February 9, expecting to change Sacramento's coach for the third time in Vivek Ranadivé's three-year ownership. Divac revealed he needed until day's end to make a decision.

Karl promptly took his staff for what many assistants expected to be their final lunch together. An obvious tension blanketed the meal. One coach finally asked Karl to end their state of purgatory. He phoned Divac, but there was no response. Karl took the call outside when Divac rang back a few minutes later. Assistants watched him through the window.

When Karl returned to their table, he shrugged. "They're keeping us," he said.

Some coaches groaned, having come to terms with their once-destined finality. "Fuck," one responded. "Let's get this shit show over with."

They rallied to beat the Sixers that evening, somehow entering the All-Star break with a victory and their job status intact.

Kings staffers sorely needed a reprieve. Only when Vance Walberg returned to Sacramento's facility the following Wednesday, 24 hours before the February 18 trade deadline, Divac ordered the assistant into his office.

An hour before Kings practice, Peja Stojaković and assistant general manager Mike Bratz sat on hand as Divac announced, "We're going to fire you, Vance." Walberg asked for their reasoning, and Divac explained Ranadivé had ordered for somebody on Karl's staff to be cut. "We decided it should be you," Divac deadpanned.

"To let George know that they're in control," Walberg says.

Another power struggle unfolded in Orlando. Across the NBA's race to the bottom, it seemed only Boston had emerged from the crop of rebuilds, launched by burgeoning analytical executives around the league, as a sturdy playoff contender by the spring of 2016. It's no coincidence Celtics ownership empowered Danny Ainge back in 2003 and haven't meddled in front office power dynamics since.

Magic general manager Rob Hennigan had filled Jacque Vaughn's head coaching vacancy with the hard-nosed Scott Skiles, whom Hennigan thought could provide structure for the franchise's inexperienced, yet talented roster. Skiles signed on after Hennigan pitched the coach an integral role determining which young pieces to keep building around.

There were few plans to cut any big checks just yet, but Orlando did re-sign Tobias Harris for four-years and $64 million. If the 23-year-old continued his progression—scoring 17.1 points and grabbing 6.3 rebounds per game on 36.4 percent shooting from deep in 2014–15—he would likely outplay that contract by the end of its second season. But despite the financial commitment, Harris remained just one of several poles for Orlando's offense.

"Again, we still didn't know who the man was," says forward Channing Frye. "Was it Tobias, was it [Nik Vučević], was it [Aaron Gordon], was it Elfrid Payton?"

A former Magic point guard himself, Skiles naturally rode Payton and Victor Oladipo harder than most, and the coach's demanding training camp was followed by a surprising 19–13 start for Orlando. From the beginning, Skiles believed it was Oladipo who possessed All-Star potential capable of leading a contending franchise, but his staff also needed to prioritize Harris' development, in hopes he'd be worth that contract, either on the Magic's roster or for Hennigan's front office on the trade market.

When Orlando dropped four straight, falling to 19–17, Skiles began growing concerned how naturally the young Magic accepted defeat; it didn't sting more than winning thrilled. And an eight-game drought in January soon sunk Orlando to 20–25. Agents phoned Hennigan to reiterate their clients' complaints that Skiles' rigorous midseason practices left them drained for games. "As a vet, you understand his toughness," Frye says. "He was trying to teach discipline in us and try creating a culture of winning and hard-nosed toughness."

Yet every Magic player was already plastered on banners across their Amway Center concourse, despite none of their young phenoms having yet to even compete for the playoffs with Orlando. "When a guy's a rookie and he's being treated like a Super Bowl MVP every single day, but not winning the game, playing to win the game is not the top priority," says one Magic staffer. "You're playing with fire eventually."

The first flame crackled on February 16. Two days before the trade deadline, Orlando abruptly shipped Tobias Harris to Detroit for point guard Brandon Jennings and forward Ersan İlyasova. Skiles had coached both Jennings and İlyasova in Milwaukee, and many within Orlando believed he forced Harris out of Disney World in favor of veterans to regroup for a postseason run. "Skiles wanted to win and bring in more vets and winners, when [the front office] were like, 'Hey, we're gonna play these guys because they're talented, and see who pops their head up first,'" says Channing Frye.

Harris' production had dropped noticeably after his payday. The front office saw Jennings' expiring contract as a way to create financial flexibility for 2016–17 and believed İlyasova's perimeter presence could fill Frye's void—Hennigan also sent the veteran forward to Cleveland to chase a title. No matter; uncertainty still lingered from who had truly pulled the trigger on moving Harris. Some young Magic players hardly spoke to Jennings and İlyasova. They lost trust in Skiles, fearing they too could be next sent out of town. "It was such a bad experience," İlyasova says. "I wish it never happened."

Meanwhile, Ryan McDonough attempted to diffuse the tension in Phoenix's locker room by moving Markieff Morris to Washington, banking a top-nine-protected 2016 first-rounder in return.

Three years after McDonough's initial roster purge for draft capital, he was still chasing picks and salary relief. Jeff Hornacek once found surprising success with young contributors in this regime's first year, but had they merely endured so much whiplash of a point guard roller coaster simply to return back to the same starting point? With all their machinations, the Suns were destined for the lottery once again, and not nearly high enough to land a generational difference maker. If any teams were stuck on the treadmill of mediocrity, look no further than the Suns, Magic, and Kings.

Sam Hinkie's rebuild, on the other hand, stood nowhere near NBA purgatory, on pace to potentially set the league record for fewest wins in a season. Unlike previous dizzying trade deadlines, Philadelphia's president swung just one trade before the February 18 horn sounded. To help facilitate Houston trading 7-footer Donatas Motiejūnas to Detroit, the Sixers planned to absorb Joel Anthony's $2.5 million salary to land another 2017 second-round pick. Hinkie waived JaKarr Sampson to create a roster spot despite the swingman's promise.

Detroit hoped Motiejūnas' shooting finesse would blend with center Andre Drummond, but the Pistons were dubious of the big man's bothersome back. Sure enough, their doctors ultimately failed Motiejūnas' physical and rescinded the three-team swap. "He's never been able to get back to where he was," Detroit president and coach Stan Van Gundy says. Indeed, Motiejūnas only played 37 more games in his NBA career.

In Philadelphia, Sixers players celebrated the deal's err. Without Anthony's contract, veteran forward Carl Landry explained to his naive teammates, Philadelphia remained around $3 million below the league's salary floor of $63 million that season. If the Sixers' payroll didn't exceed that minimum threshold, by rule, that $3 million difference would be evenly dispersed amongst the players on Philadelphia's roster at season's end. For those signed to Hinkie's minimum specials, another $200,000 would have been manna from heaven. "Getting some extra cash would have been pretty cool," T.J. McConnell says.

When news broke of the trade falling apart, the Sixers' group text message fluttered with cheers. "Everybody was like, 'We want our money! We want our money!'" Ish Smith recalls.

Philadelphia coincidentally visited Detroit the following Wednesday on February 24. Landry flagged Anthony down during warmups.

"Bro, it would have been great to have you, but we are so happy you didn't come," he teased.

Throughout the contest, Landry called down to the end of Philly's bench, leading a coordinated cheer.

"Do we want Joel Anthony on this team!" he bellowed.

"Hell no!" his teammates chanted.

"Do you want Joel Anthony on your team!" Landry cried.

"Hell no!" the chorus responded.

"Everyone was so hyped we weren't getting Joel Anthony," Nik Stauskas giggles now.

Elton Brand joined the cheers, but he remained adamant the Sixers wouldn't be getting cut an additional check. Too many weeks separated them from the end of the regular season. "Management's not gonna give us extra money for being as bad as we are," Brand warned.

The players' celebration indeed ended on March 7, when Sam Hinkie claimed forward Sonny Weems and his $2.8 million salary off waivers. Brett Brown's unit was more than accustomed to welcoming new faces, but this time few Sixers players embraced Weems' arrival. "It was just a situation where, yo, my palms was itching!" Ish Smith says. "I thought it was gonna work out."

When Hinkie waived Weems just a few weeks later, it further stunned the once-hopeful youngsters on Philadelphia's roster. "We all felt that we were the ones going through it all year, we were the ones going through a lot of bullshit, it kind of sucked to see they signed a guy for 20 days and we all could have split the $3 million," Stauskas says.

On the surface, Hinkie and Jerry Colangelo seemed like the NBA's most unlikely odd couple. Philadelphia's president still navigated his cap sheet with a thin razor. "Everything seemed okay with Jerry," says one Sixers scout.

But behind closed doors, Colangelo had asked Hinkie for a list of personnel men he'd like to work with. Colangelo and ownership wanted to hire essentially an equal for Hinkie, someone to balance decision-making and personalities on a more established basis than Colangelo. It would have created an unheard-of even split of power atop an NBA front office.

With Hinkie's suggestions supposedly considered, the Sixers' list of candidates "was very quickly whittled down to two," one Sixers staffer says, by Colangelo, ownership, and CEO Scott O'Neil. Only Danny Ferry and Colangelo's son, Bryan, emerged as serious contenders. Joshua Harris had met with Ferry previously back in 2012, before the executive took Atlanta's general manager job. Bryan had interest but preferred to pursue Brooklyn's vacancy. The Nets had parted ways with Billy King's regime to begin 2016.

Not only was Brooklyn lottery-bound, but the struggling Nets owed their pick to Boston from the fabled 2013 trade for Kevin Garnett and Paul Pierce, though neither remained on the roster. Rebuilding the Nets into a contender presented the perfect uphill battle for Bryan to escape his father's shadow. Even after winning NBA Executive of the Year in Toronto in 2007, where the Raptors won 47 games following a 27–55 season in 2005–06, his No. 1 pick in the 2006 NBA Draft, Andrea Bargnani, fell far short of expectations, and drew harsh criticism until Bryan ultimately stepped down in June 2013.

Brett Brown remained fiercely loyal to Sam Hinkie, and championed Danny Ferry for the role. Brown had overlapped with Ferry back in San Antonio and they had maintained a friendship. Ferry also played his college ball at Duke.

Ferry spoke with Hinkie throughout the winter, hashing out the particulars on how their partnership could function. Hinkie came to like Ferry but struggled to find a division of responsibility that didn't seem like a full loss of his influence. "For him to even consider being co-GMs was ridiculous," says one Sixers staffer.

Philadelphia kept losing all the while. The Sixers dropped 11 straight after returning from the All-Star break. Then Brooklyn chose another Spurs disciple, Sean Marks, to pilot its basketball operations instead of Bryan, and the younger Colangelo eagerly reentered his name into the field.

Ferry at one point had appeared like the clear frontrunner, but then management began discussing the executive's full history. Ferry was only available for Philadelphia after parting ways with Atlanta in June 2015, eight months after he took a leave of absence for making racially insensitive remarks about Luol Deng on a conference call. "I believe Danny Ferry would have been the No. 1 guy for that possible stop had that tape not come up," says one Sixers official. Jerry Colangelo soon began pushing ownership on Bryan's behalf, and by late March, they were in contract negotiations.

Whispers of the arrangement finally trickled throughout Philadelphia's facilities. With Jerry having ownership's ear, Hinkie would be outvoted on any potential disagreement with Bryan. "It was a ludicrous proposition that it would work," says one Sixers official. All the while, Brett Brown's group was stuck at nine wins, one shy of avoiding the worst record in NBA history, 9–73, set by the 1972–73 Sixers.

They nearly captured a 10th victory on March 23 in Denver, but Emmanuel Mudiay's prayer at the buzzer, from just inside half-court, flipped Philly's two-point edge into a one-point defeat. "We were like, 'Maybe it's just not meant [to be],'" says rookie Richaun Holmes.

Elton Brand felt his teammates didn't recognize their dire circumstances. Only a handful of games remained for the chance to avoid eternal infamy. Every time a future team was mired amid a poor season, these Sixers would be the comparison as the golden standard of NBA losing. "We were running out of time," Brand says.

Most players circled their April 5 home match with New Orleans as a winnable battle. The Pelicans were badly injured and also headed to the lottery. "They pretty much had a D-League squad," says guard Nik Stauskas.

One practice during the days before their matchup with New Orleans, coaches and players arrived at PCOM to see a banner stretching across their entrance to the facility. "Congratulations 2015–16 Philadelphia 76ers Worst-Team in NBA History" it mockingly read. Each team employee's name was printed on the signage, from the injured Joel Embiid to equipment manager Scott Rego. "Who put this shit up here!" fumed Embiid.

Other players matched his contempt. "It was awkward, people not really knowing how to take it," says Lance Pearson, the analytics staffer. Finally, Elton Brand revealed he'd been behind the stunt.

The veteran's message was meant to be motivational, but it was New Orleans that took a 29–21 lead later that night. Perhaps thoughts of Brand's banner fueled Philadelphia's comeback, though, as the Sixers outscored their visitors by 23 points over the second and third quarters and never looked back. "Everybody came in with some juice," says Ish Smith. The Sixers would hold on 107–93 for that elusive 10th win.

In the morning, Hinkie met with Christian Wood and his agent to make good on his word. He signed the potential-packed big man to another non-guaranteed, multi-year deal that, with only four games to play, essentially doubled Wood's 2015–16 earnings to north of $300,000.

The 20-year-old returned home, smiling over such a fortuitous payday, and was surprised to see Hinkie ring his cell later that afternoon.

The executive suddenly began apologizing. "I'm not going to be a part of the team anymore," Hinkie began. "I know you're a great talent. I'm going to be watching out for what you can do."

Hinkie soon after submitted a 13-page resignation letter to Joshua Harris' ownership group. "I no longer have the confidence that I can make good decisions on behalf of investors in the Sixers," he penned. With Bryan Colangelo's imminent arrival, Hinkie knew his regime's style of operations was all but over.

"Once that was the decision handed down, naturally Sam was out," says a Sixers official. "He wasn't willing to have his influence compromised to that degree."

"Clearly it was out of his control at that point," says one Sixers scout.

By that evening, someone leaked Hinkie's manifesto to ESPN.com. Many traditional thinkers across the basketball community jeered the obscure references littered throughout the writing, such as the extinction of a flightless New Zealand bird species called the moa.

Hinkie was stunned to see his private thoughts aired to the public. Perhaps his miscalculation of that possibility emphasized the media defiance that ultimately derailed his tenure. Had he placated the local columnists who called for his head with interview access, had he spoken to the press in the aftermath of Jahlil Okafor's Boston incident, perhaps he'd still be running the 76ers.

EPILOGUE

The day following Sam Hinkie's resignation, Sixers owner Joshua Harris gathered Philadelphia's full basketball operations staff on the court at PCOM. Rows of folding chairs topped the hardwood as Harris rambled for 10 minutes, tossing platitudes about not wanting Hinkie to leave.

Technically, history should agree. Harris, however, never acknowledged to the assembled Sixers employees how each of his ownership group's reactionary decisions, from December 2015 through March 2016, diminished Hinkie's agency, and ultimately encouraged his resignation. Because by week's end, they were already introducing Philadelphia's new president and general manager, while his father, Jerry, conveniently stepped down as chairman.

Bryan Colangelo equally prided himself on his connections and scouting ability. Unlike his father, Colangelo did say he'd come to appreciate the value of analytics and sports science. Yet Philadelphia's new president hardly ever noted the Sixers' 26.9 percent chance to land the No. 1 pick that May was both in thanks to Philadelphia's 10–72 league-worst record that Hinkie's moves garnered, as well as the Sixers' additional 1.9 percent chance thanks to Hinkie's pick swap with Sacramento from acquiring Nik Stauskas. The Sixers organization hardly ever mentioned Hinkie's name again.

Still, anticipation across the Delaware Valley had reached a fever pitch by the day of that May's lottery. And then hours before the actual drawing, former 76ers center Dikembe Mutombo infamously tweeted congratulations to Philly for winning the top spot in June's draft. With conspiracy theories intertwined throughout the lottery's 30-year history, dating back to that 1985 frozen envelope, online skeptics began claiming this very drawing was also rigged, new commissioner Adam Silver purportedly following suit of his predecessor, offering a reward, perhaps, for Sixers ownership ostensibly pushing Hinkie out of office.

Mutombo quickly deleted the post after realizing his error. NBA PR had emailed Mutombo the message to tweet if—and only if—the Sixers did win the first pick. Mutombo misread the request as something to do immediately. But when Philadelphia did in fact land the No. 1 choice that evening, the whispers of collusion only found greater wind.

Inside PCOM, there was only jubilation. "There was a huge sense of relief," says one Sixers scout. After three years of misery, Philadelphia would finally have the chance at the draft's top prospect. That year's: LSU star Ben Simmons.

Silver would order Mutombo into the NBA's offices. His internet err was a critical mistake from an official league ambassador. Mutombo even had to passionately fight to keep his role. "I almost lost my job," Mutombo says. As part of the incident's resolution, he decided to no longer operate his social media accounts moving forward. "It was so embarrassing," Mutombo says. "It changed the way I tweet."

Philly's outcome also marked the second straight lottery where the NBA's worst franchise landed the top pick. And by the following May, Boston also drew the No. 1 selection, utilizing their final pick swap with the now lowly Nets, thanks to Brooklyn's 25 percent lottery odds as the league's bottom-feeder.

Before this three-year streak—Minnesota in 2015, Philly in 2016, and then Boston by way of Brooklyn in 2017—the previous team with the worst record that claimed No. 1 was Orlando, way back in 2004. The string of successive results, though, did nothing to quell the concerns mounting from league headquarters to many team front offices, traditionalists fretting NBA stratagem's growing appeal for tanking. It wasn't just Philadelphia with Joel Embiid and Ben Simmons. Come June 2017, Boston was slated to add another future superstar thanks to yet another tanking-created top choice.

The Celtics traded away Hall of Famers and intentionally fumbled the 2013–14 season, then kept choosing at the top of the draft while owning

Brooklyn's additional lottery tickets. Two choices after Simmons went to Philly in 2016, Boston nabbed Cal swingman Jaylen Brown at No. 3. And winning the 2017 lottery ultimately added Duke phenom Jayson Tatum to the Celtics' rebuild. It took a lot of roster mixing and matching, but Tatum and Brown quickly bloomed into All-Stars, a bona fide dynamic duo that would help lead Boston to three conference finals appearances between 2017 and 2020, before the tandem starred among the Celtics' breakthrough 2022 NBA Finals appearance.

And when Joel Embiid finally debuted for Philadelphia during the 2016–17 season, his thrilling first campaign flashed obvious All-Star capabilities. The center posted 20.2 points, 7.8 rebounds, and 2.5 blocks per game, looking everything the part of a young, new-age Hakeem Olajuwon, as promised. Embiid and Simmons became mainstays of the February All-Star Game, too, first leading Philadelphia into the second round of the playoffs by 2018, where the Sixers became a fixture of the Eastern Conference post-season right alongside Boston. Embiid would fully morph into a perennial MVP candidate, with giant shoulders strong enough to carry a franchise for the better part of a decade.

"People [started] talking so much more about lottery reform and structural things as a result of that," says Celtics assistant general manager Mike Zarren.

When the NBA's Board of Governors did regroup in late September 2017, much of the discussion indeed centered on reforming the draft lottery once and for all. League officials pushed a cleaner version of flattening the worst teams' odds that was suggested back in 2014. "It was a priority for the NBA," says then Pacers executive Peter Dinwiddie.

"The league really wanted to pass it," adds one general manager, "so we wanted to be supportive."

In the end, Oklahoma City represented the lone vote in opposition to reform. Even Joshua Harris had curiously aligned with Adam Silver's cause. "The race to the bottom, and having a 25 percent chance versus a 14 percent chance, some teams were making a mockery of the season," says Elton Brand. By that fateful vote, Brand had fulfilled his own manifest destiny and joined Philadelphia's front office, en route to becoming the team's general manager.

The lottery changes wouldn't actualize until 2019's May drawing, affording clubs a brief window until the three worst teams began inheriting an equal 14 percent chance at the top pick. The new system also introduced a fourth drawing in addition to the first three picks. Then all remaining teams would be slated Nos. 5-14, by record. When the results were announced, Daryl Morey facetiously tweeted at his old colleague, "@samhinkie tanking is solved."

No league personnel expected their reform to completely abolish tanking, but they hoped flattening the odds would at least help dissuade any years-long futility that Hinkie's Sixers, and the rest of the NBA's tanking era, had so famously demonstrated.

"If it didn't happen, there would have been no reason to change the lottery rules," says Mavericks owner Mark Cuban.

"The advantage to being extremely bad is [now] lower," says one team executive. "So if the goal was to eliminate the media coverage of it, you could argue they succeeded in that so far."

The response to tanking escalated even further. Come 2021, the league introduced an annual NBA Play-In Tournament—only complete, of course, with naming rights for a lucky corporate sponsor. Under this new calendar format, the 10-seed and 9-seed in each conference now suddenly clinch spots in a nationally televised elimination game. The loser of that battle heads home, and back into the lottery drawing room where they belong. The winner, in what became a controversial twist, plays the loser of another Play-In Tournament bout between each conference's seventh and eighth seeds. From there, just 48 minutes separate the two remaining teams from clinching the final spot in their half of the postseason bracket.

The league surely expected more teams to fight for the postseason than greater lottery positioning—especially with those lower odds. Two more teams were inheriting a shot at a playoff spot. And in the first two seasons of the Play-In Tournament, the Western Conference saw one team from the newfound 9-vs.-10 games improbably surge into the playoffs. It's created a must-see television event with massive stakes, the NBA's miniature rival to March Madness.

All this change, however, still hasn't completely quelled dilapidated franchises, desperate for their prodigy who can lift them out of NBA purgatory, from racing to the league's bottom. Once the Thunder's title window officially slammed shut in Oklahoma City, Sam Presti traded off his remaining All-Stars and sunk right back to the depths of the standings just as the Thunder had in the past. Even with lottery reform and the Play-In, OKC nosedived into the 2020s with a record chest of draft capital, and no rush to launch back toward contention anytime soon.

Smaller markets, like Oklahoma City and Minnesota, have little margin for error in roster construction. Those franchises don't boast the luxuries that befit Los Angeles, offering superstar free agents the allure of Hollywood and a rich championship history to boot. The Lakers can bounce back from a few years of futility, unlike less-glitzy franchises such as Orlando and Sacramento—the other case studies of this league-wide rebuilding experiment.

The Timberwolves, for example, never built a true contender around Kevin Love in the mid 2010s, and promptly sunk to the league's basement after trading him. Because even if a top pick, even *the* top pick like Andrew Wiggins, flounders within his first playing environment, teams are still gambling on rare talent to eventually mold into winning skill sets. Wiggins only made one postseason appearance with the Timberwolves. But after a mid-season trade to Golden State in 2020, Wiggins emerged as the second-best player in the Warriors' 2022 championship run behind only Stephen Curry. And after the Timberwolves stumbled their way back to the No. 1 pick in the 2020 NBA Draft Lottery, Minnesota emerged with a young, charismatic phenom named Anthony Edwards from the University of Georgia, who almost-instantly helped Karl-Anthony Towns power the Wolves back into the playoff picture.

Drafting a one-day superstar can mask many a franchise's missteps. By October 2018, Phoenix owner Robert Sarver axed Ryan McDonough. The Suns appointed a total of five different play callers during McDonough's four-year tenure. Phoenix's own analytical executive fumbled the team's head coaching post, ultimately traded Eric Bledsoe in November 2017 at the point guard's request, and later moved Brandon Knight after injuries riddled his

Phoenix tenure. How ironic that, one week before the start of the 2018–19 season, McDonough's staff was fired for ultimately failing to supplement Devin Booker, by then a budding All-Star, with an adequate starting point guard. Phoenix's three-headed dragon had been slain.

But Booker slowly bloomed into one of the league's most dangerous scoring threats. When the Suns plummeted their way into the No. 1 pick in the 2019, they selected Arizona center Deandre Ayton to pair with Booker in the pick-and-roll. And by 2021, Chris Paul saw a full-formed rotation around the Suns' two young stars—Mikal Bridges and Cam Johnson marked two more successful Phoenix lottery picks—and Paul made sure he could be traded to join such a promising upstart. The Suns went on to win over 70 percent of their games in those first two seasons with Paul, with a 2021 NBA Finals appearance on their résumé, all despite Sarver's whimsical decision-making, and a toxic workplace culture that would come to light in future reporting.

Measuring an organization's stability and success starts at the top. Vivek Ranadivé's basketball operations antics in Sacramento has played quite an integral factor in the Kings' elongated postseason drought. Tanking doesn't pay dividends amid a franchise's never-ending cycle of musical chairs.

Sacramento did mercifully fire George Karl at the end of the 2015–16 season, mere 16 months after terminating Mike Malone before him. The next head coach, Dave Joerger, then lasted only three seasons himself. No matter who led Ranadivé's bench or inhabited his front office, infighting seemed to persist. Even Vlade Divac eventually lost his good standing with Ranadivé.

After Sacramento traded DeMarcus Cousins to New Orleans in February 2017—effectively netting sharpshooter Buddy Hield plus 2017 first- and second-round picks—Joerger and Kings assistant general manager Brandon Williams squabbled over the coach's 2018–19 rotations favoring veterans, versus developing Sacramento's young lottery selections. Both men would be gone from the Kings come season's end. By 2022, Ranadivé's stewardship had fully created NBA infamy. The Kings set a league record for the most consecutive seasons without a playoff appearance.

With Rob Hennigan's Magic, Orlando compiled multiple future All-Stars and contributing veterans, but his regime failed to match Oklahoma City's prolific rise with Kevin Durant, Russell Westbrook, and James Harden. Orlando's own turnstile of coaches kept confusing organizational messages. Scott Skiles abruptly resigned after the 2015–16 season, the final result of those lingering frustrations with the front office. The following year, Orlando ousted Hennigan as general manager, in April 2017, without a playoff appearance on his résumé.

By the 2021 trade deadline, the Magic's new front office opted for what any analytical acolyte would choose for a franchise mired in mediocrity, what any team without its central star would sensibly decide. Orlando first moved Aaron Gordon to the Denver Nuggets for a young recent first-round pick named R.J. Hampton and a future opening-round selection. They shipped out Evan Fournier for two second-rounders, and Orlando hit the jackpot dealing Nikola Vučević for two-first round picks plus a young prospect in Wendell Carter Jr., the talented former Duke big man.

In that May's draft lottery, Orlando slipped to No. 5 thanks to the newer, more volatile odds. But the Magic still came away with a highly regarded point guard out of Gonzaga named Jalen Suggs. And only one year later, Orlando lucked into the No. 1 pick at the 2022 NBA Draft Lottery in Chicago. The Magic would famously keep their selection under wraps until the final hour before they went on the clock. While the entire league, and betting marketplace, long expected Orlando to select Auburn forward Jalen Smith, the Magic shocked the basketball world by choosing another Duke prodigy, a 6-foot-10 versatile threat named Paolo Banchero.

Will Banchero and Suggs be able to lead Orlando as far as Embiid has taken Philly, or Booker has powered Phoenix, or Tatum and Brown have spearheaded Boston? That all remains to be seen as of this writing. But you can rest assured the Magic are fully on board with tanking and taking its rewards. After Orlando's front office, by then led by Jeff Weltman and John Hammond, sold off Gordon, Vučević, and Fournier, Magic ownership extended their lead executives' contracts through the 2025–26 season.

The Lakers always existed as the independent variable of the NBA's tanking era.

Palace intrigue may have shrouded the Lakers more than anyone. The Buss siblings couldn't agree. The coaches and front office quibbled over playing style. Instead of maintaining financial flexibility to supplement Kobe Bryant, Los Angeles upheld his astronomical salary and mired its chances at signing LeBron James and Carmelo Anthony back in 2014 free agency, months before it ever began. They then lost out on LaMarcus Aldridge in 2015 and failed to even land a meeting with Kevin Durant in 2016. As a result, Jeanie Buss dismissed her brother Jim as Los Angeles' vice president and Mitch Kupchak as general manager in February 2017.

Yet lo and behold, just four years after the Lakers botched his 2014 availability, LeBron James planted his flag in Southern California during 2018 free agency, as intrigued by Hollywood's screen opportunities as the roster's stockpile of young lottery selections—from four years of inadvertently tanking. With James on board, winning a title once again became the Lakers' immediate expectation. No matter Los Angeles' errs, Mitch Kupchak and Jim Buss were somewhat vindicated, for believing a superstar would once again be attracted by their city's bright lights.

"The Lakers [were] way more poorly managed than any team," says one rival executive.

They will, however, always be the franchise for icons. And while the Lakers flubbed Bryant's final three seasons, their loyalty to their superstar and his glamorous final jaunt around the NBA in 2015–16—capped by a remarkable 60-point game—spoke to alphas like LeBron James. "You can screw up, but if you have the market and the brand, people are still gonna be attracted to you," says the exec.

As NBA payrolls approached $100 million starting in 2016—due to the league's 2014 $2.6 billion television deal—players also began changing teams far more frequently, sometimes earning as much in one season as an equivalent player would have grossed from a three-year contract in the early 2000s. The next decade, team payrolls would continue soaring toward $200 million, leaving some veteran franchise faces earning over $50 million a season.

All-Stars kept leaving their incumbent franchises to fortify title contenders elsewhere. Like LaMarcus Aldridge left Portland for San Antonio, Kevin

Durant eventually departed Oklahoma City for Golden State, and then left Golden State to team up with Kyrie Irving in Brooklyn. Kawhi Leonard flocked to the Clippers in 2019, where Paul George joined him. Whenever a situation grows stale, teams with cap space are eager to offer these talents another max contract. "There's only so many All-Stars," says Kentucky head coach John Calipari.

And whether clubs tank to acquire those alphas with a top pick, or luck into an MVP like the Bucks did with Giannis Antetokounmpo at No. 15 in 2013, if they can't support him with a contending cast, organization after organization falls prey to All-NBA talents like Anthony Davis requesting to play elsewhere. The appeal of joining forces with another superstar always allures. "The best way to add a max free agent is to have another one already," says one Pelicans executive.

Of course, the cleanest way to "have another one already" is…by landing him in the draft. "I think tanking has kind of been a part of putting the super-teams together to a certain extent," says John Hammond, now Orlando's general manager. With franchises so willing to throw away seasons, just for the mere chance to draft a player of Davis' quality, those superstars naturally gained greater influence in the NBA ecosystem.

By the time Davis made his trade request in 2019, he only had eyes for joining Los Angeles, which in turn limited the quality of offers New Orleans first received for its centerpiece. The jury was out. "Anthony wanted to go there because LeBron was there," says the Pelicans official. Like Kevin Love and so many others before Davis, no rival team would trade for him knowing he planned to bolt for the Lakers in 2020 free agency, if Davis wasn't in fact sent to Los Angeles.

And when the new lottery system improbably handed Los Angeles the fourth pick, it brought one last piece for the Lakers to offer in exchange for Davis.

Because just like New Orleans, the Lakers had rested James, hampered by a supposed injury, during the final stretch of the 2018–19 regular season, vying for greater lottery positioning. They'd had years of practice losing games. Lineups and rotations quickly grew thinner and thinner. "They weren't trying to win anymore," says Hawks general manager Travis Schlenk.

Los Angeles had just a 2.8 percent chance at landing that fourth pick. Plus, under the old lottery system, they wouldn't have lucked into that slot, because the Smartplay device would have only auctioned off the first three choices.

"The Lakers fell ass-backward into No. 4 and used that for the Anthony Davis trade," says another rival executive.

To obtain Davis, Los Angeles surrendered its newly acquired 2019 fourth pick; Brandon Ingram, its No. 2 choice in 2016; Lonzo Ball, the No. 2 pick in 2017; Josh Hart, selected 30th in 2017; plus the Lakers' top-eight-protected 2021 and unprotected 2024 first-rounders, and the right to swap firsts in 2023. New Orleans then moved No. 4 to Atlanta for the Hawks' picks at Nos. 8, 17, and 35 in the 2019 draft.

The Pelicans' new surplus of assets suddenly challenged any potential trade package for the next disgruntled superstar of Anthony Davis' caliber. New Orleans used two future picks to acquire CJ McCollum at the 2022 trade deadline, who helped shoot the Pelicans into the playoffs, by way of the Play-In Tournament, mind you. And New Orleans stood in prime position to throw a hoard of picks at Brooklyn the moment Kevin Durant requested a trade from the Nets, mere hours before free agency began that June, perpetuating the vicious cycle of NBA superstar turnover. Dizzying, right?

Sixers ownership decided to build their new headquarters along the Camden, New Jersey, waterfront, which allowed for their $82 million, 125,000-square foot complex that now houses both corporate and basketball operations, hoping to one day help lure stars like LeBron James or Kevin Durant. Natural light now pours across two sparkling practice courts. State-of the-art training equipment borders the hardwood. As Sam Hinkie once envisioned, the building's structure funnels Philadelphia's roster from their players' entrance, to the kitchen, to the locker room, and so on, gradually shifting their focus toward the court. Philly's skyline, from across the Delaware River, emerges above the treetops rooted behind the players' parking lot. The team's business operations are located in another shimmering glass building across the Sixers' grassy campus.

EPILOGUE

They've erected statues along the pavement that connects the two buildings, dubbing it Philadelphia's "Legends Walk." The Sixers have immortalized Wilt Chamberlain, Julius Erving, and others. They honored Charles Barkley with his own bronze commemorative in September 2019.

A cheery mood filled the noon event. Joel Embiid and Ben Simmons had cemented their All-Star footing that previous winter. Only a dramatic buzzer-beater that swung Game 7 against Toronto in the second round ended Philly's inspiring 2018–19 season. The Sixers billed as bona fide contenders. Hinkie's meticulous orchard was now bearing its fruit, despite his glaring absence.

He settled in Northern California, dabbling in myriad venture capital and data projects, while teaching business courses at Stanford, such as "Negotiation Dynamics in Sports, Entertainment and Media." Ordering 50 pizzas for free doesn't seem to be on the syllabus.

Hinkie wonders how the basketball community discusses his legacy without mentioning his Houston years. He's inextricably linked to Philadelphia's polarizing process, but hardly ever acknowledged for his critical role in landing James Harden with Houston, where the guard blossomed into a historic scorer. His naysayers always retort that Michael Carter-Williams, Nerlens Noel, and Jahlil Okafor were failed selections, even though Hinkie, frankly, accepted that outcome as a possibility.

He never professed a perfect draft record. He openly sought more darts to toss at the board than his opponents, expecting there could be a few misses along the way. The lottery, for all its benefits, regardless of its format, has always complicated matters for even the most thorough of tanking teams. No matter your scouting, rebuilding through the draft ultimately comes down to a matter of chance. Zion Williamson would have otherwise been a Knick. That's why David Stern first introduced the drawing in 1985. Houston's blatant tanking effort in pursuit of the 1984 No. 1 pick, where the Rockets drafted future Hall of Famer Hakeem Olajuwon, first set the wheels in motion, just like Hinkie's rebuild eventually sparked Adam Silver's lottery reform over 30 years later.

The Rockets stood 24–37 way back on March 6, 1984, three games above the lowly San Diego Clippers. Remember, before Stern's novel lottery, the

NBA awarded the first two picks by coin flip between the two worst teams in each conference.

Then Sixers owner Harold Katz anxiously followed San Diego's and Houston's race to the bottom of the West. Philadelphia held the Clippers' pick thanks to a previous trade, and seemed destined for a top-two selection, guaranteeing either Olajuwon or the dynamic North Carolina wing named Michael Jordan.

But Houston went just 5–16 to close out the regular season, while San Diego somehow notched a season-high 146 points for its 30th win on the final night of the year. The 29–53 Rockets managed to sneak into that fateful coin flip, while the Clippers would only net the No. 5 selection for Philadelphia. That's where the Sixers drafted Charles Barkley.

Former 76ers head coach Billy Cunningham narrated this tale during Barkley's Legends Walk ceremony that September afternoon. He remembered the Sixers' confidence just 10 days before the Rockets finished with only 29 wins, before Houston head coach Bill Fitch helped effectively steal Philadelphia's top-two selection. "They dumped every game, which allowed them to get Olajuwon," Cunningham recalled. "So Charles, you might not have been sitting here if they didn't dump those games. We might have had Olajuwon or Michael Jordan here."

Barkley laughed at his old coach's ribbing. He's always been one to take well to a joke.

Philadelphia's then-active play caller took the podium.

"I can't believe that Coach Fitch dumped games to get high draft picks," Brett Brown teased.

He paused as giggles crept through the crowd. Standing before a Sixers backdrop, nearly identical to the one during his 2013 introduction, Brown's beard was now grayed. His sandy brown hair had aged like a United States president's before-and-after photo.

"Can you believe that? Somebody, to get high draft picks, dumping games?" Brown grinned. "I don't know what you're talking about."

ACKNOWLEDGMENTS

I'll always remember the cups shaking. It was May 2014. Lottery night. Miller's Ale House in Northeast Philly. With each envelope that NBA deputy commissioner Mark Tatum opened, the gathered listeners of *The Rights to Ricky Sanchez* podcast, and readers of *LibertyBallers.com*, screamed "No! No! No!" in unison. Once Tatum revealed another team had been awarded that pick, keeping the Sixers fans' dreams of the No. 1 choice alive, the room erupted into a delirious cheer.

They stood on tabletops and balanced above barstools. During the commercial break ahead of announcing the top three picks, that portion of the bar bounced like an earthquake. I can still see it: the cups of beer shaking and jumping and spilling over the edge.

That's when I first thought this was a story. The idea evolved and pivoted and expanded over time—it took years before I realized it could be a book—but there was something obvious rippling throughout the NBA, and especially Philadelphia, that spring.

At Summer League 2018, somewhere along the Las Vegas Strip, I met Sam Hinkie again, this time for breakfast. He'd since shaved his head, but still dressed in his customary blazer and jeans. When I told him I was thinking about writing this book, he politely declined, as always, to speak on the record. Later, all of Danny Ainge, Mitch Kupchak, Rob Hennigan, Ryan McDonough, and Pete D'Alessandro did so as well. But over the next two years, I spoke to over 300 figures around the NBA—both for attribution and on background—to compile this anecdotal history of what I like to call the NBA's tanking era, and hope to have chronicled such an era in an informative and entertaining narrative. To whomever purchased the copy you're holding in your hands, I'm truly grateful.

It's quite cliché but *Built to Lose* genuinely would not have been possible without my agent, Joe Perry. I don't know how he stumbled across a college basketball story I wrote for SI.com in March 2019, about a national "fraternity" of walk-ons, like Kentucky's legendary Tod Lanter, but Joe emailed me shortly after. We bet on each other. I kept reporting, and then wrote a terrible proposal. It waxed and waned in 17,000 directions. And Joe thankfully helped steer me in the right path, one that Triumph Books was fortunately interested in publishing.

To Josh Williams, and everyone else on the Triumph Books acquisition team, thank you for giving this book a chance to grow into what it became. Adam Motin, bless you for reading through the cluttered first manuscript I submitted, helping organize all of these thoughts and anecdotes, and always looking out for what I was hoping to accomplish during this project. To Bill Ames, Sam Ofman, and Jen DePoorter, this whole thing didn't really seem real until the marketing and publicity began. Thanks to everyone at Triumph for all your efforts that helped *Built to Lose* reach readers everywhere.

Some special shoutouts to my former *Sports Illustrated* friends and colleagues. Pete Thamel, it has been a true privilege to have you in my corner. You're a hack in pickup basketball, but a remarkable reporter to learn from. Lee Jenkins, Chris Ballard, Ben Golliver, and Rob Mahoney, thank you as always for the time, and the example, you afforded me while we overlapped at *SI*, and since. It's a shame none of you worked out of New York. Jeremy Woo, you're the best NBA draft insider there is, and I've only grown from covering them at your side. Rohan Nadkarni, did I get enough Miami Heat and Dwyane Wade references in here for you?

I remain indebted to Mark Bechtel, for instructing a naive hotshot on how to actually write something that made sense. Thanks to Matt Dollinger, Ryan Hunt, and Chris Stone for approving obscure story pitches most outlets would never think of running. B.J. Schecter, you will forever be the key that got me in the door. I wish you nothing but success at *Baseball America* and Seton Hall. Greg Bishop, Emily Kaplan, Tim Rohan, Ben Baskin, Alex Prewitt, Alex Hampl, Lee Feiner, Dave Seperson, Maggie Gray, Dave Scipione, Kenny Ducey, Steph Kaufman, Gabriel Baumgartner, DeAntae Prince, Lorenzo Arguello, Eric Single, Mitch Goldich, Charlotte Carroll, Luis Echegaray, and too many more to list—I'm grateful for everything.

The nights and weekends staff was truly the backbone of that place. Mike Harris, Mike Blinn, Molly Geary, Jarrel Harris, Amy Parlapiano, Adam Pincus, Ben Estes, Kellen Becoats, Kristen Nelson, Connor Grossman, thank you guys for being the family that you are.

Bob Holmes, the esteemed former *Boston Globe* high school editor, you are nothing short of a pro's pro, and I'm beyond lucky our paths crossed. Same goes for Ben Osborne at *SLAM* magazine. Chris Trenchard, my editor at *Bleacher Report*, you have been an invaluable colleague and friend.

Nicole Crawford taught me how to write. Greg Gagliardi taught me how to report. Our teachers never, ever get the full credit and recognition they deserve. I'm beyond grateful for your guidance.

A sincere thank-you to the Brooklyn Nets public relations team, especially Aaron Harris and Eli Pearlstein. Many of the anecdotes in these pages came from locker room conversations inside Barclays Center during the 2019–20 season, my first as an independent author. Your help was, and is, greatly appreciated. The same goes for the other PR professionals around the league, agencies, and elsewhere who assisted along the way. To those who were willing and interested in speaking for this project, I offer perhaps the sincerest thank-you. It goes without saying, these pages would have been blank without your time and candor.

Eric Kessler, you were obviously not a conventional choice to be a fact-checker, but it was an absolute joy to go through that process with one of my oldest and closest friends. New York City will be happy to have you, for however long you'd like to stay. To all in my life who have supported this book, and my overall career, thank you. I can't write it enough: thank you.

My family, of course, rounds out this list of appreciations. Freddi and Sophie; Jack, Chloe, and Olivia, I love you guys. I have the coolest aunts in the world, Elizabeth and Nancy. I hope this work has made Papa Roy, Mhana Rhona, Papa Dave, Uncle Robert, and Grandma Joan proud.

Caley and Jameson, you're the best siblings I could ask for. Thank you for your unwavering support and listening to me ramble on about this project. Peter and Betsy, I ultimately write for my parents. I hope this one lands with you two most of all.

Built to Lose was written in its entirety during the early months of the Coronavirus pandemic. And as this terrible plague blanketed my home city and stalled the globe, it was an absolute gift to have such a project to work on each day, at worst a distraction from the madness raging outside our windows. The book was released on May 4, 2021, and I hope it's just a small, small item among the many things created during quarantine, that can help spin us all forward.